The World as Sacrament

An Ecumenical Path toward a Worldly Spirituality

Michael P. Plekon

LITURGICAL PRESS
Collegeville, Minnesota

www.litpress.org

Cover design by Monica Bokinskie.

Mid-Hudson Bridge from Walkway Over the Hudson, Poughkeepsie, NY, oil on canvas by Jeanne Plekon, 2016, www.jeanneplekon.com/upcoming /41/.

Excerpts from *The Church of the Holy Spirit* by Nicholas Afanasiev, edited by Michael Plekon, translated by Vitaly Permiakov, are used with permission of the University of Notre Dame Press.

Scripture texts in this work are taken from the *New Revised Standard Version Bible*, © 1989, Division of Christian Education of the National Council of the Churches of Christ in the United States of America. Used by permission. All rights reserved.

© 2017 by Order of Saint Benedict, Collegeville, Minnesota. All rights reserved. No part of this book may be reproduced in any form, by print, microfilm, microfiche, mechanical recording, photocopying, translation, or by any other means, known or yet unknown, for any purpose except brief quotations in reviews, without the previous written permission of Liturgical Press, Saint John's Abbey, PO Box 7500, Collegeville, Minnesota 56321-7500. Printed in the United States of America.

Library of Congress Cataloging-in-Publication Data

Names: Plekon, Michael, 1948– author.
Title: The world as sacrament : an ecumenical path toward a worldly
   spirituality / Michael P. Plekon.
Description: Collegeville, Minnesota : Liturgical Press, 2017.
Identifiers: LCCN 2016048935 (print) | LCCN 2017006449 (ebook) |
   ISBN 9780814645567 | ISBN 9780814645819 (ebook)
Subjects: LCSH: Spiritual life—Christianity. | Sacraments.
Classification: LCC BV4501.3 .P634 2017 (print) | LCC BV4501.3
   (ebook) | DDC 248—dc23
LC record available at https://lccn.loc.gov/2016048935

"With *The World as Sacrament*, Michael P. Plekon solidifies his reputation as a world-renowned spiritual guide. He leads us to the company of a cloud of Christian witnesses, women and men, of different Christian traditions, and hailing from diverse cultures and countries. I know of no richer treasure of spiritual insights than this book to feed our spiritual hunger from the lives and teachings of the saints—canonized or not—and to experience God's gracious presence in everything of the world."

— Peter C. Phan
Ellacuría Chair of Catholic Social Thought
Georgetown University

"Reading Michael Plekon's essays is like being told by a trusted mentor, 'Come and meet some of my friends.' Warm, wise, and conversational, this book unveils the habit of holiness right in the thick of things. You'll come away richer for the experience."

— Sarah Hinlicky Wilson
Institute for Ecumenical Research
Strasbourg, France

"*The World as Sacrament* bears witness to the truth of a Russian proverb, 'The walls we build on earth do not reach to heaven.' Michael Plekon's life has provided him with a grand tour of Christianity, Catholic, Protestant, and Orthodox. In crossing borders, he has locked no doors. Among those lighting his path have been the remarkable people he writes about in these pages. All of them men and women with souls on fire who sought God in everyday experience; all of them a challenge to each of us."

— Jim Forest
Author of *The Root of War Is Fear:
Thomas Merton's Advice to Peacemakers*

"In *The World as Sacrament*, Michael Plekon portrays thirteen women and men who embody well the essential Christian truth that even the most quotidian of moments is imbued with sacrament. In unique ways they experience, in Plekon's words, the 'collision constantly occurring between God and the lives of ordinary people.' Without Plekon, these ordinary Christians of various backgrounds would not have otherwise been placed into conversation with each other. But, happily, their juxtaposition brings a vividness to the reality that the everyday is, by its very nature, ecumenical. Furthermore, these women and men remind the rest of us to experience the world as sacrament not only in the spectacular moments of life but also at the stoplights."

— Carrie Frederick Frost, PhD

"To read Michael Plekon is to enter a world in which holiness is not an abstract concept but a characteristic of real, albeit pretty special, human beings. Some of the people profiled here are well known while others are future old friends, and *The World as Sacrament* tells us just enough about each to motivate further acquaintance. Plekon has been around the ecclesial block and brings a strong and refreshing ecumenical sensibility to his work. The result is a collection of heroes who invite each of us, in delightfully diverse ways, to move deeper into the God they knew deeply themselves. The organization into meaty but manageable chapters makes this an excellent book for individual or group reading."

— Susan R. Pitchford, TSSF
University of Washington

"Michael Plekon's diverse and ecumenical company of spiritual teachers includes monks, priests, nuns, and lay people. But what they all have in common is a call to plumb the sacred depths of ordinary existence. We don't have to escape to a special 'religious' place to find God. As Merton exclaimed, 'The gate of heaven is everywhere!'"

— Robert Ellsberg
Author, *Blessed Among Us*

"Written in a time of turbulence, as radical ideologies isolate people and the churches turn to sectarianism to seek refuge from the world, Michael Plekon pulls together diverse voices from West and East to remind us that some of the most profound contemporary Christian thinkers called on Christians to engage the world and discover the joy of the incarnate Christ in our very midst. Traditional, yet contemporary, *The World as Sacrament* is a must-read for those who continue the hard work of ecumenical dialogue and those who have prematurely pronounced ecumenism to be dead. Only a thinker whose personal journey offered him the privilege of living with Christians of many traditions and sharing their joys and sorrows would be capable of producing such a marvelous volume. Plekon's groundbreaking book suggests that the long winter of ecumenical spirituality may be turning to spring in the coming years."

— Nicholas Denysenko, PhD
Associate Professor of Theological Studies
Loyola Marymount University

Contents

Introduction vii

Prologue
Ecumenical Journey 1

Chapter 1
**To Become Permeable to Christ:
Elisabeth Behr-Sigel's Worldly Spirituality** 15

Chapter 2
**"The Sacrament of the Brother/Sister":
Mother Maria Skobtsova** 35

Chapter 3
**"Christianity Is Only Beginning . . .":
Alexander Men and Living Faith** 51

Chapter 4
**"The Power of Love": Nicholas Afanasiev's
Radical Vision of Community** 67

Chapter 5
Limitless Love: Lev Gillet's Generous God 85

Chapter 6
**God's Love Is Foolish, We Become What We Pray:
Paul Evdokimov's Vision** 105

Chapter 7
"Seeking the True Self":
Thomas Merton, Living and Praying in the World   127

Chapter 8
"I Sense a Sacredness in Things":
Marilynne Robinson and the World of *Gilead*   147

Chapter 9
"Everything Belongs":
Richard Rohr's Active Contemplation   165

Chapter 10
"Finding an Altar in the World":
Barbara Brown Taylor's Everyday Liturgy   183

Chapter 11
"Passion for God, Life, and Justice":
Joan Chittister's Prophetic Way   201

Chapter 12
"Quotidian Mysteries": Kathleen Norris and the Struggle with Everyday Demons   219

Epilogue
"The Liturgy after the Liturgy":
Michael Plekon, Learning to Be a Pastor   233

Introduction

God calls to us at every moment, and God is life, *this* life.[1]
— Christian Wiman

Faith, in the World

We know God is everywhere, present beyond the church services and walls, Bible and prayer book pages, beyond our icons and crosses. We know the Holy One is there, in every corner of our busy, messy lives. "For everything that lives is holy, life delights in life," as the mystic and poet William Blake said.[2] We also somehow are drawn to specifically sacred locations, to distinctive religious contexts, somehow feeling that as in the Jerusalem temple with holy of holies and altar of sacrifice and the ark of the covenant, God is more intensely present in those places, so God promises. As Solomon says, in his prayer while dedicating the temple in Jerusalem, no building can contain God; in fact, even heaven cannot (2 Chr 6:18).

Jesus spends most of his time, in the gospels, out on the roads and in the villages. He visits and teaches in the towns of Galilee, in the squares and fields and in people's homes. We see him in synagogues in his hometown of Nazareth and Capernaum and in the precincts of the temple, but only briefly. So much of the material of his teaching he draws from life, from the chores of ordinary housekeeping—baking and preparing

---

[1] Christian Wiman, *My Bright Abyss: Meditation of a Modern Believer* (New York: Farrar, Straus and Giroux, 2013), 8.
[2] "America: A Prophecy," Plate 8, 10.

meals, cleaning house, and the work by which people support themselves—farming, fishing, carpentry, and other crafts. His parables and healing encompass not only great events like weddings and funerals but also the humdrum tasks of homemakers, managers, and local officials.[3]

Perhaps the relentless challenge of his teaching lies in its being so mundane, secular, and not what one might expect to find as "religious." Jesus is absolutely immersed in the faith of his tradition and people. He blesses the bread and fish before distributing it to the hungry out in the fields; he says the blessing as he breaks bread with his fellow travelers in the inn on the road to Emmaus. He knows about legal definitions of what can and cannot be done on the Sabbath, of what family obligations mean as well as the spiritual extension of the law. Not only in solitary locations and at night is he one with his Father in prayer. The Father and Jesus are always one. And after, his followers found it natural to gather, break bread, eat, pray, and learn at home, as people did each Sabbath and at Passover and other festivals. In the words of one of our writers listened to here, they understood the temple to be everywhere, the altar to be in the world, where all was worship, in spirit and in truth.

Not a few figures—writers, poets, activists, teachers—have focused on the presence of the Holy One in the ordinary, on the many possibilities of worldly spirituality. In recent years, in teaching, writing, and pastoral work, I have been exploring the search for God in the lives and thinking of some remarkable persons of faith in our time.[4] While I began with a few

---

[3] Amy-Jill Levine, *Short Stories by Jesus: The Enigmatic Parables of a Controversial Rabbi* (San Francisco: HarperOne, 2014).

[4] Michael Plekon, *Living Icons: Persons of Faith in the Eastern Church* (Notre Dame, IN: University of Notre Dame Press, 2002); *Hidden Holiness* (Notre Dame, IN: University of Notre Dame Press, 2009); *Saints as They Really Are: Voices of Holiness in Our Time* (Notre Dame, IN: University of Notre Dame Press, 2012); *Uncommon Prayer: Prayer in Everyday Experience* (Notre Dame, IN: University of Notre Dame Press, 2016).

theologians and pastors, I immediately widened the list, simply because church people, at least in New Testament perspectives, have no monopoly on holiness. But the impulse came from some of those most closely connected to the church. They themselves wanted to return to the early church's sense of God acting in the world, of worldly ways of praying and living. It seemed important to include others, less attached, or not attached to church at all, making the journey in the spirit on their own.

So here are the origins of the book. It is an exploration of women and men looking for God in everyday experience. The takeaway is how their actions and thinking could be used by those of us seeking a life with God today. I do not have in mind recipes or formulas from these persons of faith. That would be too easy. Their witness is far richer and more complex. I think they give us fresh, distinctive ways of seeing and of living spiritually today. I invite readers to encounter them with me, to listen, and be moved.

What connects the voices is precisely the awareness, on the part of these women and men, of the everyday world as the place of encounter with God—the world as sacrament. Some lived through revolution, emigration, two world wars, the Great Depression, and in some cases Nazi occupation or Soviet oppression. So, some were part of the tumultuous twentieth century in Europe. But others are still with us. They know well the American context, a society of great opportunity but also great emptiness, need, and anger.

Further, the persons of faith to whom we listen here come from both the Western and Eastern church traditions. I believe this makes the book distinctive. It is therefore an ecumenical encounter—increasingly rare these days. And it is worth noting that among them—these persons faith, these uncanonized saints—most of them were aware of what still holds Christians together, despite their differences. A number of them actively worked for the reunion of the churches.

"The World as Sacrament"

> Sacrament is movement, transition, passage, Pascha: Christ knows the way and guides us, going before. The world, condemned in its old nature, revealed as life eternal in its new nature, is still the same world, God's good work. Christ came to save it, not to allow us means of thankful escape before it was discarded as rubbish. Thoughts of the "life to come" can be misleading. In a sense, we have no other world to live in but this, although the mode of our occupying it, our whole relationship to space and time . . . will be very different when we are risen again in Christ. . . . Our lives are congested and noisy. It is easy to think of the church and the sacraments as competing for our attention with the other world of daily life, leading us off into some other life—secret, rarified, remote. We might do better to think of that practical daily world as something incomprehensible and unmanageable unless and until we can approach it sacramentally through Christ. Nature and the world are otherwise beyond our grasp; time also, time that carries all things away in a meaningless flux, causing men to despair unless they see in it the pattern of God's action. . . . [W]e should concentrate upon this world lovingly because it is full of God, because by way of the Eucharist we find Him everywhere.[5]

"The world as sacrament"—what does this mean? It is the title of an essay by Eastern Orthodox theologian Alexander Schmemann. The citation above comes from his discerning look at how liturgy and life are entwined. It has also been used by Ecumenical Patriarch of Constantinople Bartholomew to refer to the sacramentality of all creation, this in that "Green Patriarch's" series of writings calling for a spiritual approach to saving and preserving the environment.[6] There are still

---

[5] Alexander Schmemman, "The World as Sacrament," in *Church, World, Mission* (Crestwood, NY: St. Vladimir's Seminary Press, 1979), 226–27.

[6] See https://mospat.ru/en/2010/05/26/news19252/; Bartholomew (with John Chryssavgis), *Cosmic Grace, Humble Prayer*, 2nd ed. (Grand Rapids, MI:

others who have used this expression, or one very close to it, to express the sacramental theology of various authors.[7]

Here in this book, "the world as sacrament" has to do with the worldly, everyday quality of spiritual life. This is what the writers have discovered in their own experience. And this is what I want to convey—they found interaction with God in work, friends, and family; in ordinary tasks like preparing meals; in conversation and care for others; and in the passage through life—problems of loneliness, estrangement, conflict that are relational and personal, as well as those we all eventually face: of aging, loss, sickness, and death. Beyond this, each faced the larger challenges of social justice and suffering to which Pope Francis has responded.

The figures I present and reflect on here offer perspectives that while ancient, may be new to many readers. This is the second feature that holds them together. They are from both the Eastern and Western churches. They are remarkable for their openness both to the other churches and unity in the faith. All were ecumenical, bridge-building both in their thinking and action. What is more, they all felt it crucial to revisit the Christian tradition, and in so doing, found that our sense of maintaining the legacy was sometimes misguided. Their findings on the power of love, on equality and community as

---

Eerdmans, 2009); *On Earth as in Heaven: Ecological Vision and Initiatives of Ecumenical Patriarch Bartholomew* (New York: Fordham University Press, 2011); *Toward an Ecology of Transfiguration: Orthodox Christian Perspectives on Environment, Nature, and Creation* (New York: Fordham University Press, 2013).

[7] Mathai Kadavil, *The World as Sacrament: Sacramentality of Creation in the Perspectives of Leonardo Boff, Alexander Schmemann and St. Ephrem* (Leuven: Peeters, 2005), http://www.peeters-leuven.be/boekoverz.asp?nr=7957; see also https://mospat.ru/en/2010/05/26/news19252/; David J. Leigh, "Toward a Sacrament of the World," http://opcentral.org/resources/2015/01/13/david-j-leigh-toward-a-sacrament-of-the-world/; Stephan Van Erp, "The Sacrament of the World: Thinking God's Presence beyond Public Theology," https://lirias.kuleuven.be/bitstream/123456789/490209/2/Van+Erp+-+Sacrament+of+the+world.pdf.

necessary in the faith, make them especially relevant voices for us today. They were also convinced that the Gospel was to be lived out in everyday life.

Finally, the name, and thus the preaching, of the bishop of Rome (as he prefers to be called), Pope Francis will appear quite often in these pages—and not by accident. As it turns out, the awareness that we are always forgiven, loved, and sustained by God's mercy is a realization at the heart of almost every writer to whom we will listen. I cannot pretend to have selected them for that reason, any more than I can take credit for their profound sensibility to grace everywhere. But from Nicholas Afanasiev to Mother Maria Skobtsova, from Marilynne Robinson and Richard Rohr to Thomas Merton, each was shaped by the mercy of God, "mercy within mercy within mercy."

This book is rooted in my experience of a number of women and men we will shortly meet. But it is also from my experience as a pastor, a teacher, and scholar. In each chapter, I try to go behind the ideas to the experiences in the lives of these individuals, deliberately connecting their encounters with God in the people around them to the landscape of our lives today. Biography and narrative are powerful spiritual tools. Simply put, the thoughts of the persons of faith with whom I reflect here are not the only "texts." Their lives, as well as our lives, are also texts about looking for and following God in everyday existence. Given my own pastoral experience of over thirty years, I also have offered some insights from that in a chapter.

I have taught honors courses both on contemporary persons of faith and on writers and their spiritual journeys for several years at the City University of New York, a context at once both intensely diverse as well as secular. I bring that experience to this book. I have also given numerous retreats on some of these figures, as well as papers at scholarly conferences and other publications. This book derives from the research and the interactive experience in these classes and the other venues mentioned. This book could be the basis of an adult study class or a retreat and is a rich resource for personal spiritual reading—*lectio divina*. A photo gallery of the faces of the voices listened to is essential for me. It enables readers to connect the face of the person to whom they are listening. I cannot stress enough that my reflection on and engagement with the writers here is only a start, an invitation, as it were, to feast on their fiction, poems, memoirs, and other writing. There is no replacement for that. Thus I feel strongly that readers should be provided resources for further reading, both online and hardcopy sources. So I have provided generous references that are bibliographic notes, with further recommendations for reading.

Our Persons of Faith

> The great lessons from the true mystics, from the Zen monks, is that the sacred is in the ordinary, that it is to be found in one's daily life, in one's neighbors, friends, and family, in one's back yard, and that travel may be a flight from confronting the sacred. To be looking everywhere for miracles is a sure sign of ignorance that everything is miraculous.[8]
>
> —Abraham Maslow

The perennial wisdom of Abraham Maslow is captured in those lines. While none of the writers we will listen to here are Zen monks, a few are indeed monastics, and several are mystics. They are, by intention, ecumenically diverse and diverse in other ways—from both the Western and Eastern churches, women and men, some ordained clergy, others laypeople. Some are from Europe and earlier, in the past century. Others are from America and still active today. So, in each chapter, we will look at leading themes in a person's writing as well as the ways in which life experiences framed their vision—and what this has for us to ponder and follow now.

---

[8] Abraham Maslow, *Religion, Values and Peak Experiences* (New York: The Viking Press, 1964), xii.

"To Become Permeable to Christ"—Elisabeth Behr-Sigel's Worldly Spirituality. Elisabeth was a theologian much ahead of her time, among the first women to study theology both at the University of Strasbourg and the St. Sergius Institute in Paris. She was also an early pastoral associate in her local church. She first wrote on the actual history of saints' lives and later had much to say on spirituality for everyday living. She also explored the place and work of women in the church and served for years in the leadership of Laity and Clergy against Torture.

"The Sacrament of the Brother/Sister"—Mother Maria Skobtsova. Mother Maria was a poet, a political radical, married several times, divorced, and a parent of three. She was also a nun, a social activist, and a martyr for hiding victims of the Nazis. Extroverted and persuasive, her perspectives on love and care for the neighbor remain striking, as does her indictment of self-centered religiosity. She was recognized as a saint, along with several coworkers, by the Russian Orthodox Archdiocese in Western Europe, her "local church," and was canonized in 2004.

"Christianity Is Only Beginning"—Alexander Men and Living Faith. After years of having to do underground publishing, the end of the Soviet era enabled Men to become the leading voice of faith in Russia, only to be struck down by an assassin a few years later. Yet his lectures, preaching, and writing contain one of the most realistic appraisals of the decline of institutional religion and yet the possibility of authentic faith in our time.

"The Power of Love"—Nicholas Afanasiev's Radical Vision of Community. Church historian, canonist, New Testament scholar, liturgical specialist, Afanasiev's rediscovery of what held the ancient church together—love and mutual accountability, is a radical challenge to faith communities and individuals today.

"Limitless Love"—Lev Gillet's Generous God. Lev Gillet was a Benedictine who became an Eastern Catholic then Orthodox

monk-priest. A mystic and activist plagued by depression all his life, his vision of the God without limits and loving faith without boundaries decades ago speak directly to the twenty-first-century situation of believers in a diverse world that does not want to just be condemned for its sin.

"God's Love Is Foolish, We Become What We Pray"—Paul Evdokimov's Vision. Spouse, widower, parent, layperson, theologian, social activist, Evdokimov had, as the theme of all his teaching and writing, the necessity of a spirituality rooted in our era, a worldly faith, not a museum-object of piety from the past. God's suffering with us and our making all we do our prayer are major forms this spirituality of our time takes shape.

"Seeking the True Self"—Thomas Merton, Living and Praying in the World. Merton has to be one of the best-known spiritual writers of the past century. He left Columbia University graduate work to become a Trappist monk and spent the last half of his life at the Abbey of Gethsemani near Louisville, Kentucky. Enormously productive as a writer—volumes of his journals, letters, poems, books, and articles on the spiritual life have been published—he died in an accident while traveling and lecturing in Southeast Asia. Known also for his commitment to the antiwar and civil rights movements of the 1960s, he was silenced and constrained by his superiors but allowed to write in freedom again in the last few years of his life. He offers us a sense of the integration of life, the location of the true self in God and in the joining of prayer and life, of contemplation and action.

"I Sense a Sacredness in Things"—Marilynne Robinson and the World of Gilead. Robinson is without doubt one of the most celebrated writers of the last fifty years. A careful craftsperson, she takes years to create her narratives. In *Gilead, Home,* and *Lila*—her recent trilogy—without any pretension or contrivance, she reveals the movement of grace in everyday life, the

collision constantly occurring between God and the lives of ordinary people.

"Everything Belongs"—Richard Rohr's Active Contemplation. Franciscan friar and priest Richard Rohr has become one of the most highly regarded teachers of the spiritual life in the past two decades. Having served as a prison chaplain, educator, and pastor, he also was involved in an experiment to gather a community of Christians committed to prayer and social justice. This, and the profound impact of Merton's writings, led to his opening the Center for Action and Contemplation in Albuquerque, New Mexico, and to a substantial stream of books, articles, and online posts. With his long pastoral experience, his training as a friar in community life, and his use of psychology alongside the Scriptures, Rohr offers a distinctive vision of contemplation put into practice, a worldly spirituality that refuses to divide the sacred from the ordinary.

"Finding an Altar in the World"—Barbara Brown Taylor's Everyday Liturgy. Taylor was one of *Time* magazine's one hundred most significant Americans in 2014. She has been acclaimed as one of the country's finest preachers. In recent years, in three volumes, she has described her failure as a parish pastor and her disenchantment with the institutional church. Even more importantly, she has shared with us her rediscovery of God in everyday life and her encountering the darkness that all of us face in our lives.

"Passion for God, Life, and Justice"—Joan Chittister's Prophetic Way. Benedictine monastic, writer, and teacher Joan Chittister is one of the most prolific spiritual writers and powerful voices of Christian women and religious sisters in the past half century. Not only has she been a powerful voice for women in the church and for the renewal of religious life, she, like so many others here, focuses on the presence of God in the textures, in the struggles and joys of living.

"*Quotidian Mysteries*"—Kathleen Norris and the Struggle with Everyday Demons. Poet Kathleen Norris has been a riveting, discerning voice on the spiritual life for the past thirty years. She not only connected many with monastic life and spirituality but also allowed us into some of the pain and challenges of her own life in a study of *acedia*, or spiritual apathy.

"*The Liturgy after the Liturgy*"—Michael Plekon, *Learning to Be a Pastor*. Drawing on my own experience in parish ministry, I reflect on popular, that is, humane faith in everyday life. Most of the narrative is drawn from my early days as a pastor, over thirty years ago, visiting elderly and shut-in parish members and visiting and doing services at local skilled nursing centers. Simple as all this pastoral work was, the power of the encounters remains with me, decades later.

A Feast of Writers and Their Works

It is no surprise that frequently, Jesus describes the kingdom of heaven among us as a gathering of friends to feast—a wedding or dinner party or some other feast.[9] What I offer here is that, but in words and images. I can well imagine, for myself, the kingdom of heaven being at a party with the women and men in this book, with plenty of wine and good food!

The invitation list is based, as I said, on my own reading and study. But it is also based on teaching experience, on seeing and hearing students open up and respond powerfully to writers who challenged them with the spiritual life. Most of these were authors who they were encountering for the first time. Unlike the religious culture in which I grew up, really none of these writers are interested in prescribing religious beliefs or practices. One need not be an observant religious individual, a churchgoer, to be challenged by these persons of

---

[9] Levine, *Short Stories by Jesus*, 107–25, 279–82.

faith and their voices. I think the most wonderful thing is the diversity of their backgrounds. This is really a rich, ecumenical gathering. There are ordinary women and men, laypeople, a couple of monastics and pastors, a scholar and teacher here and there, also folks who raised families, struggled with paychecks, difficult spouses and friends, aging parents, and more. I invite you to the feast!

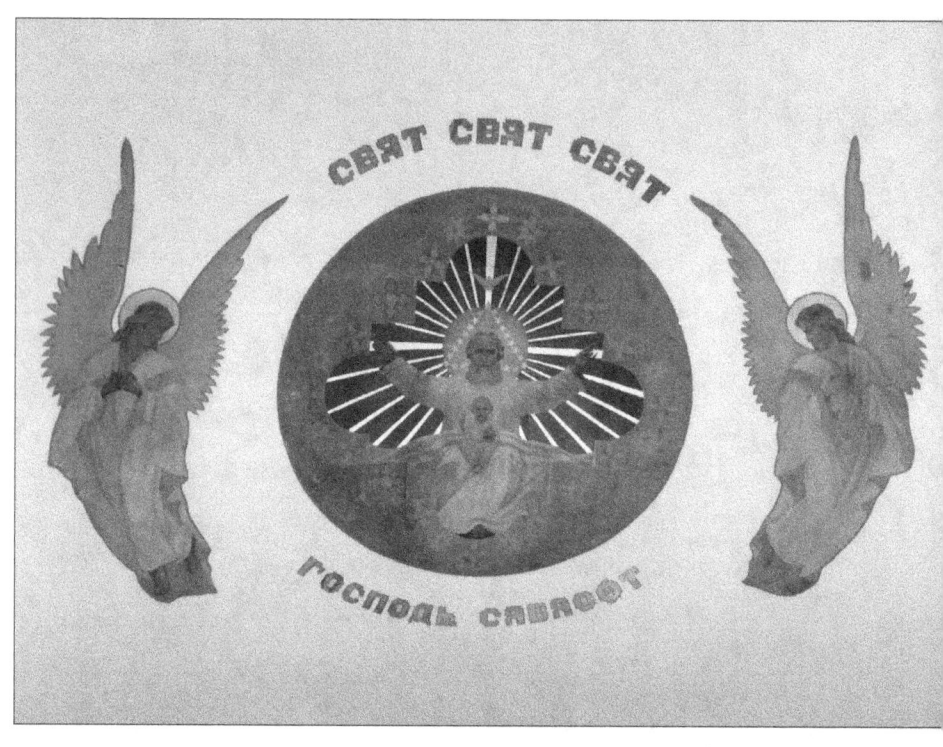

"The Ancient of Days": God the Father, the Son, and the Holy Spirit.
Inscription: "Holy, holy, holy, Lord of Sabaoth."

Photo from the former St. Michael's Ukranian Greek Catholic Church,
Yonkers, New York.

Prologue

Ecumenical Journey

Immigrants and a Pilgrim

What I will share with you at the start comes from my life. There will be a similar sharing at the end, an epilogue that draws on my experiences some years ago, learning pastoral care as a newly ordained person, often by trial and error.

Just as with the other writers to whom we will listen in this book, I hope these personal scenes will connect you to the world as sacrament, that is, some of the many encounters with God in everyday life. Another way to describe this is a worldly spirituality, one in which God is attended, listened to in the course of very ordinary activities and encounters with those around us. It is a more secular, mundane, even profane following of the Spirit's lead, without at all being antireligious.

I believe there are some good things to share from my experience. The one I put before you now is the ecumenical journey I have experienced. I have had the great gift of a number of different church homes over the years, from childhood on through adulthood. And it shows in what I think, say, and do. I experienced grace and wisdom within all of these churches, learned the Scriptures and liturgy, if slightly differently, in all of them. I know, from the years of formation in them and much subsequent research, that all of these churches have produced women and men of holiness, saints, both officially recognized and saints of more ordinary, hidden holiness. The ecumenical character of this book is a further consequence of this happy experience, with reflections on writers from both the Western and the Eastern church. Other books I have written contain many more, and from writers outside the church as well.

I did not plan on being a pilgrim of sorts among the churches. First of all, I have to blame my family of origin. I say this with love and no scorn. All of my grandparents came from the same Ternopil province, or oblast, in what is today western Ukraine. Three of the four were from the same small town, Burkaniew. I have been there, even had to wait in the car for the cows to file back to their respective barns. The town was small, rural, just a short walk from a major shrine of the Mother of God, Zarvanytsia, where both grandmothers went frequently when young. When they all migrated to the United States, before the First World War, the entire area was the province of Galicia in the Austro-Hungarian Empire, its identity changing numerous times over the last several centuries.

On both sides of my family of origin, there were ethnic diversities, that is, people were both Polish and Ukrainian in language and ethnicity. This also meant that there were both Roman/Latin Catholics and Ukrainian Greco-Catholics in the families. There were Orthodox villagemates as well as Jewish and some Protestant neighbors. The Ternopil province was an area of migration and, thus, mixing. My grandparents were, like all inhabitants of this region, taught German in the few grades of school they attended. In addition they were literate, according to their basic standards, in both the Cyrillic and Latin alphabets. They could manage, I counted once, somewhere between six and seven languages in various degrees of fluency. Because my maternal grandmother's family ran a store, she seemed to be the most gifted of these polyglots.

These grandparents came as immigrants in the first decade of the twentieth century, all locating with relatives in neighborhoods where there were others from the same province. Ethnicity comes later, anthropologically. First and most important was locality, people who were your former neighbors, roughly speaking. A good twenty-five years after the migration, my maternal grandmother was moved by the voice of the young priest assisting the pastor of her Ukrainian parish in Yonkers, New York. This was at Easter services. In the Eastern church, the services are chanted and sung *in toto*. When she approached him about the familiarity of his voice, she learned the reason. His father had sung in the parish choir with her growing up—Iwan Plekhan. Later John Plekon, here in the United States, my father's father. Eventually, this priest, Father Myron Plekon's younger brother Henry, was introduced to my maternal grandmother and her daughter—my future mother. That daughter, Helen, and Father Myron's brother, Henry, children of immigrants who grew up in the same village, would marry after World War II ended—my parents.

I should also add that I saw my maternal grandmother, the one who lived with us, pray and light candles at whatever church was accessible—Roman Catholic, Greek Catholic, Orthodox. She seemed not to recognize any difference—only the same God and Holy Mother honored in them all. The same would be true for my own parents who attended a neighbor's funeral at Yonkers' oldest Episcopal church, going up for communion as if they had attended there all their lives. Later they would come up to receive in the Lutheran church where I served in the same unaffected manner, assuming that if communion was being distributed they could, would, and should receive.

Both my parents were born in the United States. My mother's and my father's parents were married at St. George's Ukrainian Church on the lower East Side, 7th Street. My mother's family settled in New York City, then New Haven, Connecticut, and finally in Yonkers, New York, where I was born. My father was from Nanticoke, Pennsylvania, close to Wilkes-Barre, in the coal region of northeastern Pennsylvania. Even in the boom time of the anthracite industry, you got out as quickly as you could. Miner's lung, asthma, emphysema, alcoholism, heart disease—all accompanied mining, and even for those who left the work, the life of many Eastern European immigrants (especially the men) was made brief. Both of my grandfathers were dead by their very early fifties.

All of the boys in my father's family got out of the region, in one way or another. One moved away to the West and was never heard from again. Another spent his entire working life at a Ford factory in Mahwah, New Jersey, returning on the weekends. Still another one of my father's brothers became a priest in the Ukrainian Greek Catholic Church. He is the one referred to just above, the reason for my parents meeting each other. He was not allowed to marry, the result of a Vatican decision in the late 1930s that affected Eastern Catholics in communion with Rome. Thus, like most Catholic priests, my uncle was moved around quite a bit, from parish to parish, primarily in the region. For some years, when she could no longer manage on her own, my father's mother also lived with my uncle. Thus our visits were to both when I was growing up. I served as an altar boy for Fr. Myron, and visiting at his house, the parish rectory, gave me some sense of what priests did when they were not at the altar in their vestments. I have a number of his service and ritual books, some full of sermon notes and other jottings. You can tell by the finger stains what pages he used most.

I didn't get the idea of becoming a priest just from this uncle. He was originally very friendly but grew more distant and difficult to be around as he aged. In the last decade of his life we no longer saw him much, with my grandmother being gone and with health issues of his own increasing. I recall he supplied me with a lot of religious books, crosses, and other things and encouraged me to become a priest in the Ukrainian Church. I think my grandmother or one of his parishioners made me a little vestment with which to "play priest," something boys did, not so different from cowboys and Indians, playing cop or fireman or doctor.

As my parents distanced themselves from the Yonkers Ukrainian Church, and I leaned toward trying religious life in the Latin Catholic Carmelite Order, he seemed to also grow more distant to us. For him, religion as well as priesthood was very much tied up with Ukrainian identity. Vatican II was a huge disappointment and obstacle to him, as was life after the 1960s. Unlike other clergy, he refused to switch to the use of more English. He had a stroke at the altar during the words of consecration and died a couple days later, a fitting way to go as a priest, some would say. But his last parish was a handful of retired folk, and I think his last years were ones of frustration, seeing the Ukrainian Church shrink.

I have taken you on this journey of immigration, ethnic identity, and family because all of these, as well as other non-religious, certainly nontheological, factors play into priestly and religious vocation. What is more, I have come to realize just how rooted in everyday life was the faith that had been passed on to me from grandparents and parents, how much they found and served God at work, on the block, with their relatives and neighbors.

When my parents decided to attend the Roman Catholic parish just a couple blocks from our house, the Ukrainian world and language started to disappear, completely going as the last of my grandmothers died. I found myself as a kid as one of the few Eastern Europeans in a predominantly Irish-American parish. In time, this would change into a mostly Italian-American parish, with further migration up from the Bronx and other boroughs of the city. Today the parish has a sizeable Latino component.

Smells, Bells, Images

At the most sensory level, I was exposed to a lot of wonderful details of Christian existence. This too made for the experience of the sacramentality not only of liturgy but also of all that surrounds and flows from it. Easter is not just the many lessons of the vigil and the singing of "Christ is risen." Easter spills over into aromas and tastes that remain vivid.

With my nose in the Ukrainian and then the pre–Vatican II Roman Catholic churches and later the Eastern Orthodox, I associate services with a haze of incense, a dazzle of lit candles, and the stare of faces of saints looking down at me from fresco and panel icons all over the walls of the church. Also the saints looked at me from the icon screen that delineates the nave from the altar area in Eastern churches. Later in the Catholic Church, I was surrounded by life-sized statues of St. Joseph, the Virgin Mary, John the Baptist, the parish patron saint, and other beloved holy ones in the Catholic tradition such as Jude Thaddeus and Anthony of Padua—all inhabitants of the cathedral-like building I attended for many years on Yonkers Avenue.

I remember as a child not following the Latin Mass very closely, as I understood not a word. The same had been true in the Ukrainian church, St. Michael's, in which Slavonic was used. Rather, I let myself get lost in the extraordinary color and detail of the stained glass windows that line St. John the Baptist Church. I lost myself in the flowers, plants, and even the blades of grass and the donkey in a bucolic scene of Joseph, Mary, and Elizabeth at the visitation at the latter's home in the country. In the windows of the presentation of Jesus in the temple, of Pentecost and the annunciation of the angel Gabriel to Mary, the interiors of the rooms were sumptuous and often opened to a landscape beyond. There was a glorious, very large, mainly blue window covering the complete western end of the nave over the organ and choir loft, with the Virgin and child, king David and John the Baptist, Mary's parents Joachim and Anna, Joseph her husband and Elizabeth her cousin and John the Baptist's mother. Matching it, on the eastern end over the main altar was a dramatic and huge window of Christ's crucifixion. I am sure the profusion of icons and frescoes in the Ukrainian church and then the stained-glass windows and statues in the Roman church formed me into the extremely visual teacher and scholar and preacher I later became.

Prologue: Ecumenical Journey   7

Very deeply lodged in my memory are the images of God the Father in both of these churches. He was depicted as the "Ancient of Days," complete with triangle in the halo behind his head, with long, silver hair and beard. In St. John's, God the Father stretched out his hands in blessing above his crucified son and the Spirit in the form of a dove. In the Ukrainian church, the exact same "old-man-as-God" presided over all the rest of the apse fresco icons and the icon screen, arms raised in blessing of all the world and of us gathered far below. Around him were the words "Holy, holy, holy, Lord God of Sabaoth," in Slavonic.

There was an amazing symmetry in both the Latin and Byzantine iconography as far as the Father Almighty was concerned, and even as I age, it is impossible to dislodge that primary, very basic image of God from my earliest childhood. When we came, my family and I, to the Roman Catholic Church, the same Father way up at the top signaled we were home. Those from low church backgrounds with stark, imageless church interiors are usually visually and to some extent psychologically challenged by the image-rich ecclesiastical adornment of Eastern/Byzantine, Roman Catholic, and for that matter, many Anglican and Lutheran sanctuaries.

But it was not just the profusion of images of the Virgin and saints that shaped me. There were many other sounds and sights . . . and smells and tastes! There was the nearly overwhelming, powerful fragrance of flowers—the lilies and hyacinths when you came back into church after the procession at the Easter Vigil. May was Mary's month, with processions, recitations of the rosary, hymns, and the May crowning by a girl chosen to put the flower crown on her statue, surrounded by lilacs and roses. There were also the subtle, intoxicating whiffs of anointing oil and the sweet wine at communion time in the Eastern Church (as well as the Lutheran).

While all kinds of olfactory memories of Christmas and Easter dinners mark childhood and later recollections of these feasts, I am still wafted away each year when the Eastern delicacies of the paschal table of Eastern Orthodox and Catholics are unleashed—the piquancy of the smoked ham, the garlicky explosion when the kielbasa is sliced, the heady mix of spice and fruit and yeast in the dense, sweet kulich/Easter bread, not to mention the cloves forming a cross in the butter and the creamy tall unbaked cheesecake, or Pashka. The shouts of *Hristos voskhres'* /"Christ is risen" all through the services of Easter night, the paschal troparion sung over and over again: "Christ is risen from the dead, trampling down death by death, and upon those in the tomb bestowing life!"

I am not ignoring the wursts, sauerbraten, and beer of Oktoberfests, the pancakes and doughnuts of Fastnacht, nor the glorious hymns we sang all through the church year in the Lutheran church. So much of family and of religion is entwined with food and smells and tunes and colors. But for all the supposedly, definitive doctrinal divisions, the one Christ remains in them all. As Sergius Bulgakov said in his famous essay, the gifts of what unites us remain despite the divisions.[1] Gerard Manley Hopkins's lines from "As Kingfishers Catch Fire" ring true:

> For Christ plays in ten thousand places,
> Lovely in limbs, and lovely in eyes not his
> To the Father through the features of men's faces.

But this path, of immigration and of various church homes, is more than another American tale of mobility and melting pot. For me, it is a profoundly spiritual narrative, showing the presence of Christ in many different places, really an experience of the world as a sacramental encounter. I am sure that it laid the foundation for the rest of the ecumenical journey that would follow.

---

[1] Sergius Bulgakov, "By Jacob's Well," in *Tradition Alive: On the Church and the Christian Life in Our Time*, ed. Michael Plekon (Lanham, MD: Rowman & Littlefield, 2003), 55–65.

Vocation—Becoming a Pastor

When I was growing up, there was a great deal of encouragement and pride in daughters and sons pursuing vocations in religious and priestly life. Richard Rohr and Joan Chittister both witness to this, remembering their childhoods in the church.[2] Priests in the parish close to our home encouraged vocations to the priesthood and religious life, as did the Franciscan sisters who taught us in the parish elementary school. Eventually, I followed a not unusual path for the early 1960s and went off to a boarding high school that was a "minor," or "junior" seminary, a stage of preparation for the priesthood. I have written about this and the subsequent decade I spent in and with the Carmelite Order elsewhere.[3]

I was a friar, more precisely, a student friar, both in the novitiate part of formation and for several years afterward, during undergraduate studies as well as for a year as an intern, teaching in a diocesan high school in Pottsville, Pennsylvania. But I came to realize that living as a friar, more particularly, as a celibate in a community, was not what I really wanted or was gifted to do. I did love the religious life and always have, feeling a kinship with various communities to which I have become close, such as those of New Skete. But it did become clear to me that God did not want me in this life—a most discerning older friar told me that if I was no longer at peace in it, neither was God. So I requested to be dispensed from my vows and after the year of internship, I left, with sadness but also hope and anticipation.

---

[2] See Tom Roberts, *Joan Chittister: Her Journey from Certainty to Faith* (Maryknoll, NY: Orbis Books, 2015), 11–44; Richard Rohr, *Falling Upward: A Spirituality for the Two Halves of Life* (San Francisco: Jossey-Bass, 2011), 25–51; and *Eager to Love: The Alternative Way of Francis of Assisi* (Cincinnati, OH: Franciscan Media, 2014), 52–60.

[3] Michael Plekon, *Saints as They Really Are* (Notre Dame, IN: University of Notre Dame Press, 2012), 105–50.

When I left, it was still the period of the draft and selective service for the Vietnam War. So I went through the process and was granted status as a conscientious objector. I was told to find acceptable alternative service work to do. For almost two years, I served as a teacher and then head of a Head Start center in Old Bridge New Jersey, housed in a Lutheran church educational building. During the week, Head Start occupied the classroom space, while on Sundays the same space was used for coffee hour and church school. The pastor of this parish, William Mitschke, befriended me and invited me, a Ukrainian Greek Catholic, then Roman Catholic, former Carmelite friar to become a member of his Lutheran parish. So my ecumenical journey continued. In retrospect, I am sure he recognized my training and inclination to church service. And already while in Washington, DC, I had a good deal of ecumenical contacts.

But it was not until several years later that anything more happened with respect to pastoral vocation. Starting during my alternative service and extending for another five years was graduate study, various exams, thesis and dissertation writing, and in a terrible academic job market, a miraculous hire to a tenure-track position. Forty years later, after tenure and promotions, many years of teaching and publishing, I am coming to retirement, having served at the City University of New York's Baruch College both in the department of sociology and anthropology and the program in religion and culture.

Close to the start of this career, however, after a fellowship year abroad in Copenhagen working on Søren Kierkegaard and several years of teaching and the birth of our son, I was ordained in the Lutheran Church in America, one of the bodies that merged later into the Evangelical Lutheran Church in America. Still later, I would be received and reordained in the Orthodox Church in America. I cannot say I have been a pastor or presbyter in all three major traditions, Catholic, Protestant, and Orthodox, but two out of three is close, having been a friar or brother in the third, on the way toward ordination.

How and why my church journeys occurred is, on the one hand, complicated, and on the other, at least in retrospect, easy to grasp. After so many years, the last almost thirty-five in ordained ministry, I see that I have truly been at home in all of those church traditions. At different periods of my life, each one shaped me. As a young adult, the Carmelite way of life offered me structure, important spiritual perspectives, and tools. Richard Rohr is quite right in saying that we need to be formed by rules and structures in the first half of life—this he experienced himself as a Franciscan friar. But the later 1960s were also a time of foment and change. I was also much shaped by the commitment to renewal and the sense of simplifying and getting back to the sources that so characterized Vatican II: a simpler, beautiful but accessible liturgy, service shaped by the Gospel, close to everyday life, less clerical distance and more incorporation into the whole of the people of God, the church.

These are strong themes that have characterized women and men seeking to teach, to preach, to offer pastoral care and share in the liturgy and sacraments in the past half century. Names across the ecclesial landscape come to mind—the great returners to the sources—Schillebeeckx, Congar, Dix, Thurian, and Küng—from the time before and after Vatican II. Then there are the amazing thinkers I have read, written about, and from whom I have received so much inspiration—Bulgakov, Mother Maria Skobtsova, Afanasiev, Schmemann, Meyendorff. Then a parade, a truly holy one, of others—Bonhoeffer, Rowan Williams, Thomas Merton, Elisabeth Behr-Sigel, Alexander Men, and Dorothy Day.

Of course, some of these are the very figures discussed in this book and, I can tell you, they appear, along with others like Sara Miles, Barbara Brown Taylor, Mary Oliver, and Mary Karr, in my other writings. That so many of all of these writers are in the progressive if not radical and liberal categories says a lot about them . . . and me. That for all the theologians and clergy, the larger list would have many women and men both not ordained and, if ordained, in some tension with the institutional church, also is telling, again both about these writers and myself.

This book then is unusual, distinctive. In it, a diverse and ecumenical group of writers is brought together. Given what has happened to the ecumenical movement, a kind of "winter" dormancy rather the hopeful "spring" at the time of Vatican II, seems to have set in. The present state of official ecumenical relationships among the churches is bleak, cold, without any sign of life. It could also be said that lines of division and the sense of separation have reintensified, say among the Orthodox and Catholics and Protestants. The reassertion of the idea of a "Russian world" of civilization and religion has emphasized the differences and distance between East and West, the latter cast as too tolerant, liberal, secular. The former is held to be holding on to the true Christian tradition. One also sees this in the now regular sniping at and criticism of Pope Francis by traditionalist or more conservative Catholics. While the "culture wars" of the 1980s cannot be said to be continuing in their older forms, there is still, at least in the political landscape, profound clashing between progressives and conservatives on LGBT marriage and legal rights, not to mention the perennial issues of abortion and gender definition and situation.

On the grassroots level of parishes, a number of church bodies have declared themselves to be in communion with one another and so now have ordained ministries that are interchangeable (at least in principle) and recognize and admit each other to the Eucharist. Across some churches, such as the Orthodox, Catholic, and Protestant, this has not yet happened, and the prospects for church unity are becoming less encouraging.

As the writers to whom we will listen make clear, however, we all inhabit the same world, face the same challenges, search to find God in pretty much the same everyday experiences—and suffer the same frustrations and challenges in doing so.

Many of the writers you will encounter here got out of their own church homes and worked, studied, and prayed with Christians from other backgrounds, even those where there had not yet been any breakthroughs in recovering unity/communion. This was the case for every one of the Eastern Orthodox figures, Nicholas Afanasiev and Lev Gillet in particular, who address division and unity in their writings, but also Elisabeth Behr-Sigel, Paul Evdokimov, Maria Skobtsova, and Alexander Men, who behaved and wrote as though there were no divisions among Christians. Thomas Merton came to the same conclusion. And it is hard to see what in their faith could possibly divide Kathleen Norris, Barbara Brown Taylor, Richard Rohr, Joan Chittister, or Marilynne Robinson from members of church bodies other than their own. Just as with Pope Francis, there is a unanimous awareness of the mercy of God among all these thinkers, whether Western or Eastern church. Equally, one will hear from everyone one a passion for the serving of the neighbor in need.

There is no dispute among these diverse Christian authors when it comes to our time. We again need to recognize that "the church has left the building," is no longer equivalent to this consecrated space or model of congregational organization with which we were accustomed. When I recall the languages of liturgical worship I have lived with, from Slavonic and Latin to English, the styles of singing from Lutheran chorales, American spirituals and gospel, from Byzantine and Gregorian chant to folk songs, there is but one Christ, one baptism, faith, Word, and Eucharist no matter the state of ecclesiastical and doctrinal agreements. Here in this book we need not be disturbed by differences or division at all. We will all be drawn together by the encounter with the one world as sacrament, as the place of God's presence and work.

Elisabeth Behr-Sigel
Photo by Jeanne Bergreen Plekon.

Chapter 1

To Become Permeable to Christ: Elisabeth Behr-Sigel's Worldly Spirituality

Elisabeth's Love of Life and of the World

It is rare to actually know important figures that you study or write about. Often we are separated by years and miles. But Elisabeth Behr-Sigel is one of the spiritual giants I have had the privilege of knowing personally. I remember well when Jeanne and I met Elisabeth.[1] We drove round and round the Paris suburb in which she lived, in vain, trying to find her apartment building, not even finding street signs. When somehow we located her, several floors up, I mentioned our troubles. Her response, with a lot of laughter, was that since everyone knew where they lived and their address, there was no need for street signs! How very French, and how very much the personality of Elisabeth!

Having read almost everything she had written and having heard a great deal about her from friends, Fr. John Breck and Lyn Breck, I did not expect the devilish sense of humor that seemed almost to enjoy our being lost, worried, and late. As I got to know Elisabeth over the last few years of her very long life, I came to realize that this was but one aspect of a rich and complex personality, intellect, and soul.

---

[1] This chapter is based on several earlier pieces by the author, including a part of *Hidden Holiness* (Notre Dame, IN: University of Notre Dame Press, 2009), and an essay in *The Ecumenical Review* 61, no. 2 (2009): 165–76, among others.

Anyone who met Elisabeth instantly knew she was a free spirit. She routinely challenged clergy, political leaders, and other scholars. She was indefatigable, an incurable optimist, but equally a relentless critic, even in her late nineties. Her life covered most of the twentieth century, and in it, she saw numerous wars, social upheavals, and personal sufferings. Elisabeth was fearless. When the Moscow patriarchate began to attack her home diocese, she put out an open letter boldly calling out this hostile activity. She signed several petitions asking for reinstatement of women to the diaconate in the Orthodox Church. She played an important role in the process that led to the canonization of Mother Maria Skobtsova and her companions. Mother Maria was a longtime friend and collaborator, especially during the Nazi occupation of Paris. I think you will soon see why Elisabeth offers such a strong, empowering vision of faith in action—both in her thinking and in her life—what we are looking for in this book. For her, the world was very much a sacrament of God's presence and of opportunities to love.

Elisabeth died in her own apartment on boulevard Foch in Épinay-sur-Seine—the address we found hard to locate. It was in her sleep, in her own bed, with books, journals, letters, and other work spread out around her. She held on to her driver's license well into her nineties, though it was hard for her to see the road any longer due to her shrinking height. I recall when we visited her that after some conversation, she finally broke out the port bottle and glasses and asked if we minded her smoking. At her age, why not? Around the room were icons by Joanna Reitlinger and Gregory Krug and others who led the renaissance of icon painting early in the last century. There were also paintings of her home city of Strasbourg and one of her as a very young woman. And then quite a few photos of all the friends she treasured, really a who's who of important religious thinkers in the first half of the twentieth century: Lev Gillet and Sergius Bulgakov, Paul Evdokimov and Vladimir

Lossky, Metropolitan Evlogy, and Mother Maria and so many others. She knew them all, she said, gesturing toward all the images. She was aware that she had surely known some great people in her life.

Elisabeth's life was both colorful and untypical for a theologian. For much of it she did not teach theology. Rather, she administered a secondary school in the state system. A student of historian George Fedotov (noted for using historiographic methods for studying the lives of saints), she wrote a master's thesis that was one of the first Western efforts to examine the lives and outlooks of Russian saints. For most of her career as an educator, she was unable to devote herself to research and writing. Toward its end, however, she began what became a second career as a writer and teacher. She wrote a fascinating biography of her friend Lev Gillet.[2] Also later in life, she completed her doctoral dissertation on the nineteenth-century Russian theologian Alexander Bukharev. Later she wrote a number of biographical essays on him, Fr. Lev Gillet, and Mother Maria Skobtsova.[3] Eventually she collected all of her writing on women in the church.[4] She did an autobiographical piece as well, though she had to be nudged to write about herself and her own life.[5] Olga Lossky, herself a writer and the great-granddaughter of theologian Vladimir Lossky, was

---

[2] Elisabeth Behr-Sigel, *Lev Gillet: A Monk of the Eastern Church*, ed. Sergei Hackel, trans. Helen Wright (Oxford: Fellowship of St. Alban and St. Sergius, 1999).

[3] *Alexandre Boukharev—un théologien de l'église orthodoxe russe en dialogue avec le monde moderne* (Paris: Beauchesne, 1977); see also *Discerning the Signs of the Times: The Vision of Elisabeth Behr-Sigel*, ed. and trans. Michael Plekon and Sarah E. Hinlicky (Crestwood, NY: St. Vladimir's Seminary Press, 2001), 41–80.

[4] See the introduction to Elisabeth Behr-Sigel, *The Ministry of Women in the Church*, 2nd ed., trans. Steven Bigham (Crestwood, NY: St. Vladimir's Seminary Press, 2004), 1–24.

[5] We included it in *Discerning the Signs of the Times*, 5–11, as we did Lyn Breck's biographical essay, "Nearly a Century of Life," 125–36.

entrusted by Elisabeth's family with the task of organizing Elisabeth's papers. Olga became herself very close to Elisabeth in what would be the last years of her life. Both the papers and their many conversations helped Olga produce a magnificent biography.[6]

She eloquently sums up Elisabeth's personality and spiritual vision.

> "Let yourself be astonished," Elisabeth would say philosophically. "Thank God for the beauty of the world," she would add theologically. To examine one's life in order to discern the presence of God there—this was her dynamic depth. This was the spirit she showed throughout all her reflections in response to my questions whenever we met. Elisabeth grappled with the question of how it was possible to integrate the Gospel in one's life if one did not hear it in the Church's preaching. How could you live out Christ's words: "All will know that you are my disciples, if you love one another," if our divisions reached down even to our own bishops? How can there still be discrimination toward women, she wondered, women made in the image of God just like men? Surely one can review all the different dimensions which evolved in Elisabeth's work, in particular the dialogue among religions and the place of women in the church. But beyond all the specific themes, it seems to me that her principal, her unique contribution was anchored above all in what she saw as the one thing necessary, namely to go into the depths of oneself, to make one's being, with all one's singularity and personal history, permeable to Christ in order to witness to his existence to as many as possible. For me, this is really Elisabeth's legacy.[7]

---

[6] Olga Lossky, *Vers le jour dans déclin: une vie d'Élisabeth Behr-Sigel (1907–2005)* (Paris: Cerf, 2007), English translation, *Towards the Day without End: A Life of Elisabeth Behr-Sigel; 1907–2005*, trans. Jerry Ryan, ed. Michael Plekon (Notre Dame, IN: University of Notre Dame Press, 2010).

[7] "'Rendre son être permeable au Christ': Entretien avec Olga Lossky sur Elisabeth Behr-Sigel," *Contacts* 220 (2007); see also http://christophe.levalois.free.fr/fichier/Ent_Olga_Lossky.pdf.

A Life Permeable to Christ

Most of the concerns Elisabeth had, all of which became themes in her writing, are mentioned here. With her friends Paul Evdokimov and Lev Gillet, she did not so much see the church as the primary location of spiritual searching. Rather, as she experienced in her own life, it was the struggles of everyday existence—the challenges of a marriage, raising children—that were the primary arena of spiritual engagement. Then, given the historical period in which she lived, war and its accompanying terrors—oppression of ethnic and religious groups, torture—became realities of existence in the modern world with which one's faith had to deal. These were not just ideological causes but the real suffering of sisters and brothers. And all the struggles Elisabeth experienced as a woman in the church eventually made her one of the most insightful critics and commentators on gender and religion.

With Olga Lossky's fine biography, it is not necessary to retell Elisabeth's life story. Yet several elements of it help to flesh out her sense of finding and witnessing to God-permeability—in the world, in one's ordinary work, and the details of one's life.

From the start, Elisabeth lived a context of complexity, of mixed identities. Born in Schiltigheim in Alsace-Lorraine on July 21, 1907, she would always have both French and German language and cultural roots. Her mother was from a nonobservant Jewish background, her father likewise from a nonobservant Lutheran family. Yet Elisabeth was baptized in the Lutheran church, and her mother did pray with her every night. Later Elisabeth herself asked to be enrolled in classes in order to be confirmed. And while an undergraduate, she joined the World Christian Student Federation. From this point onward, she became a practicing church member.

She was in the first few classes of women allowed to study theology at Strasbourg. Meeting émigré Russian students there, she was powerfully drawn to the Orthodox Church and its liturgy. When she transferred to Paris, she went to Lutheran and Orthodox services on alternating Sundays. Eventually, before marrying Andre Behr, an émigré Russian engineering student, she was received into the Orthodox Church by Fr. Lev Gillet, himself a former Catholic Benedictine monk. He assured her that her Lutheran past would never be eclipsed by her entering the Orthodox faith, something Gillet himself believed about the communion of faith in the churches that transcended divisions. The vision of "one Lord, one faith, one baptism," of a unity that survives despite the historical divisions among the churches, was discovered by many notable figures as they experienced the person and the faith of Christians from other church bodies than their own. The émigré Russians encountered this among Roman Catholics and Protestants who welcomed and assisted them in Paris, but they also met the same with Anglicans who invited them to establish the very first ecumenical association, the Fellowship of St. Alban and St. Sergius in Great Britain. The list of those who came to see, as did Fr. Lev Gillet, the continuing unity of faith included Fr. Sergius Bulgakov, Lev Zander, Anton Kartashev, Nicholas Afanasiev, and Paul Evdokimov, among others. Later it would also include Yves Congar, the Chevetogne Benedictines, and Thomas Merton from the Catholic tradition, as well as Max Thurian and Brother Roger of Taizé. As noted in the prologue, the turns in my own life constitute an ecumenical pilgrimage through the churches, East and West, that have planted firmly in me this same vision of oneness in faith in the one Christ. When I met Elisabeth, she squeezed my arm as we were leaving her flat. Winking at me, an Orthodox priest, formerly a Lutheran pastor, she in turn assured me: "We'll always be Lutheran Christians, won't we?" This was enormously encouraging to me, something I will discuss further in a later chapter. But there is more in this amazing woman's life.

Upon completing her theological studies, Elisabeth was asked to do something most unusual. With the approval of the Orthodox archbishop, Evlogy, Fr. Lev Gillet, and Fr. Sergius

Bulgakov, she agreed to a request from the superintendent of the Reformed Church in Alsace. Well ahead of most other churches, that church body had, by synod decision in 1926, authorized women to serve both as assistants and as "consecrated," that is, fully ordained pastors. Thus, from 1931 to 1932, Elisabeth was "delegated," though not ordained, to serve as a "helping pastor" (*suffrageante/aide de pasteur*) in rural Ville-Climont.[8] This was an emergency situation, given the clergy shortage after the war, but it was at the urging of well-known ecumenically minded Pastor Marc Boegner. And it was a most significant moment in Elisabeth's experience, to be asked by the superintendent, supported both by Protestant and Orthodox clergy, and to be in a church body whose vision and decisions were decades ahead of their time for women serving in the ministry. As a "pastoral assistant," she preached and led Sunday services, taught Sunday church school, visited the sick and elderly, and buried the dead. She was not allowed to celebrate the sacraments or marry. But she was otherwise in reality the only pastor these rural parishioners had. Years later, when I met her, Elisabeth still treasured this experience of pastoral ministry, something not fully available to Lutheran women at the time and still not fully possible in the Orthodox Church.

Ecumenical almost from the start, Elisabeth naturally joined the Russian Christian Students Movement and was close to many of the major figures of the "Paris school," an ecumenically minded and progressive group of émigré Russian scholars teaching at St. Sergius Institute in Paris between the wars. Later she also joined the first ever ecumenical association, the Anglican-Orthodox Fellowship of St. Alban and St. Sergius. She and her husband, along with the Losskys, Evdokimovs, and other notable members of the Paris émigré community,

---

[8] Elisabeth Parmentier, "Elisabeth Behr-Sigel's Ecumenical Formation in Strasbourg," paper given at the September 2011 conference on Elisabeth Behr-Sigel at The Institute for Ecumenical Research in Strasbourg, http://www.strasbourginstitute.org/en/elisabeth-behr-sigel-conference/.

founded the first French-speaking Orthodox parish there, with Lev Gillet as their pastor.

Elisabeth's experience of ministry as a woman and as a Christian straddling two different churches was pivotal. It shaped how she viewed all of the Christian faith, certainly the churches, but even more importantly, how one lived out the Gospel. For us, here in this book, this vision is a great gift. Although the rules and the church divisions and barriers did not disappear, she was able to see that in our time, these could no longer stop the passion for doing the work of Christ, whether hiding those pursued by the Nazi occupiers or later the victims of torture.

Eventually she and André moved to Nancy where he worked as an engineer, and Elisabeth continued her career as an educator and administrator. They had three children, two daughters and a son. During World War II the ecumenical group to which they belonged became part of the resistance, sheltering those fleeing Nazi persecution in the time of occupation, Jewish people in particular.

Elisabeth had begun writing before the war.[9] Her first major work did not come out, however, until after the war.[10] Yet, even in her early work, she was intent on Fedotov's aim of seeing the human, the ordinary, in the lives of persons of faith.[11] Her early focus was what Western readers could learn from the Eastern church saints.[12] It was in what would be the last de-

---

[9] "La sophiologie du Père Serge Boulgakoff," *Revue d'histoire et de philosophie religieuses* 2 (1939): 130–48, republished in *Le messager orthodoxe* 57, no. 1 (1972): 21–48.

[10] *Prière et sainteté dans l'Église russe* (Paris: Cerf, 1950, rev. ed. Bellefontaine, 1982).

[11] "Notes sur l'idée russe de la sainteté d'aprés les saints canonisés de l'Église russe," *Revue d'histoire et de philosophie religieuses* (1933): 537–54; "Études d'hagiographie russe," *Irénikon* 12, 13, 14 (1935–1937): 242–54, 225–37, 363–77.

[12] Elisabeth Behr-Sigel, *The Place of the Heart: An Introduction to Orthodox Spirituality*, trans. Stephen Bigham (Torrance, CA/Crestwood, NY: Oakwood/St. Vladimir's Seminary Press, 1992).

cades of a long life, however, that she turned to what would make her best known, namely numerous lectures and papers, eventually all collected and published, on the place and the role of women in the church.[13] This was followed by her last work, the question of the ordination of women in the Orthodox Church.[14] On her ninety-third birthday, in 2003, a substantial collection of essays was published in her honor.[15]

The Place of Women in the Church

Consistent with the aim of bringing historical study to the lives of persons of faith, Elisabeth painstakingly combed through the New Testament and patristic literature to trace the roles of women in Jesus' ministry. She found that early on, the communities established by Paul knew no discrimination on the basis of gender. Women and men were heads of household-based church groups. Women as well as men were called "coworkers" in the Gospel by Paul—Thekla, Phoebe, Lydia, Junia. Women disciples worked with others in supporting the ministry of Jesus. A number of these were the first to witness the empty tomb and resurrection and became the "apostles to the apostles." There were subsequently, even after the exclusion of women from ministry, great examples of proclaiming the Gospel by such figures as Nina of Georgia, Juliana the Merciful in Russia, and in our own time, Mother Maria Skobtsova of Paris. Eventually, so notable a theological voice as Kallistos Ware would concur with Elisabeth—that there really are no dogmatic or doctrinal obstacles to the ordination and service

---

[13] Behr-Sigel, *Ministry of Women in the Church*.

[14] Elisabeth Behr-Sigel and Kallistos Ware, *The Ordination of Women in the Orthodox Church* (Geneva: WCC, 2000).

[15] *"Toi, suis-moi": Mélanges offerts en hommage á Élisabeth Behr-Sigel* par la Fraternité Saint-Élie, ed. le Carmel de Saint-Rémy/Stânceni (Iaşi: Editura Trinitas, 2003), 25–44. The bibliography, which extends only to 2003, includes seven books, over one hundred articles and another two hundred essays and reviews.

of women in the church, something churches of the Reformation have now realized for over a century.

All of Elisabeth's writings on women in the church are translated and accessible. She remains one of the major voices on women in the church and in ministry. But the record of her own life is also an important text. For years, Elisabeth struggled with her husband's alcoholism and depression, often maintaining the family and an income completely on her own. After his death, with her children grown, she was able to devote herself to writing, lecturing, and activism. She became an important voice for the Orthodox in the World Council of Churches, participating in the important consultations on women in the church at Agapia, Romania in 1976 and in 1981 in Sheffield. She was a signer of a petition asking the Ecumenical Patriarchate to consider the restoration of the diaconate to women. Elisabeth also was the vice president of the Christian Movement for the Abolition of Torture (ACAT) and a consultant to the French Orthodox Bishops Conference. In 2003, she was chosen to give the keynote lecture at the annual meeting of the Orthodox Theological Society of America.[16] She was present in Paris on May 1 and 2, 2004, for the canonization services of her friend Mother Maria Skobtsova and her companions.[17] During the Nazi occupation of France from 1940 to 1945, Elisabeth and her friends in the ecumenical circle had helped get people out of Paris and into the countryside where they could be concealed from Gestapo roundups and internment in concentration camps. This included Jewish people as well as members of the Resistance, members of left-wing political parties, and others who were targets of annihilation by the Nazis.

---

[16] "The Ordination of Women: A Point of Contention in Ecumenical Dialogue," *St Vladimir's Theological Quarterly* 48, no. 1 (2004): 49–66.

[17] Jim Forest has a photo of Elisabeth after the services holding several prints of the icons of the new saints, a few of which she sent me: http://www.flickr.com/photos/jimforest/sets/164907/. We will get to know Mother Maria well in another chapter of this book.

Elisabeth remained active in her later years despite failing health.[18] She herself was a living icon of what the Gospel looks like, enacted. As a woman she was a pioneer, not only as a theologian but also in ministry. Elisabeth wrote about the encounter of the church with the world, but even more so, she incarnated it in her life. A favorite phrase of Paul Evdokimov was that we are not only to say prayers but also to *become* what we pray, become prayer incarnate. I think Olga Lossky, quoted earlier, put it well. Elisabeth was about making oneself open, transparent, permeable to Christ in order to present him to others. This she did not only in her lecturing and writing but also in every other aspect of her long life.

Looking back on her legacy, one is tempted to emphasize her concern with the place and the ministry of women in the church. This, however, does not exhaust her vision. In fact, this concern in her writing and lecturing is linked to several other aspects of her vision. As we have seen, the principal features of her vision is both ecclesial and personal. She is consistent that the church needs to be both in dialogue with and in service of the world—that is, "discerning the signs of the times." And this happened through every aspect of one's life, in one's permeability to Christ, the possibility of holiness everywhere.

The Church in Service of the World

While Elisabeth does not deal with the church in a detailed and sustained manner as did, for example, Nicholas Afanasiev, she nevertheless has the constant sensitivity to the "churching" of the world, as her friends in the Russian Christian Student

---

[18] I have a last letter from her from the United Kingdom dated November 12, 2005, just two weeks before her death. In it (typically) she laments a number of things, including not being able to present the lecture in Oxford and also her diminishing energy and age. ("I am a tired old woman.") But she also discussed, as usual, various publishing projects, as well as unfortunate situations in the churches.

Movement called it. This was the relating of everything back to the kingdom among us, as Alexander Schmemann put it.[19] Her own friends, Sergius Bulgakov and Lev Gillet as well as Alexander Bukharev, whom she wrote about, all left an imprint on her thinking. As Olga Lossky observed, the relationship of the world and every person to Christ is the central strand of her writing, whether the tracking of the Russian forms of holiness and spirituality as evidenced in the lives and sayings of holy people or the insistence on the mission of the church in and "for the life of the world."

The conversation that Bukharev sought to establish, back in the mid-nineteenth century, between the church's tradition and the consciousness of modern people—this she followed up not only in the saints, such as Mother Maria Skobtsova, but also in the pastoral openness of her friends Paul Evdokimov and Lev Gillet to the suffering of Christians of other churches and to those without any belief. She affirms this, forcefully, in her study of Bukharev. It is well worth listening to her on this.

> Bukharev's free-flowing theological reflection rooted in the tradition of the Church along with his personal spiritual experience allowed his early intuition to deepen. "God is love," . . . [he] proclaimed with the Apostle John. His love is a love of generosity or mercy that never ceases to flow out on creation to sustain it, restore it to its original beauty since its fall. This love is also a crucified love offered from the beginning and victorious in its self-giving. This is a love which is entirely concentrated on and revealed in Christ Jesus whose name, wrote Bukharev's first biographer, "never left his lips." The Lord upon whose face Bukharev gazed looked like the Christ in the Rublev icons. It was the object of contemplation for the young monk,

---

[19] Alexis Kniazeff, "L'ecclésialisation de la vie," *La pensée orthodoxe* 4 (1987): 108–35. Also see Alexander Schmemann, *For the Life of the World* (Crestwood, NY: St. Vladimir's Seminary Press, 1973), and Nicholas Afanasiev, *The Church of the Holy Spirit*, trans. Vitaly Permiakov, ed. Michael Plekon (Notre Dame, IN: University of Notre Dame Press, 2007).

a divine and human face filled with both gentleness and an infinite majesty, radiating a love stronger than death. It is in the radiance of this face that Bukharev invited an encounter with each man and woman across time, from ancient history to our contemporary world. He characterized modern man as enclosed in his own hell, in a universe of things which have become opaque to the divine light shining in the darkness that the darkness cannot overcome. The person of today is walled off, in an almost autistic way, incapable of a real dialogue with the other. Today, to become one with Christ means descending into this hell armed only with the weapons of faith, hope, and compassionate love, Bukharev affirmed. Neither crusades against the modern world nor flight nor prostration before it will change its course, but simply interior illumination enlightened by the light that lights all men coming into the world. This is the task of people of action and reflection who likewise engage in contemplation. He refers to spiritual beings who are married couples, engaged in professions, workers in the city who work with the supreme worker, servants of communion with him who wanted to be among us as one who serves. "Teach us to search out and to discover in our respective professions the divine meaning," writes a modern Orthodox monk in the same spirit. "Transform our work into a service and a gift." Such a life means to pray without ceasing and to give thanks for all things. Taking up an Old Testament command, Bukharev invites followers of Christ to "cast aside the Egyptian" (Ex. 3:22) which means to convert the idolatrous culture to its true divine-human calling: worship of the living God through service to others. Enlivened and sanctified by the Spirit, the most humble expression of work becomes noble, and the work of thinker and artist alike become eucharistic offerings of thought and action oriented towards a constant goal of the final accomplishment when God will be all in all.[20]

---

[20] *Discerning the Signs of the Times*, 76–77 (translation modified). Also see Paul Valliere, *Modern Russian Theology: Soloviev, Bukharev, Bulgakov* (Grand Rapids, MI: Eerdmans, 2000).

In this passage she echoes her friend Fr. Lev, who must have been a contemporary image of Bukharev—a person of strong emotions, often depressed and discouraged but also able to welcome any person, regardless of religious background or personal situation. In the same article she mentions by name another friend, Paul Evdokimov, whose writings about living out the Gospel in the world, about becoming what one prays in every part of everyday life, also made him a contemporary reflection of Bukharev's vision. We will encounter both of these friends of Elisabeth in other chapters of this book.

It is very much a worldly spirituality that Elisabeth presents and recommends. It is a following of Christ she knew firsthand, from her own life—struggling with a husband crippled by his illness and addiction, supporting the family financially, raising her children and postponing her own work. We also need to recall that much of this was lived during the Great Depression, not just during World War II and the German occupation of France. We know that Elisabeth and other of her friends helped Jewish neighbors and others who were targets of Nazi annihilation get out of Paris and into a network of Resistance members and others who would move them into safer hiding places.

In the Eastern church icon of the resurrection, we see what the West calls the "harrowing of hell." Christ does not simply rise up out of the tomb. Rather, the Risen One descends into hell, searching for his own, to take Adam and Eve and all their children from death to life, a new life. This, for her, was not just the Eastern church's fascination with the Easter rising of Jesus, it was the image of what baptism and the Eucharist, of what the life of faith looked like every day. Both Easter and Pentecost are permanent, perpetual. Life winning over death, heaven putting hell down—not just after death, in some mysterious premium paid after a life of virtuous living. Rather, "paradise is all around," as Thomas Merton writes. The kingdom of heaven is not off in the distant future beyond the grave.

If it is real and powerful, it is so here and now, this Monday morning when I return to work, this afternoon when the children are picked up, this evening when after all the day's demands, supper must be put together.

As for Mother Maria Skobtsova, the "churching" of life, for Elisabeth, was not about hanging up more icons or crosses on one's walls or lighting more candles before them, or even reading more prayers or volumes of spiritual writers. "Churching" meant to keep connecting Christ with the present, with the fellow workers, the students, the neighbors shopping with me in the supermarket.

The aim of "churching" the world is connected directly to the question of what the work of the church in the world is. This work is none other than that of Christ himself, the incarnation being the divine plan for the restoration of creature to the Creator, the redeeming of what was first made good and beautiful, in the very "image and likeness" of God.[21] And knowing that in the Russian tradition great ascetic saints were characterized as *prepodobny*—"very much like . . . similar to" God, the focus of Elisabeth's vision is clear. To become permeable to Christ is to see Christ everywhere, for all of life to become transparent to God.

When I think of how such a little woman as Elisabeth was, in her later years, I realize how huge her impact was, for all the subordination and neglect she experienced as a woman, both in society and in the church, for most of the last century. When she names some of the great women of the faith, I can only add her name to the list.

---

[21] See Walter Kasper, *Mercy: The Essence of the Gospel and the Key to Christian Life*, trans. William Madges (Mahwah, NJ: Paulist Press, 2014); Rowan Williams, *Being Christian: Baptism, Bible, Eucharist, Prayer* (Grand Rapids, MI: Eerdmans, 2014); Francis, *The Church of Mercy: A Vision for the Church* (Chicago: Loyola Press, 2014); James Carroll, *Christ Actually* (New York: Viking Adult, 2014).

The greatest of souls in the ancient Church recognized that the hierarchy of spiritual gifts had nothing at all to do with sex. The apostle Paul, for instance, counted among his closest collaborators in apostolic work women such as Phoebe, Priscilla, Junia, and the others named in his epistles. Basil the Great of Caesarea and Gregory of Nyssa called their sister Macrina their *didaskalos*, their master or teacher. For these brothers in their youth, she played the role, as they said, of "mother and father" at the same time. The cultural context of the age did not permit any institutional expression of such a recognized spiritual equality. Today the cultural context is much more favorable, at least in the West. Orthodoxy ought not to remain a stranger to this, as Metropolitan John Zizioulas notes. The mission of a "Western Orthodoxy," he affirms, is to "reconnect Tradition to the problems of modern Western humanity which are, for that matter, more and more the problems of humanity in the global dimension." Among the problems of modern Western man, one of the most important concerns the restoration of an authentic partnership, a true reciprocity, without loss of their identity, between men and women.[22]

Love for God, Love for the World

For Elisabeth, the issue of the ministry and place of women in the Church was never the only issue for theology in our time.[23] It was but one of a number of issues that raised the question of what really was the "tradition" of the Church—an unchanging perspective in everything or a dynamic, living vision guided by the Spirit, the "mind of Christ" that always

---

[22] Elisabeth Behr-Sigel, "The Ordination of Women: Also a Question for the Orthodox Churches," in Behr-Sigel and Ware, *The Ordination of Women in the Orthodox Church*, 43.

[23] See also the Florovsky Lecture, delivered not long before her death: "The Ordination of Women: A Point of Contention in Ecumenical Dialogue," http://orthodoxcircle.com/blog/2401/the-ordination-of-women-a-point-of-contention-in-ecumenical-dialogue-by-eli/.

"tested the spirits to discern whether they were of God" and the kingdom. This would include how the church relates to other religious traditions—no small matter today with respect to Islam. It would also force us to consider how embracing the church is (or is not) to all sisters and brothers, no matter their sexual identity or political perspective. The easiest move is, in the name of religious freedom, to divide, to exclude, to condemn. But Elisabeth's experience of the last century's wars, economic depressions, suspicions, hatreds, even torture of supposed enemies, only emboldened her conviction that the Gospel brings together, unites, forgives, establishes peace among us. These "gifts" of the Spirit can never be matters of compulsion or law (Gal 5:22–6:10).

But does this theological view of Elisabeth not succumb to the critique of many Christian initiatives of the past several decades, namely, that it is a concession to culture, that the world itself is dictating what the church should believe, teach, and do? How could this be the stance of one who not only saw the horrors of two world wars, the Nazi occupation and the Holocaust, and the innumerable local conflicts that employed both torture and genocide as in Africa but also watched the witness of a Maria Skobtsova, a person of faith in the resurrection, "whose joy and triumph the Eastern Church sings of on Easter like no other"?[24] The newness and vitality of faith is evident in what she said at the inauguration of the Cambridge University Institute of Orthodox Christian Studies:

> Does the Church's teaching change, is it called upon to change with the centuries? . . . Divine truth transcends time. The letter to the Hebrews proclaims "Jesus Christ, the same yesterday, today and forever" (13:8). And the apostle Paul exhorts the Christians "not to be like children tossed to and fro by every wind of doctrine" (4:14). . . . The task of . . . theological formation, it seems to me, is both ever the same and yet always

---

[24] Behr-Sigel, *Lev Gillet*, 129.

new, always being renewed. It consists in the faithful transmission (an action not "rational" but "intelligent," in the sense of being the "Eucharist of the mind"), of the evangelical kerygma, of the original apostolic message. To be living, this transmission, this Tradition (giving the term its active meaning) must, in fidelity to the original and fundamental message, attempt to find answers to the new questions asked of the Church in its new circumstances.[25]

When I think back on Elisabeth, I do not see an elderly woman at all. Rather, I remember someone so full of spirit and wit and energy that she could barely contain herself. She enjoyed a good drink, delighted in her friends and in lively debate and conversation. She could be persistent in letting you know what she thought. She was "forever young." Grateful for the past—you could see this in the gallery of photos of friends mounted on the walls of her apartment and her home icon screen—she was not at all trapped in it or suspicious of the world around her. She simply refused to become myopic and rigid as the years piled up. Precisely because of this, she was sought after by many young enough to be her great-grandchildren—people like Olga Lossky. This careful, questioning attitude, plus her amazing openness and energy, are more than personal qualities to admire. I really think they are virtues, ways of living to imitate as we try to find our own ways in the spiritual life.

There is, in the Christian tradition, both the paths of flight from the world and the embracing of the world. Sometimes, the flight was accompanied by fear of things worldly, even contempt—*contemptus mundi*—for the world, for marriage, family, sexuality, wealth, power, culture. It would not at all be accurate, however, to characterize this movement as completely negative and otherworldly. Many desert mothers and fathers and later imitators of their ascetic athleticism kept open

---

[25] *Discerning the Signs of the Times*, 12–14.

the doors of their communities to the sorrowing and suffering, the poor, and those seeking God. Both Elisabeth Behr-Sigel and her coworker, Maria Skobtsova, would chronicle the exemplary lives of holy women and men, particularly in the Slavic traditions, who both loved God and their neighbors.

Elisabeth Behr-Sigel's pattern, the takeaway for us, is one of *amor mundi*—of love and care for the world about us. She consistently embodied the action of God in Christ's incarnation. She made herself "permeable to Christ," and through Christ, loved and served the world.

Mother Maria Skobtsova
Photo from Antoine Arjakovsky.

Chapter 2

"The Sacrament of the Brother/Sister": Mother Maria Skobtsova

The way to God lies through love of people. At the Last Judgment I shall not be asked whether I was successful in my ascetic exercises, nor how many bows and prostrations I made. Instead I shall be asked, "Did I feed the hungry, clothe the naked, visit the sick and the prisoners?" That is all I shall be asked. About every poor, hungry and imprisoned person the Savior says "I": "was hungry and thirsty, I was sick and in prison." To think that he puts an equal sign between himself and anyone in need.[1]

Powerful Women

The figure of Dorothy Day has become more familiar in the past few years. We know of her being arrested for refusing to obey civil defense air raid drills back during the Cold War. We have seen the photo of her sitting about to be arrested for protest in solidarity with Cesar Chavez and the United Farm Workers in their union struggle.[2] There are her trips down

---

[1] "Pravoslavnoe Delo," *Orthodox Action* (1939): 30, cited by Sergei Hackel, *Pearl of Great Price* (Crestwood, NY: St. Vladimir's Seminary Press, 1981), 29–30, from Constantine Mochulsky, "Monakhina Mariia Skobtsova," *Tretii Chas* 1 (1946): 70–71.

[2] The most complete biography and collection of images of Dorothy Day is Jim Forest, *All Is Grace: A Biography of Dorothy Day* (Maryknoll, NY: Orbis Books, 2011).

South and her support of the civil rights movement, as well as her pilgrimage to Rome for peace. Dorothy was known for her ongoing opposition to war, culminating in the movement against the war in Vietnam. Robert Ellsberg's tireless editing of her letters, her diary, and anthologies of her writings have filled in the image of this writer and activist as profoundly rooted in Christian faith.[3]

She prayed the Daily Office, attended Mass, and communed every day she could. She read and constantly quoted the great Christian writers and saints. Dorothy was the fearless critic of bishops and the rest of the institutional church. But all of this work went on as she lived and participated every day in feeding hungry people, bringing in the homeless, helping bathe and clothe them in the houses of the Catholic Worker movement. Her descriptions of people lined up in the early morning winter cold for a cup of coffee and a couple slices of bread and jam, her description of the tattered, ill street people who came to Worker houses in desperation—these are among the most powerful of her writings. She has been promoted for and still is in the official process toward canonization in the Catholic Church.

For nearly the first twenty years of her endeavors at the Catholic Worker houses, she had an exact contemporary, doing much the same, but an ocean away, in Paris. This was a nun who had been married twice, had three children and then sought the habit and vows from her archbishop in the Russian Orthodox archdiocese headquartered in Paris. From her days in the Russian Christian Students Movement (RCSM) she inherited a similar combination of life defined by prayer and work. With the older order gone, there was a freedom for these émigrés to reinvent the entire experience of faith and life. Of

---

[3] Robert Ellsberg, ed., *The Duty of Delight: The Diaries of Dorothy Day*, and *All the Way to Heaven: The Selected Letters of Dorothy Day* (Milwaukee, WI: Marquette University Press, 2008, 2010).

special importance was the commitment to putting faith into practice, a focus on faith in everyday life—exactly the perspective of this book. Those advising and guiding the movement coined an expression, that while a bit awkward in English, nevertheless was powerful in the original Russian. They spoke of "churching" (*votserkovlenlie*). The term, however, was easily misunderstood. Here is Maria Skobtsova's attempt at correcting the misinterpretation of it:

> Indeed, must we attend all the church services in order to "church" our life? Or hang an icon in every room and burn an icon-lamp in front of it? No, the "churching of life" is the realization of the whole world as one great church, adorned with icons—persons who should be venerated, honored, and loved, because these icons are true images of God that have the holiness of the Living God within them.[4]

A Complicated Woman

Mother Maria, her name taken when she became a nun, was born Elizaveta Pilenko, in 1891, in Riga. She was a precocious child, gifted in drawing, painting, and poetry. Her literary talents drew her into the circles of Alexander Blok and Vyacheslav Ivanov. She was the first female mayor of her family's country hometown, Anapa, on the Black Sea. Politically engaged, her loyalties shifted in the turbulent first decades of the twentieth century. She was put on trial by the retreating White Army but was exonerated (the Whites initially assumed that a woman in the office of mayor had to have been a Bolshevik and thus their enemy). She also came close to execution by the Bolsheviks as a counterrevolutionary. Only a

---

[4] Maria Skobtsova, "The Mysticism of Human Communion," in *Mother Maria Skobtsova: Essential Writings* (Maryknoll, NY: Orbis Books, 2002), 78–79. See also Alexis Kniazeff, "L'ecclésialisation de la vie," *La Pensée Orthodoxe* 4 (1987): 108–35.

feigned connection to Lenin's wife saved her in the latter case. An early marriage ended in divorce, as did a second with the White Army officer Daniel Skobtsov, who was on the military tribunal that tried her. Three children, Gaiana, Nastia, and Yuri, came from these marriages. She would lose Nastia as a child to meningitis. Gaiana died as a young adult back in Russia, and Youri was sent to a Nazi work camp, which led to premature death. Here is what Alexander Schmemann said about her in one of his broadcasts for Radio Liberty years later:

> In those years I personally knew Mother Maria, and often visited her. An old house on a poor and run-down Paris lane, a tiny courtyard, a few scraggly trees, an old garage in the back turned into a chapel. . . . In the house day and night: crowds, activity, the poor, ragged, unemployed, forgotten and abandoned. Everyone is being fed, attempts made to find work for all, and mainly—everyone is received with love and brotherliness. In the middle of everything, a large red-cheeked, always smiling woman in monastic garb, flitting about in some unstoppable, seamless action. She is making soup in the kitchen, sweeping stairs, painting icons on the damp walls of the garage-chapel, embroidering vestments, and in the evenings sitting in the half-lit sparse living room, greedily absorbing a passionately debated lecture. What a panoply of stars met on those evenings: that's where I will always recall the Assyrian head of Berdyayev, the scraping voice—he had throat cancer—of Father Sergius Bulgakov, the fragile, tender, kind countenance of Constantine Vasilievich Mochulsky. Soup, the poor, hospitality—all this was during the daytime, but at evening—the deep problems of life, poetry, and culture. She sits embroidering under a lamp, and her vestments are always bright, paschal, radiant with flowers. There was not one iota here of anything formal or sanctimonious, or rigoristic, but always the lightness and joy of love, the freedom of faith.[5]

---

[5] Alexander Schmemann, *Sunday Talks*, Radio Liberty, trans. Alexis Vinogradov.

Mother Maria was a brilliant, forceful, and driven personality. Drawn to assist the poor and suffering in the émigré settlements of France, she asked for and received monastic tonsure and habit from the archbishop Evlogy after the end of her second marriage. He told her that the world and its suffering people would now become her monastery. First in Villa de Saxe, then in Rue de Lourmel, and with a nursing home further out in Noisy-le-Grand, she created houses of hospitality where meals, shelter, fellowship, and counsel were available to anyone in need.

In every one of these hostels, the chapel was the heart of the house and of service to the neighbor. Maria spent much time shopping and cooking for her people, but she also made beautiful vestments and icons for the chapel. There was a continuity from the table of the Lord to the table she set for the hungry who lived in her hostel. The sacrament of the Eucharist and the sacrament of the communal meal were intrinsically connected. She was always a participant in the liturgy but would leave other services early or miss them entirely to assure there was food on the table.

She saw no opposition between Mary and Martha, no distinction between the love of God and of neighbor. The two great Gospel commandments were for her just one invitation to love, and this unity of love is the dominant theme not only in her writing but also her life. I would say she gives among the most eloquent expression in our time for how to put one's faith into practice, how to show love for God in love for the sister or brother in need.

> Christ gave us two commandments: to love God and to love our fellow man. Everything else . . . is merely an elaboration of these two commandments, which contain within themselves the totality of Christ's "Good News." . . . And it is remarkable that their truth is found only in the way they are linked together. Love for man alone leads us into the blind alley of an anti-Christian humanism, out of which the only exit is, at times,

the rejection of the individual human being and love toward him in the name of all mankind. Love for God without love for man, however, is condemned: "Those who say, 'I love God,' and hate their brothers or sisters are liars" (1 John 4:20).[6]

The World as Monastery, Holiness in the World

Mother Maria's life received its best accounting in Sergei Hackel's biography.[7] It has also been covered by Hélène Arjakovsky-Klepinine, Elisabeth Behr-Sigel, Jim Forest, in a revealing memoir by Dominique DeSantis, and by Paul Ladouceur's collection.[8] DeSantis vividly recreates the complex personality of this gifted woman, someone eager to convince others of her ideas, to the point of hounding them. But we also encounter a fragile soul, a life with much loss, pain, and guilt.

Maria was at heart an artist, and she had to keep the life of the mind and spirit alive. Thus she also sponsored regular gatherings, salons, at the Rue de Lourmel hostel, with the luminaries of the Russian émigré community participating—Berdyaev, Bulgakov, Mochulsky, and many others, as Schmemann described. DeSantis gives a vivid account of the night on which she, as a teenager, and her boyfriend went to one of these gatherings, there meeting Mother Maria for the first time, surrounded by all those gigantic intellects; it was a wall of

---

[6] *Mother Maria Skobtsova: Essential Writings*, 173–74.

[7] Hackel, *Pearl of Great Price*.

[8] Hélène Arjakovsky-Klepinine, "Le joie du don," in *Le sacrement du frère* (Paris: Cerf, 2001), 15–69; Elisabeth Behr-Sigel, "Mother Maria Skobtsova 1891–1945," in *Discerning the Signs of the Times*, ed. and trans. Michael Plekon and Sarah E. Hinlicky (Crestwood, NY: St. Vladimir's Seminary Press, 2001), 41–54; Jim Forest, "Mother Maria of Paris," in *Mother Maria Skobtsova: Essential Writings*, 13–42; Dominique DeSantis, *La Sainte et l'Incroyante. Ma rencontre avec Mère Marie* (Paris: Bayard, 2007); Sainte Marie de Paris (Mere Marie Skobtsov, 1891–1945), *Le jour du Saint-Esprit*, ed. Paul Ladouceur, trans. Hélène Arjakovsky-Klépinine, Françoise Lhoest, Bertrand Jeuffrain, Alexandre Nicolsky, Nikita Struve, and Jérôme Lefert (Paris: Cerf, 2011).

noisy debate and conversation, but so exciting, she had to keep returning. A few film clips made by the YMCA, which supported her work, capture the lively eyes, the face of a woman whose passion for life and art was incandescent.

The essays from which selections are taken here stem from an ongoing debate about what shape the Christian life should take, one in which she engaged in print with, among others, Fr. Sergius Chetverikov, chaplain of the Russian Christian Student Movement.[9] Then, as today, her ideas are incendiary. Over against the very traditional piety Chetverikov encouraged, focused on personal prayer rules, asceticism, liturgical services, and, in particular, the linkage of church, faith, and Russian identity, Mother Maria's rebuttal is radical, even ruthless. In an essay, "A Justification of Pharisaism," she rejects the subservience of the church to any political authority, any ethnic or cultural context.[10] She thus condemns the subordination of the Russian Church under not only Peter the Great but also all other rulers and governments, the Soviet included.

Mother Maria rejects the myth of "holy Russia" while at the same time revering the great saints of the tradition. She bases the commandment of radical love for the neighbor in the first place on the gospels but then on the exemplary lives of such giants as of Nilus of Sora, Sergius of Radonezh, and Seraphim of Sarov. She points especially to Joseph of Volokholamsk's ideal of "non-possession." She notes the desert monastics' care for those in need as well as the work of the later monasteries serving the poor and suffering. In light of these, she is sharply critical of the monastic life of her time. She had visited several traditional women's monasteries in Estonia and Latvia not

---

[9] Antoine Arjakovsky covers Maria's distinctive personality and work in his study, *The Way: Russian Religious Thinkers of the Emigration and Their Journal; 1925–1940*, trans. Jerry Ryan, ed. John A. Jillions and Michael Plekon (Notre Dame, IN: University of Notre Dame Press, 2013).

[10] *Mother Maria Skobtsova: Essential Writings*, 114–20.

closed by the Soviets. These valued isolation from the world and pursued a comfortable life while most in the cities nearly starved. She could only see in their way of life a privileged and individualistic pursuit of holiness and an unhealthy obsession with rules and details of tradition, characteristics of Orthodox piety that she would tear apart in the essay "Types of Religious Lives" as having nothing to do with Christ or his Gospel.[11]

Yet she has many constructive contributions too, all of them rooted in her vision of the incarnation as God embracing humanity with the invitation to us to do the same. This affirmative view is to be found in essays such as "The Second Gospel Commandment," "Love without Limits," and very powerfully in her essay "On the Imitation of the Mother of God."[12] The incarnation, God's becoming human through the Virgin Mary, was her dogmatic foundation. The incarnation must then be lived out, put into practice by those who bear the name of Christ. In so doing they continue Christ's work. They "Christify," bring all creation into Christ.[13]

It is a distinctive feature of Mother Maria's vision that she does not stop with a focus on Christ but also stresses the model that the Mother of God offers, one that the New Testament, for its few references to her, nevertheless also emphasizes. Every person is not only another Christ but also an image of the Mother of God.

> [I]nsofar as we must strive to follow her path, and as her image is the image of our human soul, so we must also perceive God and the Son in every person—God, because each person is the image and likeness of God; the Son, because as it gives birth to

---

[11] Ibid., 88–101.

[12] Ibid., 43–58, 94–101, 59–72. Lev Gillet, who also spoke of God as "Love without Limits," was one of the chaplains of her Rue de Lourmel hostel.

[13] Ibid., 181–84.

Christ within itself, the human soul thereby adopts the whole Body of Christ for itself, the whole of God's humanity, and every person individually.[14]

In July 1942, almost seven thousand Jewish citizens, over four thousand of these children, were rounded up by the Vichy government as part of the Reich's infamous "solution" of the "Jewish problem." They were held in summer heat at the Velodrome d'Hiver, a cycling stadium in Paris, without food and limited water and facilities. Mother Maria was there day and night, bringing food, consoling, according to reports, smuggling out some very young children in garbage pails.[15]

One of her chaplains, Fr. Cyprian Kern, found her personality and way of life very much at odds with ecclesial tradition, while another, Fr. Lev Gillet, recognized in it the very work of Christ and joined her activity, accompanying her to the neighborhood bars to offer shelter to those hanging out there until closing time. The same was true for her last chaplain, Fr. Dmitri Klepinine. And when the Gestapo came to arrest her for hiding Jewish people in her hostels, they took Fr. Dmitri off as well, for he had completed baptismal certificates to protect them and defied the interrogating officer by pointing out Jesus' Jewishness. Both Mother Maria and Fr. Dmitri (as well as Yuri, her son) died in Nazi camps, the men from dysentery and pneumonia and slave labor, she volunteering to take the place of another woman being sent to the gas chambers on March 31, 1945, Western Holy Saturday, just weeks before Ravensbrück's liberation by the Allies. In 2004 the four were made saints by the archdiocese of the Russian Orthodox Church in Western Europe.

---

[14] Ibid., 68–69 (translation modified).
[15] See Jim Forest's exquisite children's book on this, *Silent as a Stone: Mother Maria of Paris and the Trash Can Rescue* (Crestwood, NY: St. Vladimir's Seminary Press, 2007).

While Mother Maria's urgent sense of the Gospel command to love and serve the neighbor might appear to have dominated her activity, this is not accurate. She continued her primary craft of writing, and the YMCA Press in Paris has published collected volumes of her essays, poems, plays, and other pieces. A parish in Paris has collected the icons and vestments she embroidered and painted.[16] Her rambunctious personality, nonconformist life, and radical dedication to serving the poor seem to be the stuff of which heroes are made. It was not necessarily viewed as such in her own time and milieu. Several of her colleagues who were quite sympathetic and supportive of her efforts had, at best, mixed feelings about her and her work. To still others she was a scandal, with her explosive demeanor and ragamuffin crew. Few came to her defense when she was arrested by the Gestapo. Today her writings still evoke criticism, and the process for ecclesiastical recognition of her witness and holiness has met with silence and inaction. The late Metropolitan Anthony Bloom has written that in his youth and pride, he was embarrassed by her life and work. Yet he had the courage to recognize both her idiosyncrasies and her witness, calling her a "saint of our day and for our day."[17]

The "Liturgy outside the Church"
Celebrating the "Sacrament of the Brother/Sister" in Need

Mother Maria knew and wrote about the impossibility of celebrating the liturgy without also celebrating the "liturgy outside the church," called by some, "the liturgy after the liturgy," an idea expressed powerfully by John Chrysostom.[18]

---

[16] For many icons and photos of Mother Maria, as well as of her embroideries and icons and of her canonization services see, https://www.flickr.com/photos/jimforest/sets/72157594152181792/.

[17] Hackel, *Pearl of Great Price*, xi–xii.

[18] John Chrysostom, *Homily 50 on Matthew*, 3–4, PG 58, 508–9.

"The sacrament of the brother and sister" was celebrated not on the eucharistic altar of gold or stone but now on the altar of human hearts. There could only be a liturgy that embraced the whole world and all people in praying for the peace from above, for the unity of all, feasting on the bread and cup of life.[19]

> Just as fascinating, though enigmatic, for us is the expression "liturgy outside the church." . . . [It] is our sacrificial ministry in the church of the world, adorned with living icons of God, our common ministry, an all-human sacrificial offering of love, the great act of our divine-human union, the united prayerful breath of our divine-human spirit.[20]

Mother Maria wrote a great deal about the love of God entailing, demanding, being synonymous with the love of neighbor, and she actually lived out this reality.

In "Types of Religious Lives," she described the radically different rule of the Gospel, its distinct "mathematics." Put most simply, I never lose what I give away. A loaf of bread, a dollar, love extended to another—we are never made poorer by giving. Our everyday reckoning leads us to believe this, to want to hold on to, save what is our own. How many who lived through the Great Depression or the more recent recession became hypersensitive to loss, thus guarding every penny, every item that could be used again—I grew up with a mother like that! Mother Maria insists that the spiritual "math," the law of the heart, sees it otherwise. Whatever I share with the poor, whatever I give to someone in need, I receive back in much greater measure. I become rich from giving, not poor.

---

[19] Nicholas Denysenko, "Retrieving a Theology of Belonging: Eucharist and Church in Post-Modernity," pts. 1 and 2, *Worship* 88 (2014): 543–61 and 89 (2015): 21–43.

[20] *Mother Maria Skobtsova: Essential Writings*, 79.

And, what is more, we receive gifts that cannot be lost, cannot deteriorate—the love of God, the kingdom of heaven.[21]

If we cannot love the neighbor, the sister or brother in front of our faces, then we cannot love the God we cannot see. For we have rejected both Christ's own example of love for the loveless as well as the very face of Christ in these flesh-and-blood brothers and sisters before us. Mother Maria gets very concrete about the neighbor who, though extremely annoying, is to be loved as a fellow child of God—the loud neighbor in our apartment building, the boisterous one at the café who has had one too many, nasty senior citizens who irritate us with their cranky behavior, the student who is slow or the one I know is trying to take advantage of me, the teacher, the lonely person who does not care how exhausted I am and keeps on talking her heart out. Each is a child of God. Each bears the face of the Savior. Each is a fellow member of the Body of Christ, a chance to love both God and a neighbor.[22]

Mother Maria's vision of the Gospel reveals that the greatest temptation is obsession with keeping the letter of the law in everything—rubrics, the number of prayers, prostrations, fasting days, but without any regard for the flesh-and-blood person next to us, without any sense of the God for whom all this observance is maintained—in short, without love. It is not those in good health who need the help of a doctor but the afflicted. Mother Maria reminds us that Christ never shied away from those at the margins of his faith and society—tax collectors, prostitutes, even those from outside the fold like the women from Samaria and Canaan. He welcomes these, regarded as sinners and heretics, but he confronted the leaders of the religious establishment, the Pharisees and teachers. Today, she argues, the parallel could not be clearer. Revolution has led to millions of deaths, imprisonment, torture, destruc-

---

[21] Ibid., 79–80.
[22] Ibid.

tion. Everywhere there is hatred for the other, an absence of love. And yet among the clergy and bishops, the equivalent of the preservation of the Sabbath's purity is the topic of obsessive debate. There is a massive disconnect between the institutional church and the suffering world.[23]

Living the Gospel

There is no doubt that Mother Maria was and will always remain somehow outside the mainstream—not unlike her contemporary, Dorothy Day, no matter how well-meaning people try to repackage them. A nun who continued to smoke, who visited bistros to find the homeless, and who skipped services to scrounge for groceries will always be defined as deviant from the monastic "ideal."[24]

But to marginalize her witness would be a denial of who she was and what she actually did. There are few writers who so frequently and explicitly returned to the tradition. Mother Maria usually goes first to the Scriptures, and in the New Testament, to the words and the actions of Jesus in the gospels. This profoundly shapes her vision and her action. A colleague said to me once, half sadly, "What a difference it might make if we listened to the Gospel, if we asked what Christ has to do with this. We might end up actually being Christians."

Mother Maria challenged the domesticated, traditional piety of her readers. In the hard times of the years after the Revolution and the Great Depression, one would go to church to seek peace, consolation, relief. Religion as painkiller—this she rejected. If church was really church, saying what Christ had

---

[23] Ibid., 152–53.
[24] The other nuns who originally joined her "monastery in the world" left in order to establish a more normal, regular religious community. Moniale Silouane, *Abesse Eudoxie*, trans. Laurence Gillion and Elizabeth Mouravieff (Bussy-en-Othe: Monastère Orthodoxe Notre Dame de Toute Protection, 2014).

taught, then you should be disturbed rather than comforted, indicted rather than soothed there. You would see your sins for the damage they produced—for others and yourself. You would be given a hunger, a craving for God's justice. You would be set on fire for doing what God commanded, not lulled to sleep. Rather than worldly cleverness you would become fools for Christ.[25]

Mother Maria seemed to others always somehow fired up. In response to critics of her outreach efforts, she recalled the early monastics of the deserts of Egypt and Syria, as well as later ones. What she found was the continuous line of those who worked to feed the hungry, shelter the homeless, console the miserable. This was at the core of the tradition!

Throughout the Depression and afterward, during World War II, Mother Maria was able to keep several houses of hospitality open. Years later, the poor and suffering remain. Mother Maria and Dorothy Day are gone, their images still radiant. The churches—have they learned from the example of these extraordinary women? Institutionally speaking, the same inertia and catering to middle-class sensibilities remain. But individuals have been moved and changed by the call to love God and the neighbor, one being the "pope of mercy," who continues to disrupt and disturb with his words about compassion.

Nicholas Denysenko sees Mother Maria offering a very powerful example of the belonging that liturgy creates, the community of the kingdom, so rarely found in the hard, cruel society around us.[26] For her, the people who assembled for liturgy were censed by the deacon or priest because they were as much images of God alive and active as any of the panels on the church's icon-screen or on the frescoes on the church walls. All of us, as far as she was concerned, were "living

---

[25] *Mother Maria Skobtsova: Essential Writings*, 113.
[26] Denysenko, "Retrieving a Theology of Belonging," pts. 1 and 2.

icons" of God's love and truth.[27] How central this is to a spirituality that recognized the world as God's dwelling! Maria Skobtsova always saw the world as sacrament, as the encounter of the divine and human.

---

[27] *Mother Maria Skobtsova: Essential Writings*, 80–81.

Father Alexander Men
Photo from the Alexander Men Foundation.

Chapter 3

"Christianity Is Only Beginning . . .": Alexander Men and Living Faith

I find it difficult to make a sharp distinction between what is "worldly" and what is "religious." The terms seem to me to be highly artificial. Though they told me as a child that certain things were "special," that notion came from living among people with a different cast of mind. Gradually the distinction came to lose its meaning, since everything became "special" in its own way. Every aspect of life, every problem and experience is directly connected with God.[1]

A Legacy of Openness

While I never had the privilege of knowing Alexander Men, I have met people whose lives were touched by him—I should say changed—permanently. They are educated, talented individuals, people who would have been leaders and notable professionals in any case. But their encounter with this man made them more than just concerned citizens. You could never mistake them for "Sunday Christians" or "Christmas and Easter" believers. They are striking examples of perceiving the

---

[1] Viktor A. Grigorenko, ed., *Fr. Alexander Men: The Story of His Life*, trans. Ann Shukman (Moscow: Life with God Publications/Rudomino Book Center, 2012), 31. Also see the wonderful new study by Wallace L. Daniel, *Russia's Uncommon Prophet: Father Aleksandr Men and His Times* (DeKalb, IL: Northern Illinois University Press, 2016).

world as sacrament. For Fr. Alexander, their teacher, there was no corner of existence, no profession or job, no aspect of culture, politics, art, or science that was not an epiphany, a showing of God's presence and love. Except for the last couple years of life, Men had come to this sensibility in the most antireligious of contexts—that of Soviet Russia from the 1930s on to the century's end. In what would be the last months of his life, Men was a constant figure on Russian TV and radio, in the pages of magazines and journals, and in numerous Moscow auditoriums where he spoke.

Men's life followed the flow of history in Russia from the midst of the Stalinist era until its end. At its end, the hope he spread and left behind was truly remarkable, given the restraints under which he lived. He was born January 22, 1935, in Moscow, and his parents were Jewish. Only his mother and her sister figured in his religious identity and upbringing. His mother was baptized and became an active Christian in the underground, "catacomb" church that functioned during the Soviet era. Fr. Seraphim Batiukov baptized both Elena and her firstborn son in 1935. This priest had been close to the famous monks, the "Optino elders," who were a bridge from the nineteenth century onward between alienated intellectuals, artists, and political activists. He was connected, in particular, to the monk Nektary, now canonized along with other of the elders.

The point here is that in a time, in a country, and in a church not known for openness at all, the Optino monks were unusually open individuals. They welcomed those with questions, with anger, and with no faith at all, full of welcome and acceptance. Thus the observation in a letter of Men's.

> Fr. Seraphim (Batiukov) . . . baptized my mother and me, and for many years undertook the spiritual direction of the whole family . . . my mother . . . had a great deal to do with determining my spiritual life and orientation. She lived an ascetic and prayerful life, completely free of hypocrisy, bigotry, and narrowness; traits often present in people in her state. She was

always filled with paschal joy, a deep dedication to the will of God, and a feeling of closeness to the spiritual world, in a certain way, like St. Seraphim or St. Francis of Assisi. . . . She had a trait similar to the character of the Optina elders, a trait so dear to them: openness to people, to their problems, and to their searching; openness to the world. It is precisely this quality that drew the best representatives of Russian culture to Optina. After a long rupture, Optina did in fact renew the dialogue between the Church and society. It was an undertaking of great, exceptional importance, despite the lack of confidence and opposition of the authorities. . . . This idea of dialogue with the world has stuck with me all my life; it should never be interrupted. I have always felt I should participate in that conversation with whatever meager force I have.[2]

Men learned from quite a few mentors the importance of translating religion into ordinary language, revealing how the New Testament is about life, not just services in church.

Unable to enter university because of his Jewish background, Men enrolled at the Institute of Fur, at first in Moscow, then in Irkutsk, Siberia, where it moved. At the same time, he continued theological study—the Scriptures, church fathers, Western Christian writers too, thus the roots of his great veneration for the Western churches and their saints. Not surprisingly, he was particularly devoted to the great "renaissance" thinkers—Khomiakov, Bukharev, Solovyov, and Florensky, and then many of the Paris emigration writers.

He and an institute classmate, Natalya Grigorenko, married in 1956. Though unable to complete his exams because of his ties to the church, he was ordained a deacon in 1958 and a priest in 1960. He used every conceivable opportunity for teaching and preaching in the Alabino parish, not easy in those

---

[2] Alexander Men, "Pismo k E. N." [letter to E. N.], in *Aequinox*, quoted in Yves Hamant, *Alexander Men: A Witness for Contemporary Russia, A Man for Our Times*, trans. Steven Bigham (Torrance, CA: Oakwood, 1995), 38–40.

days, where formal religious education was prohibited and church life was restricted to the celebration of the liturgy and other services. Every service was a chance to engage people about the faith, especially memorial services, the most popular and frequent held in the Russian Church. He held office hours, and while avoiding gatherings which would have raised problems with authorities, he nevertheless maintained an unusually active round of encounters with his people. The parish car made it possible for him to visit to the elderly and ill.

His last parish, Novaya Derevnya, not far from the Sergius-Trinity monastery at Zagorsk, attracted younger, well-educated people who wanted to reconnect with the church. Because of the stream of visitors, Men was regularly called in for questioning. His colleagues were like-minded younger clergy such as Gleb Yakunin and Nikolai Eschlimann. Both got into serious trouble for an open letter to the patriarch protesting the church's acquiescence to the government. The many times imprisoned Fr. Dmitri Dudko was also connected to this group.[3] This ferment was a small part of the larger unrest that would lead to Gorbachev's first relaxing of many stringent laws and then pursuing more openness, the Glasnost of the early 1990s.

Though aligned with a renewal stream among the clergy, Men avoided direct confrontation with authorities. Rather, he began to publish educational literature abroad, in Belgium, which was then smuggled into Russia. His first book, *The Son of Man*, his catechetical handbooks on liturgy, the church year, and prayer, *Heaven on Earth*, and *In Search of the Way, the Truth and the Life*, his series on the world's religious traditions and biblical studies, appeared under pseudonyms.

---

[3] A collection of these question-and-answer discussions conducted by Fr. Dudko and his parishioners both in church at in home meetings has been translated by Paul D. Garrett, *Our Hope* (Crestwood, NY: St. Vladimir's Seminary Press, 1977). This was the same method Alexander Men used.

He continued the active ministry he had begun years before. There are videotapes of his catechizing those to be baptized as adults as well as postbaptismal homilies. He attended evening meals after Saturday evening Vespers and responded to questions—these were taped, transcribed, and eventually published. The risks he took were huge, even though he did nothing to openly challenge the regime. This was a time of intense dissident activity, very public—it frequently carried with it the possibility of interrogation, imprisonment, and exile. One only has to recall the Sakharovs and Solzhenitsyn.

As creative and constructive as Men's work and writing seem today, as visionary his openness to the other churches and his sensitivity to religion and life—the living out of the Gospel—none of these are leading features of the contemporary Russian church. Both in Men's own time and thereafter, his work—his pastoral efforts, his writing, even his Jewish origins and his personality—would all be vilified, condemned, written off. It is no surprise his books were among those burned publicly by the then-bishop of Ekaterinburg, an action protested in Western Europe as well as in North America. He was in the good company of Schmemann, Afanasiev, Bulgakov, and others of the emigration.

What Men aimed at and stood for is very much at odds with the new symbiosis of church and state under Putin and Kyrill, especially the vision of *Russkiy mir*, that of a distinctive Russian religious, cultural, and political synthesis, morally superior to that of the secular, decadent West or not. Men's Russia was that of Stalin, Khruschev, Brezhnev, and Andopov. Today it is the empire of Putin, with his invasion of Crimea and pouring of troops into eastern Ukraine, his arrogant threatening of the West while the patriarch continues to vilify the West in moral and religious terms.

But at the end of the 1980s and the beginning of the 1990s, there was Gorbachev and restructuring—*perestroika* and *glasnost*—openness or transparency. Men, a priest, began to become almost a household name in a way unthinkable for decades. Church school was started at his parish, also classes for adults. Visits to hospitals, particularly the children's hospital in Moscow started, before banned. It was a tsunami of pastoral engagement on his part. From spring of 1988 until his death in September 1990, Men would present over two hundred public talks, some on television, most in schools and other accessible locales. He claimed he was more energized in his fifties than earlier in life. There was an intensity and urgency, too, about his seemingly nonstop activity in the last two years of his life. It is almost as if he somehow knew his time was limited. Now, years later, there is a bit of the classical hagiographic work evident in some publications, but the authentic portrait is of a person completely at ease in his own skin, not at all trying to look like ancient, traditional models of sanctity. In many ways, though he wore his cassock and cross and vestments at services and followed the liturgical norms, he nevertheless was a very different, human kind of priest, quite unlike most of his contemporaries. Those who knew him, and the number is dwindling, remember he was always present for them, attentive. One never felt one was watching a clerical or churchly performance.

No one has ever been arrested or prosecuted for his killing. There are various accounts of his death, but all are reconstructions as there were no witnesses except the victim and the perpetrator. Men was traveling, as he always did, to the Novaya Derevnya Parish from his home in Semkhoz. It was early on the morning of Sunday, September 9, 1990. On the path to the train platform, it seems that someone must have called out to him. His head was ripped open by a sharp instrument, likely an axe or hatchet. He fell, but he was able to somehow get up, stumble, then probably tried to crawl back toward the path and his home. His wife heard loud groaning and found him collapsed at the gate. Speculation has ranged from the *Pamiat* radicals to government agents or contractors. Assassinations have abounded in Russia: Russian-American Paul Klebnikov, head of *Forbes* magazine there, and most recently Boris Nemtsov.[4]

The "Humanity of God" and Christianity's Humanity

Alexander Men's final talk, given September 8, 1990, the night before he was assassinated, contains three important views that continue to speak to us.

> Christ calls people to bring the divine ideal to reality. Only short-sighted people imagine that Christianity has already happened, that it took place, say, in the thirteenth century, or the fourth, or some other time. I would say that it has only made the first hesitant steps in the history of the human race. Many words of Christ are still incomprehensible to us because we are still neanderthals in spirit and morals; because the arrow of the Gospels is aimed at eternity; because the history of Christianity is only beginning. What has happened already, what we now call the history of Christianity, are the first half-clumsy, unsuccessful attempts to make it a reality.[5]

The human dimension of Christianity, the necessity of this too, is one of Men's most important recognitions. He was in a formidable line in being sensitive to the human as well as the divine in the Christian tradition, a line that in the modern era

---

[4] Subsequently, several of Fr. Men's colleagues and disciples have come under fire from conservative groups within the Russian Church, most notably Frs. George Kochetkov and Alexander Borisov, who headed the Russian Bible Society and Sts. Cosmas and Damian Parish in Moscow, for liturgical and catechetical "innovations," and for ecumenical openness, especially to the Roman Catholic Church. See Service Orthodoxe de Presse, January 1995; see also http://www.economist.com/blogs/graphicdetail/2015/02/political-assassinations.

[5] *Christianity for the Twenty-First Century: The Prophetic Writings of Alexander Men*, ed. and trans. Elizabeth Roberts and Ann Shukman (New York: Continuum, 1996), 185.

stretched back to Soloviev, and to Bukharev, on to Florensky, Bulgakov, and others. Paul Valliere has examined this profound realization, that in the incarnation in particular, God took on humanity, already made in God's image and likeness.[6] Sometimes translated otherwise, Valliere argues talking about "the humanity of God," a radical challenge to religious thinking and assumptions. In the same talk on the night before he was killed, Men said:

> So if we once again ask ourselves the question, what is the essence of Christianity, then we must answer: it is the humanity of God, the joining of the finite and temporal human spirit with the eternal Divinity, it is the sanctification of the flesh, for from that moment when the Son of Man, the Human One, took on our joys and our sufferings, our love, our labors, from that moment, nature, the world, everything in which he was, in which he rejoiced, as a human being and as God-man, no longer is rejected, no longer is degraded but is raised up to a new level and is made holy.[7]

Numerous times, in lectures and interviews, Men observed that his own Russia has been Christian for but a fragment of history, the past thousand years and a few more years. Despite the dominance of the church in Russian history, he emphasized that Christianity was only just beginning, only taking its first half-clumsy, baby steps, not only in Russian but in global history. This was so despite all the tsars, all the patriarchs and monasteries, all the grandeur that passes for the legacy of "holy Russia," and the more recent image of the "Russian world."[8]

---

[6] Paul Valliere, *Modern Russian Theology: Soloviev, Bukharev, Bulgakov* (Grand Rapids, MI: Eerdmans, 2001).

[7] *Christianity for the Twenty-First Century*, 188–90.

[8] See Nicholas Denysenko, "Fractured Orthodoxy in Ukraine and Politics: The Impact of Patriarch Kyrill's 'Russian World'," *Logos: A Journal of Eastern Christian Studies* 54, nos. 1–2 (2013): 33–68; and "Chaos in Ukraine: The Churches and the Search for Leadership," *International Journal for the Study of the Christian Church* 14, no. 3 (2014): 242–59.

Men, not only in his research but also in his own experience, well understood how much of what passed for Christianity was in fact paganism, superstition, or popular culture.

> Paganism is a primitive religion. . . . [It] is born of the human psyche—the human drive to establish a bond with prevalent mystical powers. Each one of us is a pagan. At difficult times we are always ready to have our fortunes told, to forecast. The pagan lives within us because in each one of us there are forty thousand years of paganism and only two thousand years of Christianity. Paganism is always easier for us. Primitive religion is always easiest. It is natural to people, and often what passes for Orthodoxy or another Christian confession is simply natural religiosity which, in its own right, is a kind of opium of the people. It functions as a sort of spiritual anesthetic.[9]

Men was a person of deep cultural roots and commitment. His overviews of the world religious traditions make clear that faith always used culture to express itself, in literature, music, and beyond. In pointing to "natural religion" or "popular religion," he was not overspiritualizing Christianity. But he also discerned when Christianity was functioning in other ways—and when Christianity was being used. The state symbiosis with the church in the Byzantine and later Russian imperial contexts were powerful examples of religion serving other-than-religious purposes. A good anthropologist, he realized the need of humans for legitimacy, illumination, consolation in life. So much ritual, so many visions of life after death, even the imagery of God were important for these purposes.

It was one of Men's accomplishments to recover the humanity of God and thus of Christianity. So many of the writers we encounter in this book had the same aim, from Richard Rohr and Mother Maria Skobtsova to Elisabeth Behr-Sigel and

---

[9] Alexander Men, *About Christ and the Church*, trans. Alexis Vinogradov (Torrance, CA/Crestwood, NY: Oakwood/St. Vladimir's Seminary Press, 1996), 52–53.

Lev Gillet. This is evident in Men's efforts to get his parishioners thinking about their faith and connections to their lives. He consistently related what was read in the lessons or celebrated in a feast back to the ordinary lives of his hearers. This is in contrast to the use of religion as a moral tool, so prevalent today. Many writers I have been drawing on in reflection on the search for God today make a point of recognizing the negative side of institutional religion, of the church, its toxic character, the destruction it sometimes does and yet denies.[10] The ignoring of abuse and its cover-up by religious leaders for so many years has made us sensitive to religion's damaging possibilities.

To read Men is to experience something quite different. He once remarked that there was more of the splendor of God in a leaf than in many icons. All too often, what passes for Christianity is what we moral and spiritual Neanderthals feel and think. We re-create the faith in our own image and likeness. Long sermons, the reduction of Christian life to certain positions on abortion, on same-sex marriage, LGBTQ people, immigration, now Muslims. The list of pious activities goes on—reciting certain prayers and attending an endless series of Bible studies—it is hard to square any of this with either Jesus or the first communities. Men realized this and communicated it in *The Son of Man* and other writings. For him, the Sabbath was for us, not us for the Sabbath. Christianity comes across for him as freedom, joy and light, not primarily as rules or warnings about the darkness, or fear, or threat. And of all the distinguishing features of Christian teaching, the one Men emphasized most was the "new commandment," the real gift of love—love of God and love of the neighbor.

---

[10] Michael Plekon, *Hidden Holiness* (Notre Dame, IN: University of Notre Dame Press, 2009); *Saints as They Really Are: Voices of Holiness in Our Time* (Notre Dame, IN: University of Notre Dame Press, 2012).

"The Kingdom Exists, Here and Now"

> I am talking about the very essence of the Christian faith, the eternal value of the human person, the victory of light over death and corruption, the New Testament which grows like a tree out of a little acorn and . . . which permeates history, as the leaven does dough, so even today the kingdom of God is coming secretly among the people. When you do good, when you love, when you contemplate beauty, when you feel the fullness of life, the kingdom of God is already touching you. The kingdom is not something only in the distant future, in a conjecture about the future here and now. So Jesus taught us. The Kingdom will come but is already here.[11]

The presence of the kingdom of God, here and now, is another of Men's distinctive recognitions. It goes along with his vision of the human dimensions of Christianity. Of course, this is not an original insight, rather one found already in the New Testament many times over. Amy-Jill Levine, in her uncovering of the Jewish roots of Jesus' teaching, stresses how the immanence of God's rule, presence, and power would have been prominent in the Judaism of the first century CE.[12] The consequences are many. In the comments collected into the document *Credo* and in his studies of the New Testament and of the world religious traditions, Men affirms the imprint of God in all traditions of faith, in all historical periods and social situations. Here again, the legacy of openness and dialogue in which he was raised enables him to think about faith ecumenically and globally. It is impossible to conceive of Christianity as a cult that wants to separate itself from the rest of the world and humankind. Equally impossible is the idea of Christianity as a teaching and an institution that wants to obliterate and

---

[11] *Christianity for the Twenty-First Century*, 191.
[12] Amy-Jill Levine, *Short Stories by Jesus: The Enigmatic Parables of a Controversial Rabbi* (San Francisco: HarperOne, 2014).

conquer other cultures or institutions, certainly not other traditions of faith. Though unique among them, there is a recognition that wherever humanity is, there too is the Creator, there too is Christ the incarnate Word and there also the Spirit, who is "everywhere, filling all things." This cosmic dimension of Christianity is classical, there from the beginning as the Gospel reached across the boundaries of Judaism into all the other cultures of the world of the first century CE.

Perhaps the sense of the immanence of the kingdom for Men came from the experience of Stalinist terror, of the gulags and trials, the repression that made so many disappear. Unbelievable as it had appeared, all this eventually was transcended, overcome in Russia, with the end of the Soviet state. Therefore the death and resurrection and ascension of Christ and the coming of the Spirit are a victory of life over death, not just in the historical past but in one's own life and experience. As miserably as human beings can behave, as destructive as they are capable of being, still, Christ is risen. This is what one hears in Men's Lent and Easter sermons and in the conversations in people's homes.[13] At the end of the Easter season, he says that like the disciples, all of us forget the things that have happened to change everything.[14] Though they have never been outside Russia, he reminds his listeners they are part of what is by definition inclusive and open, the church of Christ, not members of a sect who fear and despise those outside their membership.[15] There are so many small asides, little connections between the texts read in church and the daily chores of parents and students. This is one of Men's great gifts, to always see the eternal in small details of home and work. Every human being fully alive, as Irenaeus of Lyons said centuries ago, is

---

[13] See Men, *About Christ and the Church; Awake to Life*, trans. Marite Sapiets (Torrance, CA: Oakwood, 1996).

[14] Men, *Awake to Life*, 86–87.

[15] Men, *About Christ and the Church*, 15–23, 55–65.

the glory of God manifest. And the story of each is part of the church's story.[16]

Christianity Is for the World, for All, for Life

Lastly, for Men, Christianity is creative and sanctifying. The previous quotations were taken from Men's last public talk, presented on the night of September 8, 1990, before he died. He was concluding a series on the world religious traditions. He had spent years producing a kind of encyclopedia of volumes on them. He was aware that no such literature was available in the Soviet period, only propaganda about religion's opposition to freedom and knowledge. His lifelong commitment to dialogue and openness made understanding these traditions very important. And upon reaching the end of the lecture series and Christianity, he did not use his own tradition to dismiss the others. Rather, he was able to show how each of them was, in a way, a kind of incarnation.

In all the traditions, God's choosing out of love to become part of space and time was evident. In Jesus of Nazareth God became part of creation, one with us uniquely. Men saw Christianity as global, not just the religion first of the Middle East and later of Europe, but a path that transcended geography and ethnicity, just as it also transcended social and economic and political differences. He wrote and lectured as though Christians had more in common than divided them. He saw faith as powerful in supporting believers in their work, in their families, in moving toward a more just world. This is a vision of Christian faith and life worlds apart from that trumpeted by so many, no matter the denominational background.

Men's work abruptly stopped with his death, and conditions in his Russia have changed dramatically. Nevertheless, there is good reason to include him when reflecting on the spiritual

---

[16] Ibid., 97–109.

life in the everyday. Here in America, there was a surge of interest in him in the late 1990s, with numerous translations of his writings, articles, and papers—there were also many conferences centered on his work. As is often the case in professional perspective—within both the academy and the church—the surge is over. He remains on the list of important figures, but there is no longer the excitement as when he was first discovered and was being presented. This does not diminish his worth, as hopefully has been shown here.

As we sense a new openness and compassion being fostered by Pope Francis, we also continue to experience backlash, those fearful of his openness and alleged lack of rigor. It is also the case that while we have had to revise our ideas about the progressive secularization of society and culture, the numbers of those who do not connect with communities of faith, with worship, continue to increase. Survey data is strangely complex. On the one hand, it appears that religion, as we have known it in its institutional structure and operation, continues to decline. The number of those religious "nones," those not identifying with or belonging to a group or congregation, keeps growing.[17] Yet, globally, it is not so much secularization but pluralism that dominates, according to my teacher, sociologist of religion Peter L. Berger.[18] Those formerly confident in traditional, evangelical communities within their cultures are no longer so sure about the absolute characteristics of their points of view. Rachel Held Evans has made many take notice of religious ferment and discontent as she documents her experience in evangelical church contexts.[19]

---

[17] Pew Research Center, "America's Changing Religious Landscape," May 12, 2015, http://www.pewforum.org/2015/05/12/americas-changing-religious-landscape/.

[18] Peter L. Berger, *The Many Altars of Modernity: Toward a Paradigm for Religion in a Pluralist Age* (Boston/Berlin: De Gruyter, 2014).

[19] Rachel Held Evans, *Searching for Sunday: Loving, Leaving and Finding the Church* (Nashville, TN: Thomas Nelson, 2015).

Pope Francis has experienced, and will continue to experience, backlash to his efforts to promote openness and compassion, this from those who fear that such will threaten truth and order. Over against both of these trends, I think Men's relentless hope is important for us today, almost twenty years after his death. His confidence that, despite all the centuries, we are only beginning to walk in the Gospel is anything but discouraging. All of the persons of faith in this book have sinned on the side of openness toward society and culture. All have believed the Gospel is not at war with the world but has the Good News of new life. They see Christ as continuing to work in the world, for the life of the world. The world for Men and them all continues to be sacrament.

Father Nicholas Afanasiev
Photo from Dr. Anatole Afanasieff.

Chapter 4

"The Power of Love": Nicholas Afanasiev's Radical Vision of Community[1]

Authority is part of the life of the Church . . . but ecclesial authority ought to conform to the nature of the Church and not be in conflict with her. If such authority claims to be superior to the Church then it must also be superior to Christ. This is why the Church can never be founded, nor her authority based upon a juridical principle, for the law is external to, outside of Love. Such authority cannot belong to the vicars of Christ on earth, since God has not delegated his power to anyone, but has put all people in submission to Christ, "put all things under his feet." In the Church, which is Love, there is only the power of love. God gives the pastors not the charism of power but that of love and, by his mediation, the power of love. The bishops who exercise the ministry of administration are the representatives of the power of love. The submission of all to the bishop takes place in love, and it is by love that the bishop submits to the faithful. Every submission of one to another is realized through the mediation of the love we have for Christ. The submission

---

[1] Earlier versions of this chapter were presented at the conference, "Friendship: An Ecumenical Value," inaugurating the first Institute of Ecumenical Studies in Ukraine at the Ukrainian Catholic University in Lviv, June 11–15, 2005, and at a conference on Sobornost', "Conciliarity and Communion," sponsored by St. Andrew's Theological College, Moscow, at the Ecumenical Monastery of Bose, Italy, October 23–26, 2008.

> of all to the bishop is actualized by the love he has for all and by the reciprocal love of the faithful for him. There can be no other foundation of power in the Church, for Christ is the only foundation of power in her. The pastors are able to have only that which Christ gives to the Church. Law cannot be the foundation of power in the Church because Christ has not given it as a charismatic gift but rather he has rejected it. "Shoulder my yoke and learn from me, for I am gentle and humble in heart." (Matt. 11, 29) The power of Christ in the Church is the power of Love, acquired by the love which he has for us.[2]
>
> —Nicholas Afanasiev

It's been said many times here in these reflections that the appeal of Pope Francis to God's mercy has been immensely encouraging. His consistent vision of God as compassion and the pattern to which we should aspire is a real invitation to reconsider what religion is truly about for so many who are alienated from it. The appeal to generosity, to inclusion and tolerance he has talked about and enacted is also deeply disturbing to others, convinced that order and the law are the most important aspects of faith. But why is the leaning toward love and compassion so threatening? Do we have any insight on the power of love rather than the rule of law in church history? A Russian émigré scholar and pastor of the earlier twentieth century has much to tell us on this score.

Nicholas Afanasiev (1893–1966) was known in his time as a multifaceted scholar, respected by an ecumenically diverse number of colleagues and honored as an ecumenical observer at Vatican II, where his thinking is reflected in *Lumen Gentium*, the Dogmatic Constitution on the Church. Today, likely very few would recall the emphasis that Afanasiev placed on the

---

[2] Nicholas Afanasiev, *The Church of the Holy Spirit*, trans. Vitaly Permiakov, ed. Michael Plekon (Notre Dame, IN: University of Notre Dame Press, 2007), 273–74.

primacy of love, on love as the bond and the impetus for the church and Christian life in the first few centuries. Those familiar with religious history, though, are not surprised by such coincidences, that of Pope Francis with his namesake, the "little poor man" of Assisi, Francis; or for that matter, of the present pope with this Russian émigré priest and scholar, dead almost fifty years.

Of all the religious writers and scholars of the Russian emigration, especially the so-called "Paris School," Afanasiev was one of the least familiar but most significant. His studies began in Russia, were continued in Belgrade, and were completed in Paris. The most important influence on him was his teacher, the great historian A. P. Dobroklonsky. Afanasiev was in a circle of students that included liturgist Fr. Cyprian Kern and exegete Bishop Cassian (Bezobrazov), both of whom would be colleagues at St. Sergius Institute. The great theologian and visionary Fr. Sergius Bulgakov was also an important shaper of his ecclesial thinking, as was the historian Rudolph Sohm. It was Bulgakov who brought Afanasiev to the St. Sergius faculty.

Afanasiev was one of those rare figures that does not really exist any longer. He was a one-man Renaissance. He was skilled in more fields than anyone is today—in biblical studies, church history, liturgical theology, canon law. The notes from his courses and outlines of the lectures he gave in his years at St. Sergius show someone at home both in pastoral work as well as the study of crucial historical documents, among other fields.

He is known as a church historian who rediscovered the "eucharistic ecclesiology" of the early church. Many of his writings are taken up with this, the two principal ones being *The Church of the Holy Spirit* (from which the citation above was taken), a work only published after his death. He planned a companion volume, *The Limits of the Church*, chapters of which exist, scattered as journal articles. He wrote a critique of liturgical practice, *The Lord's Supper*. The far more widely known work of his younger colleague Alexander Schmemann, as well as the vision of John Meyendorff, are very much indebted to Afanasiev's unassuming, humble manner and his scholarly achievements.

Aidan Nichols notes that Afanasiev's work in eucharistic ecclesiology was the only piece of modern Orthodox theological work explicitly cited in the working papers of Vatican II.[3] The texts of the Dogmatic Constitution on the Church and the subsequent "communion ecclesiology" are clearly shaped by Afanasiev's thinking, just as the Pastoral Constitution on the Church in the Modern World is marked by the contributions of another colleague of Afanasiev, Paul Evdokimov. The latter's son, Fr. Michel Evdokimov, told me the Evdokimovs and Afanasievs spent many Sunday afternoons together, and the cross-fertilization of the two St. Sergius Institute theologians' ideas is most evident. Paul Evdokimov utilized the rediscovered eucharistic ecclesiology in all of his writings, in particular emphasizing the ministry of the laity, that of the priesthood of all the baptized, so crucial in Afanasiev's vision of the church.[4]

It is also a curious thing that the critics of Afanasiev, such as John Zizioulas, Aidan Nichols, and John Erickson, among others, take him to task for positions he never maintained, such as the absolute independence of the "local church" from the rest of the churches or, in their eyes, the overemphasis on the eucharistic liturgy as the constitutive element of the church to the neglect of baptism and the work of service and outreach. Zizioulas, in particular, faults Afanasiev on the allegedly

---

[3] Aidan Nichols, *Theology in the Russian Diaspora: Church, Fathers and Eucharist in Nikolai Afanas'ev* (Cambridge, UK: Cambridge University Press, 1989), 253, 270.

[4] See Paul Evdokimov, *Ages of the Spiritual Life*, ed. and trans. Michael Plekon and Alexis Vinogradov (Crestwood, NY: St. Vladimir's Seminary Press, 1998); and *In the World, of the Church: A Paul Evdokimov Reader*, ed. Michael Plekon and Alexis Vinogradov (Crestwood, NY: St. Vladimir's Seminary Press, 2001).

diminished and unclear role of the bishop in his ecclesiology.⁵ Still others fail to see a strong enough appreciation in Afanasiev of the "universal" church, once again the "local church" being overvalued.⁶ Victor Aleksandrov has dealt decisively with the complex of problems of his critics, many of whom condemn him for positions he did not maintain, or without consulting major pieces of his research and writing.⁷ There is also the question of the extent to which Rudolph Sohm's work shaped that of Afanasiev, an issue that Stefan Barbu has most capably engaged.⁸ This is not the place to take on such varied (and in my estimation, questionable) criticism. As with any theologian, there will always be some elements to criticize. For example, I find Afanasiev's rejection of the representation of the laity and clergy in the Moscow Council of 1917–1918 both baffling and problematic, especially given the communal or sobornal

---

⁵ John D. Zizioulas, *Eucharist, Bishop, Church*, trans. Elizabeth Theokritoff (Brookline, MA: Holy Cross Orthodox Press, 2001), 17ff. Afanasiev and Schmemann are dismissed in a couple of sentences, referenced only in a few articles because of the inaccessibility of their Russian-language writings, even though by the mid-1970s Afanasiev's major work was available in French and all of Schmemann's in English.

⁶ See for example John Zizioulas, *Being as Communion* (Crestwood, NY: St. Vladimir's Seminary Press, 1988); see also Paul McPartlan, *The Eucharist Makes the Church: Henri de Lubac and John Zizioulas in Dialogue* (Edinburgh: T & T Clark, 1993), and *Sacrament of Salvation: An Introduction to Eucharistic Ecclesiology* (Edinburgh: T & T Clark, 1995); John Erickson, "The Local Churches and Catholicity: An Orthodox Perspective," *The Jurist* 52 (1992): 490–508. J. M. R. Tillard, however, was consistently positive and cognizant of Afanasiev's recovery of eucharistic ecclesiology. See his *Church of Churches: The Ecclesiology of Communion* (Collegeville, MN: Liturgical Press, 1992).

⁷ "Nicholas Afanasiev's Ecclesiology and Some of Its Orthodox Critics," *Sobornost* 31, no. 2 (2009): 45–69. Also see his "Богословие Николая Афанасьева" [The Theology of Nicholas Afanasiev] in Николай Афанасьев, *Церковь Божия во Христе: Сборник статей* [The Church of God in Christ: Collected Articles] ed. Andrei Platonov and Victor Alexandrov, with an introduction by Victor Alexandrov (Moscow: St. Tikhon's Orthodox University of Humanities, forthcoming).

⁸ Stefan Barbu, "Charism, Law and Spirit in Eucharistic Ecclesiology: New Perspectives on Nikolai Afanasiev's Sources," *Sobornost* 31, no. 2 (2009): 19–44.

character of the eucharistic assembly, the "local church" he so often describes.[9] There is also no doubt that Afanasiev was led and is now limited by the New Testament and early church scholarship of his time. Another problem is his suspicion of the *Didaché* as Montanist in origin and thus unreliable.

The Power of Love—All You Need Is Love

If the power founded upon love is insufficient in actual life, which has lost the principle of love, on the contrary it is completely sufficient in the Church where love is the first and the last principle. Juridical power is a substitute for love in actual social life, a substitute as perfect as possible in a very imperfect life. In the Church where perfect love dwells there is no need for such a substitute.

"Now as an elder myself and a witness of the sufferings of Christ, as well as one who shares in the glory to be revealed, I exhort the elders among you to tend the flock of God that is in your charge, exercising the oversight, not under compulsion but willingly, as God would have you do it—not for sordid gain but eagerly. Do not lord it over those in your charge, but be examples to the flock." (1 Peter 5:13)

To dominate or command [*katakyrieuô*] the flock of God means to use a power not based upon love. The Letter of Peter demands of the bishops who are fellow pastors that they govern by being examples to the flock [*typoi ginomenoi tou poimniou*]. They must be a model or image for the flock . . . of love by means of which they govern the flock of God. The power of love with which the shepherds or pastors are clothed is the sacrificial offering of oneself for the others and self-sacrificing ministry, of which St. Paul gives an example.

---

[9] See Hyacinthe Destivelle, *The Moscow Council 1917–1918: The Creation of the Conciliar Institutions of the Russian Orthodox Church*, trans. Jerry Ryan, ed. Vitaly Permiakov and Michael Plekon (Notre Dame, IN: University of Notre Dame Press, 2015), 174–80.

As servants of God we commend ourselves in every way: through great endurance, in afflictions, hardships, calamities, beatings, imprisonments, tumults, labors, watching, hunger; by purity, knowledge, forbearance, kindness, the Holy Spirit, genuine love, truthful speech, and the power of God; with the weapons of righteousness for the right hand and for the left. . . . Who is weak, and I am not weak? Who is made to fall, and I am not indignant? . . . For though I am free from all men, I have made myself a slave to all [*emauton edoulôsa*], that I might win the more. . . . I have become all things to all men, that I might by all means save some. (2 Cor 6:4-7, 11:29; 1 Cor 9:19, 22)

It is only in the love of Christ and in him that the charism of Love is acquired, the gift which permits one to give oneself to others so that at least some may be saved. To win all not for oneself but for Christ is the content of the power of love in the Church. The opposition . . . of domination to servitude is the opposition of the power not based upon love to the power of love. The first demands that one be served, the second serves the others. The first dominates, the second makes oneself the servant of all (Phil. 2:7). I repeat here nearly word for word the saying of Origen: "Let the rulers of nations exercise lordship over them, but let the rulers of the Church be to it as servants."[10] Such a power does not create superiors and inferiors, masters and slaves. It does not provoke division in the Church but by it all are reunited in love. It does not dominate by fear or force but "takes the form of a servant," for the fear has no love. "There is no fear in love, but perfect love casts out fear. For fear has to do with punishment, and he who fears is not perfected in love" (1 John 4:18).[11]

This is powerful. It is an indictment of law crowding out grace, no matter the legitimation. It is not at all a romantic view of love either but one that sees love in Pauline terms, as

---

[10] *Commentary on the Gospel according to Matthew* 16.8.
[11] Afanasiev, *Church of the Holy Spirit*, 274–75.

enduring, suffering patiently, putting the other first, as in the first letter to the church of Corinth. Afanasiev offers a challenging and provocative view of the church as community. I think that the masterpiece of his writing is *The Church of the Holy Spirit*, a radical examination of the church before its clericalization and domination by law. It is also a careful look at what is at the heart of the church, namely the Holy Spirit and the gift of love. I might add that a close second for the title of "masterpiece" is one of the last essays Afanasiev published, "Una Sancta," the essay dedicated to the "Pope of Love, John XXIII," still one of the clearest views of what it would take to heal the Great Schism.[12]

For those who grew up in the 1960s with the Beatles' songs ringing in our ears, the very power or rule of love was never in doubt, for as John, Paul, Ringo, and George sang, "All you need is love." I don't know if Afanasiev listened to the Beatles, living as he did in Paris in the 1960s, attending the sessions of Vatican II as an invited ecumenical observer, attending the service at which the anathemas of 1054 were put aside. He was, as his wife notes in her biographical sketch, a very busy man in those years, not only teaching and writing and advising the bishop and diocese on matters of canon law but also overseeing the institute's financial situation, a responsibility that must have greatly exhausted him.[13]

---

[12] Nicholas Afanasiev, "Una sancta," in *Tradition Alive: On the Church and the Christian Life in Our Time; Readings from the Eastern Church*, ed. Michael Plekon (Lanham, MD: Rowman & Littlefield, 2003), 3–30; see also, in the same collection, his essay on the Eucharist as both the center of continuing unity and the only way of reestablishing this in the churches: "The Eucharist: The Principal Link between the Catholics and the Orthodox," 47–49. Afanasiev here echoes his colleague Sergius Bulgakov's classic statement on the unity remaining despite the division of the churches; see again in the same collection Bulgakov's essay from 1933, "By Jacob's Well," 55–65; finally, see my essay "Still by Jacob's Well: Sergius Bulgakov's Vision of the Church Revisited," *St. Vladimir's Theological Quarterly* 49, nos. 1–2 (2005): 125–43.

[13] See Marianne Afanasieff, "Nicolas Afanasieff (1893–1966) essai de biographie," *Contacts* 61, no. 2 (1969): 99–111; "La genèse de 'L'Église du Saint-

Yet, if I may be so bold, I think that had he heard this Beatles song, he would have agreed, at least such was the spirit of his principal work on the nature of the church. And it is crucial to realize that historian that he was, Afanasiev was insistent that distancing oneself from the human or ignoring the empirical social and historical realities of the church led one immediately into the error of Nestorianism, the emphasizing of the divine to the detriment of the human. Like so many others in the emigration, he was constantly aware of the implications of the incarnation, the meaning of the "humanity of God," that was the main focus of Sergius Bulgakov's thinking as well, as Solovyov and others before him.[14]

The central message of not only the book in question, *The Church of the Holy Spirit*, but also, really, of Afanasiev's entire scholarly effort is the echo of St. Irenaeus of Lyons: "Where the Church is, there also is the Spirit of God, and where the Spirit of God is, there is the Church and all grace" (*Adversus haer.* 3.21.1). The principal gift of the Spirit is the very life of God, the charism of love. How much of the Scripture, not just the hymn of 1 Corinthians 13, lifts up this same truth! The letters of John, the Johannine gospel, and especially the eucharistic action of the washing of the feet of the disciples: "I give you a new commandment, that you love one another as I have

---

Esprit,'" in *L'Église du Saint-Esprit*, trans. Marianne Drobot (Paris: Les Éditions du Cerf, 1975), 13–23; Alexander Schmemann, "Fr. Nicolas Afanasieff—In Memoriam," *St. Vladimir's Theological Quarterly* 10, no. 4 (1966): 209; and his earlier essay, "The Eucharist and the Doctrine of the Church: On the Book of the Rev. N. Afanasieff: The Banquet of the Lord," *St. Vladimir's Theological Quarterly* 2, no. 2 (1954): 7–12.

[14] See the last volume of his "great trilogy," *The Bride of the Lamb*, trans. Boris Jakim (Grand Rapids, MI / Edinburgh: Eerdmans / T & T Clark, 2002). Bulgakov was, in turn, indebted to the earlier nineteenth-century theologian Vladimir Solovyov, really the first to speak of "divine humanity." See his *Lectures on Divine Humanity*, trans. Boris Jakim (Hudson, NY: Lindisfarne Press, 1995). Finally see Paul Valliere, *Modern Russian Theology: Bukharev, Soloviev, Bulgakov; Orthodox Theology in a New Key* (Grand Rapids, MI: Eerdmans, 2000).

loved you (John 13:34). It was the Lord showing his love for them to the end who told them that just as he washed their feet in love, they were to copy this, do likewise, for one another. I call this eucharistic because there is no institution of the Eucharist or the church in the Johannine Last Supper. Perhaps that is to be found explicitly in the bread of life discourses, after the feeding of the five thousand (John 6). For Afanasiev, the church comes into being after the descent of the Spirit at Pentecost when under the Spirit's grace, the chief apostle Peter presides at the first Eucharist after the Last Supper. Thus "the Eucharist makes the church and the church makes the Eucharist," as we have come to say.

But sadly, the celebration and receiving of the Eucharist, the ministry of the presiders and servants of the assembly, the ministry of every member of the assembly as a priest, prophet, and king by baptism—all this has been imprisoned and deformed—by the dominance over time of laws, by the emergence of a clerical caste that alone controls the bread of life, the cup of salvation, and the Word of God. In time, too, assemblies have been cut off from—no, in truth have cut themselves off from—each other. And so we now find ourselves not the community that shares the broken bread and cup poured out for the life of the world. No, we ourselves are simply broken, the communion within us and among us—broken. The royal priesthood of all the baptized people of God has been reduced to the laity who obey and pay but have nothing to say when it comes to the life of the church. The lower clergy, priests and deacons, live in fear of the hierarchs over them and of each other. Afanasiev recognizes how defective and imperfect, in practice, the church and the ministry within the church are. *The Church of the Holy Spirit*, though, is not primarily a running commentary on what is broken. Rather, throughout his examination of the church as eucharistic and communal, he constantly shows us what the church is in God's vision and plan. So, for example, rather than the insistence on one's position and the use of power, he sees in every aspect of the Eucharist, ministry, and laity the strength, the gift of community, and the only true power—that of love. It is of the very nature of the church community and its life that members are accountable to each other, are servants of each other as Christ is the servant of all.[15]

And worst of all, men and women who have been washed by water and sealed with the Spirit as Christians no longer recognize each other as brothers and sisters of the Lord but as members of this or that jurisdiction or denomination, calling each other heretics, schismatics, unbelievers, without grace. The landscape across the world of divided churches that ancient Christians saw as horrible we have come to accept as normal, even ideal. The faithful separated from the heretics. The flock dispersed. The Body broken.

In all fairness, it must be said that great saints saw this sin against love and acted boldly to counter it. St. Basil the Great sent out his assistant bishops to reconcile those cut off (in schism) by breaking the bread of the Lord with them.[16] Metropolitan Platon of Kyiv and also monks Lev Gillet and Thomas Merton of the Eastern and Western churches could not imagine that the walls of separation reached into heaven, so that the saints of the earthly church, once divided, were now together before the throne of God: Seraphim of Sarov and Francis of Assisi, Juliana the Merciful and Mother Maria Skobtsova, Dietrich Bonhoeffer and Dimitri Klepinine.

It is the Spirit's love that gives life to the church, a love that descends every time the bread and cup of the Eucharist are offered in thanksgiving to the Father. We know that the love of God is shown not only when we embrace in the kiss of peace and share the eucharistic bread and cup. But after the Lord's

---

[15] Michael Plekon, "Bishops as Servants," *Sobornost* 31, no. 2 (2009): 70–82.

[16] John Meyendorff, "Church and Ministry: For an Orthodox-Lutheran Dialogue," in Plekon, *Tradition Alive*, 123–33.

example at the Last Supper in the Gospel of John, this love is also shown when *we wash each other's feet*, that is, when we become servants of one another, in love. I think this is what Antoine Arjakovsky means when he speaks of the "ecumenism of life" as the new form we need to recognize today, an ecumenism enacted in love or a love incarnate in our relationships.

The apostle Paul warns us not to eat and drink without recognizing the body, otherwise we eat and drink condemnation to ourselves in the Eucharist (1 Cor 11: 29-30). Contrary to pious interpretations of these lines, St. Paul is not speaking about whether we have fasted or said the preparatory prayers, whether we have eaten meat, made love, smoked, had a drink, or any such thing. Not to recognize the Body of Christ is to refuse to recognize the face of Christ in the brother or sister before us. I am afraid that over the centuries, we have sinned in our excessive care for preserving the purity of doctrine, for maintaining the walls of division among us. It would have been far better had we "sinned boldly" in the opposite direction, in taking the risk of recognizing, despite the years of separation and all the anathemas and the literature of hate, that as Bulgakov observed, God had graciously left us many signs of his gift of unity, this despite our divisions: his Word in the Scriptures, prayer, the sacraments, the holy men and women through the ages.[17]

Love as Rule

To the charge that leaving the life of the community to love would result in anarchy, disorder, Afanasiev counters that love is the gift of one's self, one's service. Love thus can rule.

---

[17] Sergius Bulgakov, "By Jacob's Well," in Plekon, *Tradition Alive*, 55–66. This strong statement was originally published in the *Journal of the Fellowship of St. Alban and St. Sergius* 22 (1933): 7–17, coming from the intense discussions of that ecumenical fellowship.

> Submission to Christ and our mutual submission to one another is the love of Christ and reciprocal love. It is the same as the love shown by Christ in his ministry. "For the Son of Man himself did not come to be served but to serve, and to give his life as a ransom for many." (Mark 10:45) The same love is expressed in the service of one another, because all of this occurs in the Church for which Christ has given his life. In the Church there is no love without ministry and there is no ministry without love. Love surrounds all the members of the Church and thus ministry belongs to them all. Every ministry is charismatic for grace is one. Consequently all ministries are like in nature but different according to their charismatic gifts. The differences in the gifts creates the differences among the ministries, the importance of which is their function in the life of the Church. The hierarchical principle manifests itself in the Church in the hierarchy of ministries which is also that of love. The hierarchy of ministries culminates in that of the bishops which is the most important in the Church. As the highest hierarchical ministry, it is the highest model of love and the most complete imitation of Christ's self-sacrificing love. This is the culmination point of all ministries, their beginning and end being in love. Among the differing gifts from which stem the differences among ministries, the greatest is the charism of love and this charism belongs to all . . . (1 Cor 12:31; 13:2).
>
> Without love every ministry is nothing and is outside of the Church for the Church is love. "And this commandment we have from him, that he who loves God should love his brother also." (1 John 4:21) The ministry of administration, of direction both external and internal, would cease to be without love, for without love there is no charism, no gift. The pastoral office is by nature insofar as it is the chief ministry of the Church, the chief expression of love.[18]

If these lines from Afanasiev sound familiar, even scriptural, it is because they echo the first letter to the Corinthians and

---

[18] Afanasiev, *Church of the Holy Spirit*, 273–74.

other Pauline material. There are different gifts, different individuals, in the Body of Christ. Men and women, Jews and Greeks, slaves and masters—none of these distinctions any longer hold. And if these social, cultural, and economic distinctions are leveled by Christ, how then can there be a replacement of them with distinctions between the ordained and the nonordained? In order to dispel this empty, distorted distinction, Afanasiev tells us that the church knows no distinctions of power due to consecration or ordination. All Christians are ordained priests, prophets, and kings in baptism.

Every other Christian who is ordained for service to God and the church must first be a priest by baptism, must be a member of the community who then is called out from and chosen by the assembly to exercise a ministry, a service of love, not power.[19] For our purposes here, these would be the principal elements of Afanasiev's vision of conciliarity and communion in the church. Those who are chosen can only be consecrated by the laying on of hands for service to God and the community, and they must be from the community—their lives attesting to their faith and service previously. Ordination is not to a clerical caste, not to power over the rest of the community—whether as bishop or presbyter or deacon or any other office. The texts of the ordination prayers, even as early as those from Hippolytus, attest to this.[20] A colleague, liturgical scholar Nicholas Denysenko, underscored this, noting that:

> First, the ancient invocation, dating to the fourth century since Chrysostom mentions it, read always from a special scroll in the Eastern rites, "the grace divine." . . . [T]he point is the filling of human weakness, that the bishop is never the source of his own power, but God alone. The ancient use of a threefold "Lord, have mercy," in response to the call to prayer accentuates the same point, and thus begins the prayer. The other part is the holding of the Gospel book over the candidate's head.

---

[19] Ibid., 33–79.
[20] Ibid., 34, 60, 94–105, 231.

Numerous interpretations over the ages, but I think for our day, a motif that the Gospel is always the center of Christian life and the bishop's first responsibility is to the Lord and the Gospel, to preach it, to be an apostle who is accountable to God's word . . . no small point in our days of misconstrued ecclesial jurisprudence.[21]

The principle remains: *Lex orandi, lex credendi*.[22] The one who "presides," who "offers thanksgiving" or the Eucharist, who teaches, preaches, and oversees all the rest of the community's work—such a leader is a servant.[23] Afanasiev states it most directly: "The power of pastors considered to be vicars of Christ destroys the very doctrine of ministry in the church."[24] Submission in love to a presider/pastor is first and foremost affection for a sister or brother, for a fellow disciple and servant of God and the community. The submission, the service, the love, should be reciprocal.

It may seem counterintuitive, that in speaking of leaders of the community, Afanasiev sees these as first and foremost servants, bound to the community by mutual love and responsibility. The new commandment of love, however, so central to the Johannine texts, assumes that love will be the bond that holds the whole community together.

Even in the churches today, I am tempted to say, most especially in the churches today, there is a great deal of suspicion about love and acceptance and forgiveness. Pope Francis's off-hand comment, in a press conference on his plane, when he was asked about gay clergy—"Who am I to judge?" provoked serious criticism.[25] So did the June 2015 decision of the

---

[21] Nicholas Denysenko, personal communication with author, July 30, 2008.
[22] Afanasiev, *Church of the Holy Spirit*, 81–105.
[23] Ibid., 133–68, 169–215.
[24] Ibid., 270; see also 267–71.
[25] "On Gay Priests, Pope Francis Asks, 'Who Am I to Judge?'," *New York Times*, July 30, 2013, http://www.nytimes.com/2013/07/30/world/europe/pope-francis-gay-priests.html.

US Supreme Court recognizing the legal status of same-sex marriage. The reactions of some religious leaders and commentators were ballistic. One commentator, Rod Dreher, set off a storm of debate by urging on traditional Christians the "Benedict option."[26] This is a misunderstood version of St. Benedict of Norcia's flight from the world. Rather than separate themselves from society, political activity, all that is the world, contemporary Christians need to better discern the real vision of St. Benedict and focus on Christ and serving Christ in every other person, in every situation of daily life.

But the dependence on clerical status and on rules, on legalism, dominate even more than a controversial court decision or issues from the American "culture wars." While we have come to rely on law and authority to compel compliance and to prevent disorder, we know full well their limitations and the consequences of compulsion. Afanasiev invites us to remember that it is love that drives out fear, gives freedom, and heals what has been broken. He would concur with the ancient saying that no one can be "compelled" in the community of the church, that the use of force is always at odds with the Spirit, with grace, with the Gospel. Afanasiev does not just nod in the direction of Tertullian in titling the major work he completed *The Church of the Holy Spirit*. He knows full well that it was the Spirit that Jesus asked the Father to send down and make the disciples the community of the church. The Spirit is constantly being called down or, as Bulgakov said, the church is a "permanent Pentecost." At baptism and chrismation, in the Eucharistic Liturgy, in the ordaining of those to serve the church, also in the setting apart of a table and building for gathering and liturgy, it is the Spirit who is asked to come down. "Where the Spirit is, there is the church and all grace,"

---

[26] Rod Dreher, "Benedict Option," *American Conservative*, December 12, 2013, http://www.theamericanconservative.com/articles/benedict-option/.

in the words of Irenaeus of Lyons.[27] Likewise, as the Western church has sung on Holy Thursday evening, during the washing of the feet in imitation of Christ, "Where there is charity and love, there is God."

---

[27] Irenaeus, *Adv. Haeres* 3.24.1.

Paul Evdokimov and Father Lev Gillet

Photos from
Tomoko Faerber-Evdokimoff.

Father Lev Gillet

Chapter 5

Limitless Love:
Lev Gillet's Generous God

God is fire. God is love. God is a self-propagating emotional power, a fire that shares itself. Centuries after Moses beheld the flames of the burning bush, this same fire merged with the tongues of flame at Pentecost, and with the fire that burned within the hearts of the disciples at Emmaus. In saying that God is a fire of love we are certainly stating a truth that plays havoc with many of our ideas, in fact almost all our ideas.[1]

—Lev Gillet

A Troubled Man, a Wandering Monk

I never met or knew Lev Gillet, but I did meet and get to know one of his best friends during a long life—Elisabeth Behr-Sigel. You have already gotten to know her in this book and, even if briefly, you have likely heard the name Lev Gillet. Personally, I have a lot in common with this complicated, turbulent little man. I too was once in a religious community. I was first a seminarian, then a friar in the Carmelite Order. Later on, as with him, my life took me elsewhere, maybe even further among the churches than Lev ventured. This will be touched

---

[1] Lev Gillet, *The Burning Bush* (Springfield, IL: Templegate, 1976), 12–13.

on in a later chapter. The great gift of such ecumenical experience is that I came to experience Christ in all of them. Thus, for me, as for Lev Gillet, there is sadness when confronted with one who cannot see or appreciate Christ beyond a single set of church boundaries.

There is no doubt that God, faith, certainly the church and service in it as a priest played havoc with the life of Lev Gillet. Photos show a kindly, avuncular face, one that indeed put many troubled individuals at peace. But he was seldom at peace himself. Originally attracted toward psychoanalytic theory and practice, he became in later life a compassionate pastoral counselor and healer. Less visible, almost hidden, was his outreach, often on the streets to troubled souls. As one who suffered profoundly in life from depression and isolation, often self-imposed, he understood well the sufferings of others seemingly lost in the swirl of modern urban life. Toward the end of his life, when it seemed he had a home (a room in the old St. Basil's House in London), there was hardly anything in it, only a bed, chair and table, a few books, and his cassock. It was as if he'd just stopped off for the evening.

I think Lev Gillet is very much a figure of our time and there are three ways in which he shows us how to navigate, how to live the life of the Spirit in our time. First he offers in his own life an alternative to structure and rules. Though he was shaped by these—the structures and rules of monastic life and of the church, he showed that life was something else—movement of the Spirit. He became a kind of pilgrim among churches and shepherd of searching individuals, truly a citizen and inhabitant of various worlds. Second, he saw in the burning bush, also in his own life and the lives of others, a God larger than the exclusive boundaries we place. Third, in the suffering people to whom he ministered, he came to recognize God as having no limits, no judgment—only mercy. He came to see and preach God as "limitless Love," foreshadowing Pope Francis's amazing celebration of God, "whose name is mercy."

Life and Movement in the Spirit

Lev Gillet went from military service in World War II to graduate work in psychology, then to monastic life in the Benedictine Order and then to life with the Ukrainian Greek Catholic monks in Univ monastery near L'viv. But he actually spent only a few years in monasteries. Most of his life he was a kind of freelance pastor, mostly without a permanent parish assignment. Briefly, he headed the first Orthodox Francophone parish in Paris. Later, he was chaplain at Mother Maria Skobtsova's hostel, also in Paris. He also worked among émigré Russians in several French locations. Still later, while living in London and doing street ministry there, he traveled to Beirut and Geneva and back to France, invited by small groups of people close to him.

So, this quirky little man was both mystic and monastic. Yet for all the solidity of his faith, he was restless, his moods swinging widely, very likely one who suffered from bipolar disorder. He was never really at home in any monastery, parish, or church jurisdiction.

It is clear that Lev Gillet's public life was as turbulent as his own feelings. Always passionate for restoring the unity of the church, seeing in himself both the West and East, he collided continuously with old Catholic colleagues wary of him after his entrance into Orthodoxy. After all, he was an intensely ecumenical Christian when the ecumenical movement itself was indeed very young and not widely supported. As with other singular persons of faith, he did not have a very successful time in the institutional church. He clashed with the bishops of various Orthodox churches—the Moscow and Ecumenical patriarchates as well as those of Antioch and Jerusalem. Over and over, he encountered the inability of the Orthodox to utilize their much vaunted "economy" principle, enabling adaptation and modification for the good of the souls of those involved. More often he experienced clerics, even clerics of discernment, hiding behind church canons, worried about appearances and reactions.

Lev Gillet discovered, through his own personal torment and that of two world wars, the powerful vision of a suffering but always merciful God. He took this realization as a personal impetus to continue ministry whenever and wherever asked. The leaders of the Orthodox Youth Movement in Lebanon welcomed him and he flourished among them, giving talks and retreats, writing a number of texts for them that were later published. But even this rewarding work was cut short when the Russian Church ordered him out of the country and back to England. The number of times Lev Gillet found himself shut out, even battered, at least metaphorically, by church leaders is truly remarkable. It is miraculous that he was usually able to find some way through this ecclesiastical jungle, some permission of a bishop by which he continued to exercise, wherever and however he could, his pastoral ministry. So the profound sense of God as "love without limits" emerged from what at times appeared to be a frantic wandering, a rootless, sometimes most unhappy existence.

He used "A Monk of the Eastern Church" as his literary tag. At first this was to spare Western former colleagues both ecclesiastical difficulty and embarrassment. The pen name stuck and became part of the mystique surrounding him, something clear from even how his friends related to him. He was startlingly intimate in speaking about God (and even for God) in his writings. At the same time, compassionate as he could be for suffering people, he could be strangely remote and irritable, even with the people closest to him. Elisabeth Behr-Sigel admitted that when she most needed his support, when her marriage had fallen apart and her husband was dying, Lev did not respond to her letters and calls, remaining unreachable and detached from her troubles.

An ecclesiastical pilgrim, personally a nomad, he was nevertheless a go-between, a traveler between numerous "worlds," and a bridge builder. By the way, most all the writers we listen to in this book are themselves quite similar in this regard, travelers between churches and worlds. Gillet would use language much like that of Thomas Merton years later to describe the hidden communion behind the divisions.

> The whole teaching of the Latin Fathers may be found in the East, just as the whole teaching of the Greek Fathers may be found in the West. Rome has given St. Jerome to Palestine. The East has given Cassian to the West and holds in special veneration that Roman of the Romans, Pope Gregory the Great. St. Basil would have acknowledged St. Benedict of Nursia as his brother and heir. St. Macrina would have found her sister in St. Scholastica. St. Alexis the "man of God," "the poor man under the stairs," has been succeeded by the wandering beggar, St. Benedict Labre. St. Nicolas would have felt as very near to him the burning charity of St. Francis of Assisi and St. Vincent de Paul. St. Seraphim of Sarov would have seen the desert blooming under Father Charles de Foucauld's feet, and would have called St. Thérèse of Lisieux "my joy."[2]

He considered himself always to be a Christian among Christians who were sisters and brothers. The divisions were historical and, perhaps, at times doctrinally meaningful. He had attempted earlier in life to outline the differences and similarities between Catholics and the Orthodox in an essay now lost. But as he grew older, he moved among Roman Catholics and Protestants and Orthodox as well, in short serving all of the people of God like his friend Paul Evdokimov, as if there had never been schisms.

---

[2] Lev Gillet, *Orthodox Spirituality*, 2nd ed. (Crestwood, NY: St. Vladimir's Seminary Press, 1978), x–xi. The biographical material here is indebted to Elisabeth Behr-Sigel's masterful and extensive biography, *Lev Gillet: A Monk of the Eastern Church*, ed. Sergei Hackel, trans. Helen Wright (Oxford: Fellowship of St. Alban and St. Sergius, 1999).

Toward the end of his life, he would describe himself as "a Catholic priest in full communion with the Slavic Orthodox Church."[3] Sadly, this statement was misunderstood by some as a kind of betrayal of both churches, almost the kind of ecclesiastical espionage alleged to have been done in earlier outreach.

Like others in this book—Mother Maria, Paul Evdokimov, Elisabeth Behr-Sigel—all of whom were his friends—but also like Alexander Men and Nicholas Afanasiev, Lev Gillet was able to transcend the rigidity of church bodies. But he suffered constant disappointment and ill treatment by the institutional church, especially its leaders. For all that he wrote and thereby revealed of his inner life, for all that has been documented of his public ministry, there is still a great deal of mystery about him. The pieces do not all fit together. Lev, in the end, is an enigma, if a saintly one.

In the Presence of a God without Limits

Several of his most widely read books take the form of dialogues between an individual and the Lord, a kind of prayer "out loud." *The Burning Bush* as well as *Love Without Limits/ In Thy Presence* bring the reader very close to a God who is everywhere in the everyday world around us. Even though so much of religion seems to consist of things that must or must not be done, such rules are of no interest to this God who is love, love without any limitations. Such a God is, however, both comforting and a huge threat to religious folk. One can see this today in the negative reactions to Pope Francis.

> So then, Lord, it is this? It is truly this? It is only this? This is the whole law and all the prophets? To love with one's whole heart. . . . To love Him who first loved us, to love everything

---

[3] See Helle Georgiadis, "The Witness of Fr. Lev," *Chrysostom* 8 (1980): 235–38; and Behr-Sigel, *Lev Gillet*, 9–12, 441–42.

that He loves, all men, all women, all creatures. . . . Yes, my child, that is it, and that is all. Everything "else" has value only inasmuch as it is the expression, the carrying out—under so many various forms—of that initial impulse which is my limitless Love. . . . The heart transplants, which in our day have become possible, are a wonderful sign of a spiritual reality. To give one's heart to another, to accept the heart of another. . . . It is the parable of limitless Love's triumph.[4]

It is striking that both Paul Evdokimov and Lev Gillet discovered the image of God as one who suffers with us.[5] Lev also came to speak of God as "Love without limits" and "Lord Love." These, I am sure, were efforts to break through traditional piety and language.[6] He consistently drew on biblical images—the Good Shepherd, the burning bush, the Holy Spirit, the Lamb of God and the Rabbi/Teacher. Distinctive in his writings is the use, in many of the talks that were published, of conversation or dialogue as the form—God speaking to a person, that person speaking to God. Thus, there was a very personal character, rather than the objective sense of a more academic presentation. I also think it was a way of modeling prayer, showing how he, Lev himself, addressed the Lord and how he heard God responding.

---

[4] Lev Gillet, *In Thy Presence* (Crestwood, NY: St. Vladimir's Seminary Press, 1977), 71–72.

[5] See his preface, "Le père Lev Gillet: grand théologien du Dieu souffrant et de l'Amour sans limites," in the anthology of Fr. Lev's writings, *Au cœur de la fournaise*, ed. Maxim Egger (Paris/Pully: Cerf-le sel de la terre, 1998), 9–23.

[6] See Elisabeth Behr-Sigel, *Alexandre Boukharev: un théologien de l'Église orthodoxe russe en dialogue avec le monde moderne* (Paris: Beauchesne, 1977); Paul Evdokimov, *Le Christ dans le pensée russe* (Paris: Cerf, 1986); "God's Absurd Love and the Mystery of His Silence," in *In the World, of the Church: A Paul Evdokimov Reader*, ed. Michael Plekon and Alexis Vinogradov (Crestwood, NY: St. Vladimir's Seminary Press, 2001), 175–94; and Michael Plekon, "The God Whose Power Is Weakness, Whose Love Is Foolish: Divine Philanthropy in the Theology of Paul Evdokimov," *Sourozh* 60 (1995): 15–26.

Having been asked to give his name, the Lord first speaks most basically—"I am."

> You ask what my name is. I am Being. I am the Being whom you see in being at this very moment. Look before you. You see the bush that burns without being consumed. You see fire. The Being I am is a Being of fire. These flames proclaim my love. But look more carefully. My fire does not destroy. That which it burns it purifies and transforms into itself, makes part of itself. And my flame has no need to be fed. It imparts itself, gives itself. I am the Gift that never ceases to give itself. . . . I am Limitless Love.[7]

And here from another text:

> You call me God. This traditional name has been worshiped and blessed by countless souls, to whom it has given, and never ceases to give, depths of feeling and strength. Foolish are those who would depreciate it, and ungodly those who would reject it! It is for you, rather, to worship me precisely as God, and to venerate that name by which I am known. Nevertheless, without lessening that veneration, you recognize that, from the point of view of the word itself, this name, "God," does not have a specific content; it is lacking in precision. Those meanings people have attached to it were not all direct expressions of the word "God." For that word is so vast, so open to elaboration, that at times, because of human weakness, it can somehow seem empty.
>
> In your prayer you call me "God," "my God," "You who are God," and "Lord God." In this ancient designation, this sacred name "God," you can surely find new strength. But you can also find a fresh source of enlightenment in calling me by names that correspond more closely to your immediate experience or your immediate need. You can appeal to those aspects of my Being that are revealed by present circumstances. For example,

---

[7] Gillet, *Burning Bush*, 17–18.

> depending on what is happening in your life, you can call me "You who are Beauty," or "You who are Truth," or "You who are my Purity, my Light, my Strength." You can also call me, "You who are Love."
>
> This last expression will draw your language more closely to my heart. You can say to me, "Lord of Love." Or more simply, you can simply speak the name "Love." Here I would set before you, in your reflection and your prayer, a term which, if you so desire, can become like the sun, the sun that knows no setting, the sun of your life. My beloved ones, I am "Boundless Love," "Love without limits."[8]

And he says, this limitless Love received a personal name, that of Jesus. Love walked along our roads, became one of us without losing being God. All of the world around us is filled by, filled with this Love.[9] And it is this Love who will suffer with us and suffer for us. In another place, Lev points to the presence and pressure of this Love.

> Divine Love is comparable to the atmospheric pressure surrounding us, which sustains each being and also exerts pressure from all sides. Love lays siege to each being and seeks to discover an opening, a path leading into the heart, by means of which Love can permeate everywhere. The difference between the sinner and the saint is that the sinner closes his heart to Love while the saint opens himself to this same Love. In both cases the Love is the same and the pressure is the same.[10]

One can hear the echo of numerous, painful conversations in the way that Fr. Lev has Love speak to the heart.

---

[8] Orthodox Church in America Website, "Love without Limits (3): From Archimandrite Lev Gillet, 'A Monk of the Eastern Church'," http://oca.org/reflections/archimandrite-lev-gillet/love-without-limits-3.

[9] Orthodox Church in America Website, "Love without Limits (4)," http://oca.org/reflections/archimandrite-lev-gillet/love-without-limits-4.

[10] Gillet, *Burning Bush*, 33–34.

> The doorway of Hope is open before you, and no one can ever close it. What is this doorway like? It is the doorway of possibility that Love offers you at every moment. You trouble yourself over the missed opportunities of your life. At times you say to yourself, "Oh, if only I had known! Oh, if only I had done this or that differently. If only I could do it all over again!" We cannot redo what is already done. Yes, of course there have been missed opportunities. They are gone for good. But those lost possibilities are nothing in comparison with what is before you right now: the possibilities that I offer you, that are offered to you in this very moment.
>
> The door of present possibility, which is also the door of Hope, is open before you at every instant. It is different with each one of us. Don't just sit in front of the door, waiting for someone to come open it because you think it is closed. You only have to push against it gently, and it will open wide before you.
>
> The moment you cross the threshold, Love without limits will come to you. Since it is of me, it is more than promised Love; it is Love already given. Nevertheless, in this world, as long as you are in this life, you can always break communion with Me. Here, that union remains imperfect. For the time being, ours is only an engagement, not a full marriage. It is Hope rather than possession. But move ahead with the Hope which is yours, that youthful, spring-like Hope you already possess. Hope in your Lord of Love, even when you feel you may be crushed to death. The greatest Hope is to hope against all Hope.[11]

Does one proceed from God, from the Scriptures and liturgy, down to ordinary people? Or, as these parts of tradition themselves, can we not begin with ourselves, with our lives, our joys and our miseries, and move to God, who is limitless Love? Why not the latter? And surely this is how Love sounds so

---

[11] Orthodox Church in America Website, "Love without Limits (5)," http://oca.org/reflections/archimandrite-lev-gillet/love-without-limits-5.

human, so much like one of us. I think this is how the Russian religious thinkers' idea of "the humanity of God" has to sound—like God who as a result of becoming human is now more like us, has come to know, from inside out, how we feel, what we go through. Love cannot be anything but personal.

> My Love, Love in its incorruptible essence, Love without limits, is never entirely absent. God is never absent. At times such Love seems barely to exist, yes. It can be undetectable, covered by hatred, by all sorts of perversions, or by a layer of instinctive brutality. Yet I still work through it. No matter how deformed love may be, I can make it rise to the level of a conscious and total gift. Love has a great many different aspects, it's true. But there is only one Love.
>
> You are loved. Isn't there a place for the most "insignificant" person in the flame of the Burning Bush? A soul, a person whom I love, though, is not insignificant. You are loved. It is *you* whom I love. This is no universal affirmation; I'm not speaking here about groups of people. I am speaking about you.[12]

Even when it comes to sin, to the evil we do, Love knows no limits.

> Let me repeat, my child: I love each person both completely and yet differently. I love each one "otherwise." There is room in that Love for divine intentions and pleasures, for graces and callings, for choices that are unlike any other. You, my child, I love differently from any other person. I love you with a love that is incomparable, unique. Your sins might well wound the Love I have for you. Nevertheless, they can never diminish that Love.[13]

---

[12] Orthodox Church in America website, "Love without Limits (7): You are Loved," http://oca.org/reflections/archimandrite-lev-gillet/love-without-limits-7-you-are-loved.

[13] Orthodox Church in America website, "Love without Limits (9): You Are Loved 2," http://oca.org/reflections/archimandrite-lev-gillet/love-without-limits-9.

I will not just wonder out loud about it, I will say it with conviction. This is the unconditional, breaking-all-the-rules compassion of God that we desperately need today. When Pope Francis speaks of God in this way, as mercy, it opens doors of hearts previously slammed shut because of disappointment and rejection by the church. It does not take long, in either the online or hardcopy literature of theology, to immediately encounter the doctrinal and legal rigorists. For them, tolerance, the overlooking of the well-defined lines of what is allowable and what is not—such weakness has led not only to moral confusion but also religious weakness. What is really needed, they say, is fearless assertion of the church's teaching, no matter how condemning this may be, whether to LGBT people or to the divorced or to those who feel dispossessed because of their gender.

God as Limitless Love

Lev Gillet, I think, out of the wealth of many encounters with suffering individuals, started to speak of God in striking yet straightforward language, a Love without limits. Such a "Lover of humankind," *Philanthropos*, as the Byzantine liturgy calls God, is someone other than simply Judge of our sins and the one to mete out our punishment.

And when one thinks of the imagery in the gospels, there are to be found the shepherd who goes back for the one lost sheep, the ninety-nine safely penned in. Or of the father who forgives not only his son's wasteful selfishness but also the damage done to the entire family's security by this prodigal behavior; or the woman who slaps together so much yeast and flour that there is enough bread for everyone in town to come and take from the communal ovens, free; or when all are called to feast at the wealthy man's dinner party—friends and then even the riffraff from the streets and outskirts.

Fr. Lev pushes even further, as in *The Burning Bush*. He places God there, present, with both the sinner and the sin.

> The ethic of Limitless Love demands that we should be able to recognize the presence of God in the very sin that the sinner commits. . . . You must not think I mean that God approves of the sin or encourages the sinner. I simply mean that even in an act of sin God is, to a certain extent, present. . . . [E]verything that happens—the bad act as well as the good—has its roots in the being of God. Only because God gives us our being (or rather lends it to us) are we in existence at the very moment when we commit a sin. At that very moment God could withdraw our being from us, could destroy us. But he holds us in the existence we have received from him, even when that existence turns against him. Moreover the Lord Love, in his infinite mercy, allows sin to contain certain positive elements.[14]

It is a radical vision of both God and humanity that Fr. Lev employs. He wonders if, in a sexual encounter that is not right, if there is a moment when genuine affection, kindness, caring is experienced. This then is the spark that still burns of Love, not unlike the small morsel of bread Judas received and that stayed with him after the Last Supper. He sees that somehow the Eastern church, with a sense for healing, a feeling always for the good of the person, invokes "economy" rather than rigor. There is always a chance, another turn for us with this unlimited Love that God is. Bulgakov made room for the saving of all in Love's plan, Love's ultimate victory.[15] Evdokimov recognized this too.[16]

---

[14] Gillet, *Burning Bush*, 48–49.
[15] Sergius Bulgakov, *The Bride of the Lamb*, trans. Boris Jakim (Grand Rapids, MI: Eerdmans, 2002), 379–526.
[16] See Sergius Bulgakov, *Apocatastasis and Transfiguration*, trans. Boris Jakim (New Haven, CT: The Variable Press, 1995); and Paul Evdokimov, "Eschatology," in Plekon and Vinogradov, *In the World, of the Church*, 11–35.

The church historian and canonist Nicholas Afanasiev credited the early church, that of the first three centuries at least, with a reluctance to resort to legalism. Instead, the rule was that of love, of grace, of the power of the Spirit moving and shaping the community. There must have been some cross-fertilization in the church life of Paris, in the circles around Fr. Bulgakov, Mother Maria, Paul Evdokimov, and Fr. Lev when it came to Love at the center, when it came to God as Love.[17] The ancient saying, both from the desert monastics and the fathers, was that no one could be compelled to love, but rather, it was the contrary. Love compelled. God's sharing "the bread of our suffering," was the image of Revelation, of One who stood by the door, knocking.

> To love, with all one's heart, as oneself; the Gospel transmutes all of the law and the prophets into that . . . It is a matter of offering our whole heart to Love, a heart which is pure as a wine is pure, a heart unadulterated and whole, a heart which is not divided or shared.[18]

Purity of heart was key, not the absolute purity of every act of the body. Purity of heart is neither virginity nor heroic abstinence. What are branded still today in the "culture wars" as acts against God and God's law do not make a person incapable of loving and being loved. This holds for LGBT people, for those addicted, and those afflicted by depression and other emotional challenges, for all of whom Fr. Lev had particular compassion. We have even come to need to include all those defined as "other," marginalized by race, religion, and immigration status in a country where none of these should ever count in a person's freedom or worth. Fr. Lev saw the heart of

---

[17] Gillet, *Burning Bush*, 51.
[18] Ibid.

limitless Love as large enough to encompass every child of God.[19]

When he was the chaplain at Mother Maria Skobtsova's hostel, he would go with her to the local bistros, offering a place to stay to those nursing a glass there in order to stay indoors. On the streets of the Notting Hill section of London, close by St. Basil's House, in the area around the British Museum and in Hyde Park, who knows how many people Lev Gillet listened to and tried to comfort. There were also those who came to retreats and conferences where he spoke. Thinking of how the "barbarians" of Malta extended hospitality—a fire and food and clothing to the shipwrecked apostle Paul and other fellow travelers (Acts 28), Love without limits continues to extend the same mercy to those who survive, even if barely, all the miseries of life.

> It is not easy for us to tear down the walls we construct within ourselves. We cannot simply remove the stones, one by one. Yet the Lord of Love surrounds us constantly, patiently, doing what human hands are incapable of doing. Simple adjustments are not enough. To be set free requires a profound transformation. To roll away the stone that closes the entrance to the tomb requires a veritable earthquake. Our walls are broken down only when they are shaken at their very foundations.
>
> O Lord of Love, shake me to those foundations! By striking one stone against another we can make sparks fly. May the shock produced by the crumbling of walls of separation light within me the fires of longing, allowing me to be consumed by the Burning Bush! May every miserable barrier in my life be broken down by the assault to my depths of Love without limits![20]

---

[19] Ibid., 52.

[20] Orthodox Church in America website, "Love without Limits (11): Tearing Down the Walls of Separation," http://oca.org/reflections/archimandrite-lev-gillet/love-without-limits-11-tearing-down-the-walls-of-separation.

Many of these themes also appear in other of Lev's books.[21] His vision of God was anything but sentimental and romantic.

> Limitless Love forces open doors. Perhaps I had not achieved some sort of peaceful coexistence with God. Perhaps I had succeeded in believing that, as far as my soul was concerned, I was more or less "in good order," and so had come to feel more or less at rest. . . . And now all those presuppositions have been turned upside down by a divine intrusion. God asks something from me that I am quite unprepared for. It is like the news of an unwanted child. . . . To listen to this demand, to take the costly decision, ah, but why? Everything seemed to be going so well! Must I have new uncertainties and anxieties? And now limitless Love wants to erupt into my life. It comes to upset everything in it. It comes to break up what seemed stable and to open new horizons to which I had never given a thought.[22]

Once more, behind the lines are the women and men with whom he interacted, people struggling with the challenges of their marriages, their children, with sickness, and their jobs.[23] Here is the real gift of Lev Gillet to us about the world as sacrament—Love is present everywhere, in a look, a laugh.[24] The course of a very ordinary day reveals the presence of Love, that is, the Lord, without limits as well as our own limitless possibilities to return love in loving others. He once told some very devout people that instead of trying to keep the details of the ancient fasting rules, rules from a very different historical period and culture of the Near East, that we would do better to eat what is put before us in a university cafeteria, what the poor could afford in a coffee shop, or at the market. The times we eat each day—with whom, where, what transpires over

---

[21] Such as Lev Gillet, *Jesus: Dialogue with the Savior* (NY: Desclée, 1963).
[22] Gillet, *In Thy Presence*, 37–38.
[23] Ibid., 47–49, 54.
[24] Ibid., 56, 66–70.

the meal—all these are eucharistic moments in which Love is revealed in "the breaking of bread," just as in the city streets, in our homes, even at night as we head to bed, tired from the day.[25]

Living in the *Una Sancta*

Lastly, what stands out so strongly, particularly in our time of conflict, both in religion and politics, is Lev Gillet's radical openness, the incarnation in his thought and ministry of the freedom of the Eastern church of which Bulgakov, Solovyov, Berdyaev, and so many others knew. Many years later, in a journal entry that would find its way into his volume *Conjectures of a Guilty Bystander*, Thomas Merton would write, almost echoing Lev:

> If I can unite in myself the thought and the devotion of Eastern and Western Christendom, the Greek and the Latin Fathers, the Russians with the Spanish mystics, I can prepare in myself the reunion of divided Christians. From that secret and unspoken unity in myself can eventually come a visible and manifest unity of all Christians. If we want to bring together what is divided, we cannot do so by imposing one division upon the other or absorbing one division into the other. But if we do this, the union is not Christian. It is political, and doomed to further conflict. We must contain all divided worlds in ourselves and transcend them in Christ.[26]

In his own person and work, Lev aimed at this reunification, even though he was unable to see any actual structural divisions healed. His own nomadic existence led him to identify himself with the undivided church, much like Evdokimov,

---

[25] Ibid., 127–32, 120–26, 133–38.
[26] Thomas Merton, *Conjectures of a Guilty Bystander* (Garden City, NY: Image/Doubleday, 1968), 21.

Afanasiev, and other like-minded colleagues and friends. Those who knew him, like Olivier Clément and Elisabeth Behr-Sigel, recognized his remarkable generosity and openness, a catholicity of heart, a universality and amazing freedom of spirit. We have been greatly encouraged by Pope Francis's emphasis on mercy. For him, this means a strong sense of solidarity with the world and commitment to do what one can for the life of the world. For Pope Francis as for Lev Gillet, God suffered with the world, not just for the world's sin, but out of love.

Lev's own personal disabilities, as well as those institutional ones of the churches in which he worked, are not catalogued here simply for biographical completeness. Rather, these dysfunctions underscore the messiness of faith in the lives of each of us and the communities of faith to which we belong. Once again, Francis of Rome has numerous times noted and assailed disorder and dysfunction—clergy careerists, the privileged culture of clericalism, aloof, uncaring church leaders, intractable church bureaucracies. All of these stand in opposition to Jesus and his actions and words of mercy in the gospels. With Lev Gillet's life and frustrations, we learn that one can bring compassion, contact with the "limitless Love" that God is despite all these imperfect, defective structures—not because of them, but despite them. And that is a most valuable lesson about the world as sacrament.

Paul Evdokimov
Photo from Tomoko Faeber-Evdokimoff.

Chapter 6

God's Love Is Foolish, We Become What We Pray: Paul Evdokimov's Vision

Who Is Your God?

The Scriptures and so much of Christian tradition say that God is to be found everywhere. But is it not the case that God has become a problem for us, not God's death or absence as in the past, but rather, versions of God we cannot trust, versions of God with which we cannot connect?

We have become used to contention, even conflict, as important features of religion in America. Same-sex marriage, various kinds of entitlement assistance to low-income, chronically ill, and elderly people, the providing of health insurance to all, the role of government in all the preceding and its size—all of these have become religious issues, not just matters of policy. We routinely hear appeals made to the Scriptures for opposition to these actions and situations. Candidates fall all over each other trying to religiously legitimize their perspectives, no matter how misanthropic or selfish. One even has ventured beyond opposing immigration reform to argue that there are too many legal immigrants in the United States.

Of course, others will also appeal to the example of the Hebrew prophets in standing up for widows, orphans, the poor and hungry, and otherwise dependent. They will see the care of such people in need as central to the Christian life from the earliest days, citing passages from the New Testament Acts of the Apostles on the sharing of possessions in common and the setting apart of deacons to care for those in need.

Unlike the avoidance of religion in the public square, the reluctance to mix religion and politics, the last several decades have been an explosive time for religious alignments and appeals. For all the Scott Walkers and Mike Huckabees, the Glenn Becks and Ted Cruzes, there is the still-towering figure of a Dr. Martin Luther King Jr. and, on the international stage, the Dalai Lama, Archbishop Desmond Tutu, and, most recently, the "pope of mercy," Francis, with his appeals to God's compassion as the model for our thinking and behavior.

As we listen to voices of the writers here in this volume, though, we will hear the theme echoed—that of the mercy of God trumping everything else in the spiritual life—God as forgiveness, God as welcoming the stranger, the outcast, God siding with the marginal, preferring the oppressed. Paul Evdokimov, a lay person and theologian of the Russian emigration in Paris, was a strong, eloquent spokesman for such a view of God and the corresponding attitudes and actions we should take on ourselves. He directs us to a vision of God we don't often encounter. So the central gift we receive from him, quite like that of Lev Gillet, is not only an image but also an understanding and relationship to a God who is above all, love.

> The idea of God as all-powerful imprisons his vision in blind alleys, ready made in advance. Evil becomes an inevitable smudge in creation which God tolerates without recognizing Himself as responsible, the shadow accenting the light. . . . It is the passage from Philippians 2:6-11 which is the keystone and which speaks of the veritable alienation of God from Himself: "*He emptied himself,* taking on the form of a *slave* . . . making himself obedient to death on the cross." The divine omnipotence is freely emptied, renounces all power, above all, even the will to power. "I am in your midst as one who serves" expresses a total otherness with regard to all human under-

standings. God is more than Truth, for he is incarnate in making himself "other," in emptying himself of himself. The omnipotence of the "foolish love" of God does not simply destroy evil and death but assumes them: "by death he has conquered death." His light shines forth from Truth crucified and risen. It is this light which faces the suffering of the innocent, of handicapped children, of absurd accidents, it is here where we can apply to God the most paradoxical concept of invincible weakness. The only response adequate is to say that "God is weak" and that he cannot but suffer with us because suffering is "the bread that God shares with man." He is weak, to be sure, not just in his express omnipotence, but in his Love which freely renounces his power.[1]

Evdokimov found the idea of God's foolish or absurd love in the writings of a fourteenth-century Byzantine court official who also was a spiritual writer, Nicholas Cabasilas.[2] This is precisely the God who throughout the Hebrew Bible kept pursuing Israel, the people God created and chose, despite their continued lack of faithfulness. And it is the same God who eventually became one with creation, one in and with humankind in being born of a woman, growing, living, rejoicing, grieving, suffering, and dying as one of us, for us. So, when the question is raised of how God can permit so much suffering and terror down through the centuries, so much evil, when God is supposedly so good and so forgiving as well as just—a real twist in the whole drama appears. God is not just the imperial ruler requiring subservience and submission. We know that in God's name enormous oppression has occurred. And we know that today, God's name is invoked for all kinds

---

[1] Paul Evdokimov, *In the World, of the Church: A Paul Evdokimov Reader*, ed. and trans. Michael Plekon and Alexis Vinogradov (Crestwood, NY: St. Vladimir's Seminary Press, 2001), 192.

[2] Nicholas Cabasilas, *The Life in Christ*, trans. Carmino J. deCatanzaro (Crestwood, NY: St. Vladimir's Seminary Press, 1974), 164; also 173, 178–79.

of cruelty, hatred, and prejudice. Somehow, it is "godly" to despise refugees and immigrants, and an entire tradition of submission to God—Islam—all this and more, allegedly, in name of God.

Because, in part, of the misuse or abuse of this God, there is understandable, widespread revolt against this God. Better, there is a pushback against what this God's followers have preached and done in this God's name. There is a wholesale rejection of the God who legitimizes patriarchal power, political hierarchy, misogyny, slavery, genocide, religious and ethnically based violence, homophobia, and numerous other toxic perspectives and behaviors. Despite the previously mentioned "religious right" appeals to a God of law and order for the status quo, it is not just agnostics, atheists, and critics of religion who condemn religious legalism and formalism. The sensationalized warning of some political/religious figures that Christianity is under siege, being "persecuted" by a secular, liberal state and the media is understood by most as hyperbole. On the other hand, as Robert Putnam and recognized in their study, *American Grace*, there has been a cumulative drift away from the political use of religion by conservatives. The number of Americans of all religious backgrounds who want same-sex marriage legal continues to rise. Conversely, over 20 percent of Americans are religious "nones," that is, nonparticipants in religious communities and events, and they note intolerance and prejudice among believers as reasons.[3]

Seeing God's Beauty, Living a Life of Service in the World

Like his good friends Elisabeth Behr-Sigel and Lev Gillet, Paul Evdokimov lived through much of the turmoil of the last

---

[3] Pew Research Center, "America's Changing Religious Landscape," May 12, 2015, http://www.pewforum.org/2015/05/12/americas-changing-religious-landscape/.

century. Also like them, he did not spend his life in a monastery or parish rectory. He was a father, a spouse, and then a widower who remarried. With his family, he fled the Russian Revolution, settling in Paris, where like many other impoverished immigrants, he worked at whatever jobs could be found. Scholarships enabled him to complete his undergraduate education at the Sorbonne, and he was in the first graduating class at the St. Sergius Institute.[4] He was a student and then a young scholar in a depression-wracked Europe where there were no positions for teachers or researchers.

Although described even by intimates as an elegant St. Petersburg patrician, reserved and remote, he was nonetheless in behavior and writing a passionate and compassionate voice and, even more so, teacher and counselor. He was able to relate to Third World immigrants and alienated young people in the hostel he administered and in the academic life of Paris in 1968. He was sympathetic to the rebellious young people of 1968, frustrated with corporate greed and inequality, much as today. Earlier he noted the distrust and disgust of many for the black-robed clergy who seemed joyless enemies of change.[5] Knowledgeable about literature, philosophy, politics, music, and art, he was also at home with the diverse people—immigrants, students, activists, and others who lived in his hostel. He was at home in the liturgy and icons of the Eastern church, but as with Mother Maria Skobtsova, he never took them as a refuge or retreat from the world of people in pain.[6] Lev Gillet observed

---

[4] See the photo gallery in Antoine Arjakovsky, *The Way: Religious Thinkers of the Russian Emigration in Paris and Their Journals; 1925–1940*, trans. Jerry Ryan, ed. John A. Jillions and Michael Plekon (Notre Dame, IN: University of Notre Dame Press, 2013).

[5] Evdokimov, *In the World, of the Church*, 49–60; see also Paul Evdokimov, *Ages of the Spiritual Life*, trans. and ed. Michael Plekon and Alexis Vinogradov (Crestwood, NY: St. Vladimir's Seminary Press, 1998), 13–17.

[6] Olivier Clément, *Orient-Occident, Deux Passeurs. Vladimir Lossky et Paul Evdokimov* (Geneva: Labor et Fides, 1985); see also the many remembrances of Evdokimov gathered in the special commemorative number of the French Orthodox periodical *Contacts* 73–74 (1971), as well as Evdokimov's own brief

in the homily at Evdokimov's funeral that he was completely at home in the "kingdom of the invisible ones, of divine realities." But the reason we are listening to him here is that he was equally at home in everyday life. There was never anything sectarian or cultic about his faith. For him, as we shall see, the world truly was sacrament.

Evdokimov points us, not only by his writings but also by his own example, to an eminently practical, this-worldly life of holiness. As a teacher and scholar, he challenges political and economic thinking when it comes to inequality, when it comes to the more than 99 percent who do not share in the wealth and the less than 1 percent who control an enormous amount of the same.[7] He likewise confronts religious traditionalism with the need to change.[8] And rather than hold up just the past historical patterns of holiness, he argues for new ones for our time.[9] He insists on the inseparability of liturgy and life, on the linkage between prayer and service of the neighbor. His lifelong ministry—in the hostels, later in theological schools and ecumenical institutes and journals—is the lived-out liturgy on the "altar of the neighbor's heart," in St. John Chrysostom's phrase, one that Mother Maria Skobtsova also used, the "liturgy after the liturgy."

It is instructive to read Clément's biography of Evdokimov alongside Elisabeth Behr-Sigel's biographical study of his close friend, Lev Gillet, as well as Olga Lossky's biography of Elisa-

---

but poignant biographical essay, "Quelques jalons sur un chemin de vie," in *Le buisson ardent* (Paris: P. Lethielleux, 1981), 13–26.

[7] Evdokimov, *In the World, of the Church*, 61–94.

[8] Ibid., 49–60.

[9] Ibid., 95–154; see also Paul Evdokimov, *The Sacrament of Love*, trans. Anthony P. Gythiel and Victoria Steadman (Crestwood, NY: St. Vladimir's Seminary Press, 1995), 61–62, 92–94; and Michael Plekon, *Hidden Holiness* (Notre Dame, IN: University of Notre Dame Press, 2009); *Saints as They Really Are: Voices of Holiness in Our Time* (Notre Dame, IN: University of Notre Dame Press, 2012).

beth, herself a lifelong friend of Evdokimov. In their lives we see the untypical ways in which they found their footing in the tumultuous world of the twentieth century.[10] Evdokimov was an "ecclesial soul" or, as he also described it, a "liturgical being." He was a member of the church yet completely a citizen of his world and time. For him, living out the Gospel did not mean reproducing the spiritual life of another age. This is the thrust of his best-known book, *Ages of the Spiritual Life*. The same rooting of the Gospel life in the everyday permeates his writing, from his study of marriage as "the sacrament of love" to his many essays on God's solidarity with us—God's suffering with us—in love. Everywhere Evdokimov finds the incarnation, the embodiment of the Good News in one's own time. Living tradition looks like this—finding that God is present in yourself as well as in others and the world around you, finding the world as sacrament.

Leaning on the rediscovery of baptism and of the early church's eucharistic communalism by his friend and colleague, St. Sergius professor and scholar Nicholas Afanasiev, Evdokimov championed the universal priesthood of all. Holiness, as the ancient church and, most important, the New Testament witness, is the vocation of all Christians. This is one of the most important realizations in the last century, grasped by Dorothy Day and Thomas Merton, by Yves Congar and Hans Küng, Maria Skobtsova, and Elisabeth Behr-Sigel, as well as Evdokimov and Afanasiev. Vatican II incorporated this evangelical principle into several of its documents, especially the constitutions on the church and its place in the world, *Lumen Gentium* and *Gaudium et Spes*. Scholars believe one reads in these

---

[10] See Clément, *Orient-Occident*; see also Elisabeth Behr-Sigel, *Lev Gillet, A Monk of the Eastern Church*, trans. Helen Wright (Oxford: Fellowship of St. Alban and St. Sergius, 1999); Olga Lossky, *Towards the Endless Day: The Life of Elisabeth Behr-Sigel*, trans. Jerry Ryan, ed. Michael Plekon (Notre Dame, IN: University of Notre Dame Press, 2010).

documents the impact of both Afanasiev and Evdokimov's thinking and presence as official ecumenical observers.[11]

If holiness is a universal call, then the tools of the spiritual life are for all, not just for ascetic specialists and heroes. Evdokimov goes further. He notes the extreme forms of mortification, deprivation, and fasting prevalent in the early centuries of the church and observes how rooted these were in the culture of the time. But then he asks whether or not there are new, contemporary forms for these? Of course there are, he says, and he proceeds to reflect on fasting from noise and overindulgence in technology, not just types of food or music. Work is addictive, as are information technologies. We have no reason to see asceticism as demanding that we stop working. Rather, we try to return to a balanced, humane, spirit-filled way of integrating work and information into life, along with the relationships and obligations we have to others. We can fast from the tendency to want to distance ourselves from those in need and reach out to help feed those who are hungry, work for laws that extend benefits to the chronically ill and elderly.

Opportunities to serve God in the neighbor abound. Given the political climate, not to mention the recent damage of the recession, attending to inequality, to the deeper economic and social inequities, are important paths of ascetic possibility in our time. Put simply, there is no need to copy ascetical patterns from the past, such, in fact would be spiritual sickness. The kingdom's door, paradise is present everywhere. Evdokimov holds out the truth of the patristic adage, "See your neighbor. There is God." His vision of the spiritual life is neither romantic nor nostalgic. It is as gritty, everyday, and worldly as Mother

---

[11] See Clément, *Orient-Occident*, 115; Evdokimov, *In the World, of the Church*, 199; and Aidan Nicholas, *Theology in the Russian Diaspora: Church, Fathers, Eucharist in Nikolai Afanas'ev; 1893–1966* (Cambridge, UK: Cambridge University Press, 1989), x–xiv, 60.

Maria Skobtsova's feeding the hungry in her hostel and hiding there, the targets of Nazi oppression.

God, the Lover of Humankind

Throughout his essays and books, Evokimov deals with so many aspects of the Christian tradition. Yet at the core is the challenge of living out the Gospel in our time. Crucial to this is coming to terms with the mystery of what appears to be God's absence and silence, especially given the atrocities and sufferings of that last century and the present—the Holocaust and other genocides, the random violence of terrorists, the sufferings of the defenseless, the apparently irremediable poverty and disease that afflicts so many. Is it really that God allows or even wills all the pain and destruction? More and more, people of conscience and discernment leave God out of the formula. But this is never sufficient for him. Unexplainable injustice and suffering continue to cry to a supposedly just and loving God. And so, Evdokimov returns, many times, to the God that later Thomas Merton and now Pope Francis point to, the one who is "mercy within mercy within mercy," the God who is absurd in giving of Himself, foolish in emptying Himself, limitless in loving and forgiving us.

The sources for his thinking about God's identity as Lover of humankind are first and foremost the Scriptures. God is the Bridegroom, the Beloved singing to the Beloved. God is the faithful spouse of the unfaithful. God makes Himself small and defenseless, "the Lamb immolated from before the foundation of the world," suffering for us in his weakness. God is all powerful but is self-limiting, allowing the finite—a tent, an ark, words from a prophet—to contain the infinite. God is the shepherd looking for the sheep that have lost their way, the farmer hunting out the treasure somewhere buried out in the field. Evdokimov, like other Russian writers, is profoundly shaped by the passage in the letter to the Philippians, in which

Christ is described as taking on the identity of a slave to love and save us, "emptying himself" (*kenosis*).[12] Closer to our time, Dostoevsky enables him to point to Christ descending into the hell of our lives, through the forgiveness and mercy of one person for another—not just at Easter, but always. Christ, the Risen One, searches for Adam and Eve and all their children, seeking us to pull all of us out into life. We replicate this in our mercy and openness toward our neighbors.

Evdokimov explores the many questions that persist for believers. Is hell forever?

Is there any hope for so many who die apparently unreconciled with their neighbors and God? Is the eternal damnation of billions compatible with Christ's resurrection victory? Might there be a place for purification and forgiveness in God for those seemingly damned? In addition to the Scriptures, he examines what a number of teachers and saints have said. He also looks at writers such as Khomiakov, Philaret of Moscow, Bukharev, Solovyov, and his own teachers, Berdyaev and Bulgakov.[13]

All these writers, as well as the church's scriptural and liturgical tradition, bring Evdokimov to the God of mercy and compassion, the "abyss of the Father," revealed in the Son who freely sacrifices himself for the life of the world. How different this vision is from the hard atonement theology of Western Christianity. In his last essays, before his death in 1970, Evdokimov pointed out the face of the loving, suffering Father in that of the Virgin Mary, who is the Mother of God.[14] Evdokimov was

---

[12] Johannes Miroslav Oravecz, *God as Love: The Concept and Spiritual Aspects of Agapē in Modern Russian Religious Thought* (Grand Rapids, MI: Eerdmans, 2014).

[13] See Paul Evdokimov *Le Christ dans la pensée russe* (Paris: Cerf, 1970); and Evdokimov, *In the World, of the Church*, 11–36, 217–30.

[14] Evdokimov, *In the World, of the Church*, 155–74; see also my essay, "The Face of the Father in the Mother of God: Mary in Paul Evdokimov's Theological Writing," *Contacts* 172 (1996): 250–69.

close to Afanasiev, and it shows in the insistence that the power of love (an important vision for Afanasiev) is at the heart of how we understand and live in relationship to God.[15]

It is God's love (and not justice) that shapes God's actions, he says, echoing Isaac the Syrian (and the more recent message of Pope Francis). It is also necessary for us to see our own projections onto God, our remaking of God in our own images and likeness. God is other than we take God to be. God is always new, always astonishing. We are consistently surprised, not just by what God does, but by who God is! The depth of God's compassion, the radical freedom of God's forgiveness and generosity surely must scandalize us, shake the very foundations of our religiosity. Thinking back to the "religious right" and the climate of fear, law, and order they foster around God, is it at all surprising that they have no feeling for the Lover of humankind, the foolish Lover Evdokimov shows us from the Scriptures on down through the Christian tradition?

We need to take seriously the claim, in the beginning of the Torah, that we are made in "the image and likeness" of God. We resemble God. God somehow looks like us—the insight of the Russian thinkers' insistence on the "humanity of God."[16] The freedom God gives us is outrageous—it has terrified many. Dostoevsky, the focus of Evdokimov's early study, pits Jesus and his freedom against the grand inquisitor, the archbishop of Seville. Of course for the sake of maintaining order and the loyalty and fear of the faithful, Jesus once more must be eliminated. It has always seemed necessary to either deny or somehow modify the radicalism of this fundamental likeness to God. Evdokimov's teacher, Bulgakov, has God bending over

---

[15] Nicholas Afanasiev, *The Church of the Holy Spirit*, trans. Vitaly Permiakov, ed. Michael Plekon (Notre Dame, IN: University of Notre Dame Press, 2007), 255–74.

[16] See Paul Valliere, *Modern Russian Theology* (Grand Rapids, MI: Eerdmans, 2000).

creation, especially women and men, from the start, assuring us that we are created out of love and that the Creator wants our love. The incarnation only makes sense for such an absurdly loving God, even the terrible suffering of the God-Human, Jesus, on the cross.

That God wants to be loved by God's creatures, that God so lowers and empties God's self to become one with them, one of them, even crucified by them, has always been threatening to us, a dangerous thing for religious ears. The prophet Jonah was not the only one to rebel against such incomparable freedom and generosity. Jonah is joined by apostles, and later, by many theologians, clergy, and laity. The church's history is littered with conflicts precisely over the outrageous compassion of God. The rejected, abused Bridegroom of Good Friday is the culmination of all the nuptial imagery of the Old Covenant, the passion of the bridegroom for his bride despite her infidelity. How many of us still recoil from the Father's unreasonable forgiveness to the prodigal son? How natural it is, like the other, "good son," to despise the feast celebrated for the returned runaway, the reconciliation and resolution of all in the great wedding banquet of the Lamb. Thankfully, there have also always been other voices who were able to receive such a tremendous gift—the absurd lovingkindness of God.

Evdokimov then, in the face of all the human horror of revolutions, wars, genocides, hatred, and greed offers us not the just Judge or the thundering fury of Sinai. Rather, he directs us to a God who gives of self, empties oneself, out of love. This is a God who is powerless over against His creatures, unwilling and unable to compel or force them to be loving. This is the authentic vision in the Scriptures, for love is only real if it is free, not if coerced or compelled. How ineffective and weak this vision has appeared to the enforcers of religion in the past, as well as to the same today. We hear the disgust, for example, of the hierarchs who detest Pope Francis's emphasis on mercy, his unwillingness to judge and condemn LGBT people, his compassion for those marginalized by official church law because of the end of their marriages. The purveyors of God's wrath and justice want to keep order, hold the doors closed, always, of course, "for the good of the church" and for "the salvation of souls." It used to be that the fire and torture were legitimized for the same reasons.

Without realizing it, Evdokimov's recovery of the Scriptures' loving God also reignites the seemingly never-ending, never-to-be-resolved debate about whether or not God can and does suffer. Faithful to the patristic tradition as well as that of the liturgy and the outlook of the Eastern church, Evdokimov does not try to distinguish between human suffering and divine impassibility—lack of suffering in Jesus or for that matter, the Father. Following his teacher, Bulgakov, *kenosis*, or self-emptying out of love, is not only the work of the Son. Those from whom he absorbed this vision of God's philanthropy—figures such as Bukharev, Solovyov, Frank, Florensky, and especially his own mentors, Berdyaev and Bulgakov—were perceived as threatening both ecclesiastical and theological order with a perspective much too free, beyond what the tradition of the Church was thought to bear. In varying degrees, all were criticized and sanctioned. Today, Evdokimov and the rest of his "Paris School" colleagues from between and after the wars are dismissed, at best, as irrelevant, time bound, or at worst, condemned by Fr. Chaplin, a leading spokesman for the Moscow patriarchate, as having held the Russian Church "captive" with alien Western liberalism and humanism! Freedom, even divine freedom, has never played well in the church.

Yet such relentless return to divine freedom, to divine pathos and philanthropy, is for Evdokimov, as for the others, only a return to the view of both biblical and patristic sources themselves. One of Evdokimov's favorite and most frequent quotes is from a Good Friday sermon of the greatest preacher of the Russian church in the nineteenth century, then-Metropolitan, now St. Filaret Drozdov of Moscow. It captures the trinitarian kenosis and compassion: "The Father is crucifying Love, the Son is Love crucified, the Holy Spirit is the invincible power of the Cross." In the light of the Gospel of John, the light shines in the darkness, even that of hell, and the darkness cannot overcome it. For Evdokimov, even Judas carries a morsel of the bread of life out with him from the Last Supper, out into the darkness of his treason.[17] This is the revolutionary vision of Bulgakov of the ultimate triumph and generosity of God, the real victory of the resurrection, in the rising of all.[18]

"God can do everything, except constrain us to love Him," so Evdokimov echoes the tradition, as he has appropriated and inherited it, on God's "limitless Love," a certainty he shared with his friend Fr. Lev Gillet.[19] All this contemplation of the boundless mercy of God was hardly academic abstraction for Evdokimov. In the essay where we began, the context is sketched in stark, realistic terms, just as in many other places in his writings. We should recognize it well. The setting was everyday life in the last century. He mentions the bomb, cancer, and draws on both psychoanalytic and Marxist theory, very much the current of the 1950s and 1960s. Evdokimov was of the opinion that a chair of atheism was necessary in every theological school. He names the films that are now classics, those of Bergman and Antonioni. The writers he cites—Freud, Sartre, de Beauvoir, Sagan, Malraux, Simone Weil—are likewise modern classics and are still read in university courses. Other modern classic thinkers are cited as well: Bultmann, Heidegger, Merleau-Ponty, Kant, Feuerbach, and Nietzsche, among others.

---

[17] Evdokimov, *Ages of the Spiritual Life*, 108, 110.

[18] See the addendum to Evdokimov's *The Bride of the Lamb*, "Apokatastasis and Transfiguration," trans. and ed. Boris Jakim (New Haven, CT: The Variable Press, 1995).

[19] Lev Gillet, *In Thy Presence* (Crestwood, NY: St. Vladimir's Seminary Press, 1977). See also Elisabeth Behr-Sigel *Lev Gillet, A Monk of the Eastern Church*, trans. Helen Wright (Oxford: Fellowship of St. Alban and St. Sergius, 1999).

Evdokimov does not avoid the atrocities and tragedies in the newspapers, on TV, outside our windows, in the streets. He engaged with the street protests in Paris in 1968, with the rebelling students and the targets of their rage.[20] The world Evdokimov addressed was not so far removed from ours today, in the next century. It was, and is, a world remarkably enlarged by technology, unavoidable, intrusive, overwhelming with its data and stimuli, full of opportunities and promise, but still oppressed by many fears: of nuclear and now terrorist destruction, and still other forms of ethnic and religiously rooted violence, of unemployment, long-term economic inequality and racism, discrimination on the basis of gender and sexual identity, and the fear of aging, of sickness, and death.

God Is "Yes" and Only Yes

Does the perspective of the "religious right" respond to all these and other fears very effectively? Is manipulating the image/figure of God for purposes political, for fearmongering (or worse), to support hatred and discrimination—have we not seen through and moved past this kind of "religion"? With Bulgakov, Paul Evdokimov recognizes that we have neither use nor respect for a "theology of terror"—God as the one to fear. If the questions and challenges, even the opposition of our time to God is met only with antagonism, pitting God against humanity and against the world, then religion is seeking to control by fear, condemnation, or divine absolutism. Evdokimov turns us toward God's freedom and unreasonable, generous love. God is neither a distant accountant, nor the impassible and infinite prime cause and vengeful judge. The Scriptures, on the contrary, present God as the One who literally wants to pitch His tent in our midst—live with us. God is

---

[20] "Réaction àla crise de mai: Discerner les esprits," (with Olivier Clément), *Contacts* 62–63 (1968): 228–32.

the Lover who incessantly knocks at the doors of our hearts, speaking even in silence, inviting us to God's table, there to break the break of our suffering with us.

We can say always "no," Evdokimov reminds us, pushing the philanthropy of God to the extreme. But there is only "yes" in God. That "yes" awaits the "yes" of others, as that of the patriarchs and prophets, the "yes" of Mary, John the Baptist, apostles, martyrs, teachers, and many other holy women and men before. And God's "yes" evokes a "yes" from each of us. Evdokimov says that the point of our prayer is *to become what we pray*, to put it into flesh and blood, enact it.[21] This incorporates us into the community of those who have done the same. At the head of this community is the one whose own fiat helped bring God to human birth, Mary, whose great "yes" forever makes her the image of God's love embodied and the love of God enacted.

The "foolishly" loving God whom Evdokimov presents is much more authentic than the distortions of the divine we have thrust upon us by politicized religious figures today. Like his teachers before him, Evdokimov took the risk of proclaiming the abundance of God's compassion rather than imprisoning God within the legalism and ritualism of institutional religion. It is not so much to satisfy contemporary skepticism, or to interest the indifferent, or even to appease the outraged that Evdokimov points to a powerless, suffering God. Rather, it is to affirm the truth about God. This is, despite his critics, what Pope Francis has been trying to do. Only such a God truly loves us, wants to be loved by us, and is worthy of our love. We, in turn, are made ever more like God by our "yes," by our love for God and for the neighbor. Evdokimov always sees the two loves, as did Mother Maria, as indivisible.[22]

---

[21] Evdokimov, *The Sacrament of Love*, 61–62.
[22] *Mother Maria Skobtsova: Essential Writings* (Maryknoll, NY: Orbis Books, 2002), 45–60, 75–83.

Evdokimov's thinking about God's radical love was based on what he experienced in his own life, in the world as sacrament. Just as with Lev Gillet and Elisabeth Behr-Sigel, his was a life full of encounters with people in need, troubled immigrants who lived in the hostels he headed, students from the Third World, and refugees in the 1960s, overwhelmed by the political terror and poverty they fled in Africa and Asia, equally overwhelmed by the turmoil of Paris and the social changes occurring there in those years.

In his youth, he himself was an immigrant, a refugee fleeing revolution who was welcomed with scholarships and the Nansen passports given in those days to refugees who had no country.[23] As a student, he worked at night and on the weekends cleaning train cars for the National Railroad, also in the Citroën plant and in food preparation at Paris restaurants. Later, he would be a house husband/stay-at-home parent, caring for his young children while his wife supported them all as a language teacher. He knew well the "liturgy of life," the many ways in which we love God and the neighbor in our daily work.[24]

After the war he worked in hostels sponsored by CIMADE (*Comité inter-Mouvements pour l'accueil des évacués*). In hostels at Bièvres, Sèvres, and Massy he and his second wife were administrators. Yet he was even more a counselor, a surrogate parent for those in the hostel. After his death, there were many accounts, moving ones too, of his tender, parental care for the communities he led.[25] He was asked to lead their evening prayers, and he developed an ecumenical service for this purpose.

---

[23] On his biography, again see Clément, *Orient-Occident*, 105–90.

[24] Ricky Manolo, *The Liturgy of Life* (Collegeville, MN: Liturgical Press, 2014).

[25] *Contacts* 73–74 (1971): 225–40, 261–67.

By the later 1950s, Evdokimov had begun full-time teaching at St. Sergius Institute and at the Ecumenical Institute in Bossey and the Institut Supérieur d'Etude Œcuméniques of the faculty of Catholic theology in Paris. He was an official ecumenical observer at the third session of Vatican Council II in 1963, and his theological influence on the council's statement on the church and the world, *Gaudium et Spes*, is unmistakable. The years following the council until his death were most productive.[26]

As mentioned already, there are numerous testimonies from former residents of his hostels, recalling his care as a lay pastor and house parent.[27] Likewise, his academic and ecclesiastical

---

[26] Although Evdokimov had published *Dostoïevsky et le Problème du Mal* in 1942 and *Le Mariage, Sacrement de l'Amour* in 1944, it was not until the later 1950s that his writing, both journal essays and monographs, began to flourish. A formidable series of publications proceeded. Of them, it is important to recognize his masterful overview of the church, her liturgy and life and theology, originally published in 1959: *Orthodoxy*, trans. Jeremy Hummerstone (Hyde Park, NY: New City Press, 2011). His study of the place of woman in the economy of salvation (*La Femme et le Salut du Monde* [Paris: Tournai, 1958], English translation *Woman and the Salvation of the World*, trans. Anthony P. Gythiel [Crestwood, NY: St. Vladimir's Seminary Press, 1994]), has been seriously criticized, but he was preparing a revision of it at his death. Evdokimov's *The Sacrament of Love* has also appeared in English under the same title from St. Vladimir's Seminary Press (1985), as has a translation (Torrance, CA: Oakwood, 1990) of his posthumously published examination of the icon and its theology, *The Art of the Icon: A Theology of Beauty*. Several studies—of Russian theologians, of the Orthodox liturgy and theology, particularly the Holy Spirit, appeared both before and after his death: *La Prière de l'Église d'Orient* (1966, Paris: Desclée de Brouwer, 1980); *La Connaissance de Dieu* (1968, Paris: Desclée de Brouwer, 1988); *L'Esprit Saint dans la Tradition Orthodoxe* (Paris: Cerf, 1969, 1977); *Le Christ dans la pensée Russe* (Paris: Cerf, 1970, 1986). There are three collections of the best of his essays: *L'amour fou de Dieu* (Paris: Éditions du Seuil, 1973); *La nouveauté de l'Esprit* (Bégrolles: Abbaye de Bellefontaine, 1977); *Le buisson ardent* (Lethielleux, 1981); *Les âges de la vie spirituelle* (Paris: Desclée de Brouwer, 1964, 1980, 1995) an insightful examination of the development of the spiritual life through church history was retranslated as *Ages of the Spiritual Life*, and a collection of essays was translated as well (Evdokimov, *In the World, of the Church*).

[27] *Contacts* 73–74, 1971.

colleagues write of him as one who listened to all kinds of people and their miseries and who made them welcome, housed, fed in the hostels as well as listened to in the classroom. The essay he wrote about the student uprising in Paris in 1968 reveals a teacher fully aware of the frustrations and impatience of young people with government and their universities, desirous of peace and the sharing of resources. Evdokimov's course on what should be the social theology of the church in the 1960s echoes the same radical criticism of capitalism and of inequality as Pope Francis recently launched on a tour of Latin America in July 2015 and in Mexico in February 2016.[28] Evdokimov proposed that the First World needed to consider long-term peace by taxing itself and using this income for health care, education, and the economic improvement of the Third World.

The world, for Evdokimov, was thus never simply a target for religious proselytism. He understood the "salvation" of the world in the scriptural sense of therapy. True religion, for him, was essentially healing, and healing in every dimension, not just the spiritual.[29] He never rejected the world as secular or essentially immoral as do so many traditionalist Christians today. Rather, since for him the world, particularly that of the suffering and the poor, had always been the location for God's unbelievable solidarity and compassion, the world was, for him, a sacrament of divine healing.

Paul Evdokimov's work and life not only opens up the beauty of the saints, of icons, and the liturgy. He is more than a curator of the past glories of Christianity. He shows how the life of prayer lived out in the church of the past can be lived by us today, not only or even primarily in the beauty and safety of God's house but also, even more so, in the sweat and grime of the streets, in the messiness of our world. His is an everyday,

---

[28] Evdokimov, *In the World, of the Church*, 61–94.
[29] Ibid., 11–36.

a worldly life in God. He fosters a very important meeting of tradition with our thinking and ways of living now in the twenty-first century. He does not allow us to forget that the life of prayer, our "liturgical being," is valid only when continued in the liturgy of lovingkindness and service to the neighbor. And at the heart of this vision lies his proclamation of the "abyss" of divine compassion, the God's whose love for us is limitless and all-powerful precisely in suffering and weakness.

Thomas Merton

Photo from the Thomas Merton Center,
Bellarmine University, Louisville, Kentucky.

Chapter 7

"Seeking the True Self": Thomas Merton, Living and Praying in the World

Thomas Merton is still one of the most influential spiritual writers in America, years after his death. In 2015, his centennial, there were numerous new publications, conferences, and documentaries. We continue to listen to him because of his honesty as well as his humanity. Like others, from Augustine to Teresa of Avila, and his contemporary Dorothy Day, there is an exuberance that makes him—and them—classics. Still provocative is his determination to continue to seek God, to come to terms with his own gifts and defects, in his commitment to continue to find his "true self," the person, the saint he was made to be.

His letters and journals are remarkable records of his experiments with ideas. They contain his rants as well as his coming to terms with crises and difficulties, of which there were many. His musings on details of everyday life brings us back to America in the 1960s. In his journals for those years, Merton has a lot to say about the civil rights movement, about the antiwar movement, and about the place of the church in the turbulence of those days. When he speaks of the president he means Lyndon B. Johnson. He is torn apart, as many were, by the assassinations, in that last year of his life, of Robert F. Kennedy and Dr. Martin Luther King Jr.

Throughout Merton's journals, in his letters, and now in sources like Michael Mott's biography, not to mention numerous scholarly articles, it is clear that for a long time Merton wanted more solitude in his life at the Abbey of Gethsemani. On the one hand, he was given positions of enormous responsibility in the formation of young monastics there, as master of novices and the director of student monks. And Merton continued to maintain an amazing volume of writing—books, articles, reviews, not to mention his journals and the huge correspondence he conducted, much of this now published. He took his turns presiding and preaching in the liturgical cycle of the monastery and also earlier directed work projects for the monks in formation under him. He had considered asking for a release to another order in which he could find more quiet, such as the Camaldolese Benedictines or some experimental monasteries, including one in Cuernevaca, Mexico. What he eventually arrived at was the possibility of a hermitage at Gethsemani. This course derived from permission he was granted to spend time out walking, reading, and praying on the extensive monastery property, then time in an abandoned shed. At last a small concrete block building was constructed not far from the main monastery buildings, for conferences and retreats—the notable gathering of peacemakers was held there in November 1964.

By the time Merton was finally allowed to live at his hermitage, he had come a long way from the idealistic author of his best-selling memoir, *The Seven Storey Mountain*. Released decades after his death, his journals show the extent to which his faith and spiritual practice had evolved. Jonathan Montaldo puts it well. Though often touted as a "spiritual master," Merton would have recoiled at such a title. The substantial record of his self-examination he left behind, his journals, when first made public, scandalized some readers. In these years of daily account-keeping of his spiritual life, Merton does not hide what he saw as his failures, his falling into despair and

"Seeking the True Self" 129

self-pity. But as with other literature of the stories of souls, the journals reveal as well how God was at work in the mess of his everyday life, in the complex personality at once writer, monk, critic, and individual looking to love and be loved.[1]

Throughout his life, Merton's pilgrimage continued. He was never content, always restless, constantly becoming—someone who knew him well described him this way to me.[2] Merton has a place in this book because not only did he work hard at it but also he was able to attain a spiritual life that was worldly while at the same time deeply in communion with God and others. I want to listen carefully to what Merton has to say about life, prayer, and his identity as he moved to a new phase of his time as a monk, that of living at the hermitage. It is most valuable for us now—mindfulness, returning to simplicity, attention to the world and oneself, doing away with dualism, all while celebrating the ordinary, the everyday, and passing on what one has received. Merton offers a distinctive approach to finding God in the ordinary, of experiencing the world as sacrament.

Day of a Hermit

While Merton had wanted more solitude, his hermitage was never an isolated retreat. It was only about a mile from the main monastery buildings. He complained about fans as well as stalkers who occasionally terrified him and became a nuisance. Yet journal entries, letters, and photos witness to the

---

[1] Victor A. Kramer, "'Crisis and Mystery': The Changing Quality of Thomas Merton's Later Journals," in *The Vision of Thomas Merton*, ed. Patrick F. O'Connell (Notre Dame, IN: Ave Maria Press 2003), 77–97; and Jonathan Montaldo, "Loving Winter When the Plant Says Nothing: Thomas Merton's Spirituality in His Private Journals," in O'Connell, *Vision of Thomas Merton*, 99–117.

[2] Very much in focus with what I am saying here, see Jonathan Montaldo, "To Uncage His Voice: Thomas Merton's Inner Journey toward *Parrhesia*," *The Merton Seasonal* 39, no. 4 (2014): 9–20.

many visitors he welcomed there.[3] It was the site for an important gathering of peacemakers in November 1964.[4]

"Sometime in May, 1965," as Merton's journal entry puts it, comes "Day of a Stranger."[5] Having recently moved into the hermitage, he wrote a description of his daily routine as a hermit. He had done a bit of this in a piece for *Holiday* magazine, "Rain and the Rhinoceros."[6] At first, he was allowed to spend part of the day at the hermitage and the rest at the monastery. Later on, more improvements would be made, such as plumbing, electricity, and a small addition for a chapel. On August 20, 1965, he would be done as novice master, and by vote of the monastery council, allowed to take up full-time residence.

Merton wrote this essay in response to his friend, the Argentinian poet Miguel Grinberg, and his request for a description of a day in the life of a hermit.[7] The first, shorter version is edgy, confrontational.[8] There was to be a second and then later a third, longer version.[9] Merton adds reflection, even a short question-and-answer exchange, as well as detailed descriptions of everyday chores ("rituals," he calls them): washing the coffee pot, approaching the outhouse carefully because of the snakes who like to lodge inside, spraying for insects, clos-

---

[3] *Meatyard/Merton: Photographing Thomas Merton*, The Fons Vitae Thomas Merton Series (Louisville, KY: Fons Vitae, 2013).

[4] Gordon Oyer, *Pursuing the Spiritual Roots of Protest: Merton, Berrigan, Yoder and Muste at the Gethsemani Abbey Peacemakers Retreat* (Eugene, OR: Cascade Books, 2014).

[5] *Dancing in the Water of Life: The Journals of Thomas Merton*, ed. Robert E. Daggy, vol. 5, 1963–1965 (San Francisco: HarperSanFrancisco, 1997), 237.

[6] *Holiday* 37 (May 1965): 8, 10, 12, 15–16. It is accessible in *Thomas Merton: Selected Essays*, ed. Patrick F. O'Connell (Maryknoll, NY: Orbis Books, 2014), 216–24.

[7] Daggy, *Dancing in the Water of Life*, 87, 89–90.

[8] Ibid., 239–42.

[9] This version was published in *The Hudson Review* 20 (1967): 211–18 and then by itself (Salt Lake City, UT: Gibbs M. Smith, 1981).

ing and opening windows for either cooling breeze or to shut out heat. These are elements of his daily liturgy of living—and lessons for all of us in mindful, prayerful existence!

Merton's very important letter to Ludovico Silva not only previews but also enlarges on what he would say in "Day of a Stranger."

> The religion of our time, to be authentic, needs to be the kind that escapes practically all religious definition. Because there has been endless definition, endless verbalizing, and words have become gods. There are so many words that one cannot get to God. . . . When [God] is placed firmly beyond the other side of words, the words multiply like flies and there is a great buzzing religion, very profitable, very holy, very spurious. One tries to escape by [words] of truth that fail. One's whole being must be an act for which there is no word. . . . My whole being must be a yes, an Amen and an exclamation that is not heard. Only after that is there any point in exclamations. . . . That is where the silence of the woods comes in. Not that there is something new to be thought or discovered in the woods, but only that the trees are all sufficient exclamations of silence, and one works there, cutting wood, clearing ground, cutting grass, cooking soup, drinking fruit juice, sweating, washing, making fire, smelling smoke, sweeping, etc. This is religion. The further one gets away from this, the more one sinks in the mud of words and gestures. The flies gather.[10]

This is Merton at his most discerning, aware of the entrapment of faith in the culture and sentimentality of the past, something of which he saw himself guilty in his earlier writings.[11] Merton lists writers who speak to him in the solitude, from the ancient Syrian mystic Philoxenus to contemporary

---

[10] Thomas Merton, *The Courage for Truth: Letters to Writers*, ed. Christine M. Bochen (New York: Farrar, Straus and Giroux, 1993), 224–25. Thanks to Jonathan Montaldo for pointing out this passage.

[11] Montaldo, "To Uncage His Voice," 13–15.

poet Nicanor Parra. He adds Asian authors, more contemporaries like Ungaretti and Zukovsky, as well as almost half a dozen women writers, including Julian of Norwich and Flannery O'Connor.

The South American destination of the piece, *Papeles*, would render "stranger" as *extraño*, and there are layers of meaning here. Merton is "stranger" to his own North American society and culture. This is stressed throughout, his sense that America would want to claim him as a citizen, a consumer, a supporter of government policy. As in the rest of his journals and other essays in the last decade of his life, he was anything but a booster of American values, politics, lifestyle, or anything else. "Wealth is poison," he shouts in the text, also decrying the pollution of water and soil. There is affluence, but also hunger and poverty in the United States, and affluence has produced "dementia" rather than peace and satisfaction.[12]

> I do not intend to belong to the world of squares that is constituted by the abdication of choice, or by the fraudulent choice (the mass-roar in the public square, or the assent to the televised grimace).
>
> I do not intend to be citizen number 152037. I do not consent to be poet number 2291. I do not recognize myself as the classified antisocial and subversive element that I probably am in the file of a department in a department. Perhaps I have been ingested by an IBM machine in Washington, but they cannot digest me. I am indigestible: a priest who cannot be swallowed, a monk notoriously discussed as one of the problems of the contemporary Church by earnest seminarists, wearing bright spectacles in Rome.
>
> I have not chosen to be acceptable. I have not chosen to be inacceptable. I have nothing personal to do with the present indigestion of officials, of critics, of clerics, of housewives, of

---

[12] Daggy, *Dancing in the Water of Life*, 240.

amateur sociologists. It is their indigestion. I offer them no advice.[13]

Merton joined the ranks of Catholics who spoke out for more freedom both in the church and the country, most notably Dorothy Day and the Berrigan brothers. He recognized the institutional power that saw such protest as great threats. He himself would experience the ostracizing and silencing of such voices of prophetic protest.

The journals document a great deal of personal struggle, failure but also the growth of the stranger in the hermitage years to follow. There were his visitors, celebrities and less known, exchanges with other writers both in letters and in person, the falling in love with "M," and so much soul-searching and anguish that surrounded it. Whatever can be said about his relationship with her, this was a life-changing encounter. It is true that we only know of it from his point of view. Yet Merton learned that he could be loved and that he could love.

Out in the Woods, Still in the World

Merton refused to be part of the American dream, of rat race between work and leisure. He had been turned inside out in an epiphany, the vision narrated in the famous passage, "In Louisville, at the corner of Fourth and Walnut."[14] He was no longer the one who had run away to the paradise of the monastery. Such was his early infatuation. By May 1965 much had changed, not just in the larger world of which he was a part, but within Merton himself as well.

---

[13] Thomas Merton, "Day of a Stranger," second draft. Typescript in the Thomas Merton Studies Center, Bellarmine University, 1–2.

[14] Thomas Merton, *Conjectures of a Guilty Bystander* (Garden City, NY: Doubleday, 1968), 156–58.

Even out in the woods, with the birds, foxes, and snakes, in silence, the world was with him, in him. And so, he carried the world and the many with whom he corresponded with him in the early hours as he read from the Scriptures and other writers. This was a huge realization for him, especially poignant in the start of this new life out in the hermitage. There was no longer separation of either the world or God from this hermit-poet.

The world intruded on Merton's "day." Overhead he saw jetliners and imagined them full of cocktail-swilling passengers en route to Miami or Chicago. With the Cold War and Vietnam alive and well, he visualized the atomic weapons in the bomb bays of the SAC planes flying above him. He lists words that penetrate the silence of his rising at 2:15 a.m. for praying the psalms. *Magna misericordia*—great mercy, also "wash me," "destroy iniquity," "I know my iniquity, "I have sinned." "Concepts," he says cynically, "without interest in the world of business, war, politics, culture, etc. Concepts also often without interest to ecclesiastics."[15]

Merton begins to sound as though he is writing in our time, not over fifty years ago, now, when we are tired of hate passing for politics, of remote, disconnected churches and overspiritualized religion.

> Blood, Guile. Anger. The way that is not good. . . . Out there the hills in the dark lie southward. The way over the hills is blood, guile, dark, anger, death: Selma, Birmingham, Mississippi.[16]

We are back in the 1960s, in the civil rights conflicts, and even closer is Fort Knox, with gold reserves and material for nuclear weapons. Maybe we are not back in the 1960s at all!

---

[15] Thomas Merton, "Day of a Stranger," in *Thomas Merton: Spiritual Master; The Essential Writings*, ed. Lawrence Cunningham (New York: Paulist Press, 1992), 218.

[16] Ibid., 218.

Just before all of this, the passage I like best.

> This is not a hermitage—it is a house. ("Who was that hermitage I seen you with last night?") What I wear is pants. What I do is live. How I pray is breathe. Who said Zen? Wash out your mouth if you said Zen. If you see a meditation going by, shoot it. Who said "Love?" Love is in the movies. The spiritual life is something that people worry about when they are so busy with something else they think they ought to be spiritual. Spiritual life is guilt. Up here in the woods is seen the New Testament: that is to say, the wind comes through the trees and you breathe it. Is it supposed to be clear? I am not inviting anybody to try it. Or suggesting that one day the message will come saying NOW. That is none of my business.[17]

This is confrontational language, startling for one who says his hermitage is "full of ikons of the Holy Virgin"![18] In a time where "finding yourself" and "being yourself" were trending, Merton retorts that he intends to forget about being himself![19]

Merton here is irreverent, smugly sarcastic, playing the proverbial wise guy, as in his letters to his friend, Robert Lax.[20] He could not have known that in the last three years of his life so much would happen. He would be given a hermitage and solitude, allowed to travel, and fall in love. As for the world beyond the monastery and so much going on in it—the Cold War's aggressive nuclear arms race, then the Vietnam War and the civil rights movement, the growing cultural upheaval of the 1960s—Merton had long before returned to this world.

---

[17] Ibid., 217.
[18] Ibid., 219.
[19] Ibid., 215.
[20] *When Prophecy Still Had a Voice: The Letters of Thomas Merton and Robert Lax*, ed. Arthur W. Biddle (Lexington, KY: University of Kentucky Press, 2001), 200; see also Michael N. McGregor, *Pure Act: The Uncommon Life of Robert Lax* (New York: Fordham University Press, 2015).

This he accomplished through extensive reading and his voluminous correspondence with writers, activists, like-minded critics of church and society, and peacemakers. Merton still wears the Trappist habit to the monastery and vestments at the liturgy, but beneath it all, not just literally, what he wears is pants. Completing the vision he has at the corner of Fourth and Walnut, he is one with his sisters and brothers everywhere. He is just like everyone else, searching for peace, for God. He has discovered the world as sacrament.

The volcano of writing continues to erupt—correspondence, essays, translations. He reads incessantly, even while walking outside. But he also makes coffee in the predawn darkness, does simple cooking to feed himself. Cleans house, does dishes. Cuts brush, stacks wood, and feeds the fireplace. All that anyone living rurally, in the woods, would do.

Mindful of the Everyday

A key feature of the "Day of a Stranger," is mindfulness. It may be trending into meaninglessness today, but for Merton, it was an important stage of growth in the spiritual life. One could also call it contemplative attention, but whatever description, it is the product of the pattern of living he also describes as his existence there. This contemplative way of being includes cleaning away a lot of the baggage of institutionalized, stereotypical religion. Getting back to basics means the psalms, the rest of Scripture—"Up here in the woods is seen the New Testament." We don't find any longer the elaboration he employed in earlier writing, like *Seeds/New Seeds of Contemplation, No Man Is An Island*, and similar books. His South American correspondent, a secular poet, would be able to understand the kind of "slow living," like today's "slow food," as more humane, basic, and attuned to the most important things in one's faith and existence.

"Seeking the True Self" 137

    This is very beautifully expressed through what Merton saw and chose to capture with his camera.[21] In the many photographs he takes, one rarely finds any specifically religious images or objects. He was not interested in writing about such details of church or monastic life and observance, nor in stock photography of monastic piety. Rather, it is the simple, worn, everyday things inside the hermitage and around it and in the countryside that he most frames in his camera lens and captures—barns, a woodpile, the chair on the hermitage porch, his kitchen and dishes, his desk, covered with books, magazines, and manuscripts. All these are the sacramental elements of his life.[22] This I take to be another facet of the living, breathing prayer he engages in and tells us about. His prayer is as ordinary as the stool, the little hermitage kitchen, the water can, typewriter, and other objects that are the markers of his space, the tools of his "day."

    What he does is live. How he prays is breathing and it is the wind, the Spirit, who blows where she wills. The spiritual life, Zen, Love—all this does not get close to the life he experiences in the cinder block walls and out in the woods. In the quiet, the words of the psalms, especially Psalm 51, are clear. Over against iniquity, sin, blood, anger, guile, and death there is mercy—the mercy of God, mercy for us, mercy that becomes ours to give and be. It is the theme that winds its way through all of Merton's pages and life.[23] In a journal entry, one of many, he expresses it.

> [S]eeing the multitude of stars above the bare branches of the wood, I was suddenly hit, as it were, with the whole package

---

[21] *A Hidden Wholeness/The Visual World of Thomas Merton: Photographs by Thomas Merton and John Howard Griffin* (Boston: Houghton Mifflin, 1979).

[22] See Thomas Merton, *Day of a Stranger* (Salt Lake City, UT: Gibbs M. Smith, 1981), 22–23.

[23] Thomas Merton, *The Sign of Jonas* (Garden City, NY: Doubleday/Image, 1956), 362.

of meaning of everything: that the immense mercy of God was upon me, that the Lord in infinite kindness had looked down on me and given me this vocation out of love, and that he had always intended this, and how foolish and trivial had been all my fears and twistings and desperation.[24]

In these few pages describing a typical course of the day in his hermitage, Merton says more than in many of his more focused pieces, ones on contemplation, what it is and is not. Quite directly, he shows how both integration and contemplation play out in daily life. In "Day of a Stranger," we find not so much a formula or program but rather a narrative of prayer lived out and the vision that such an everyday prayer creates.

The Natural World's Sacramentality

Another important aspect of life Merton shares with us is his awareness, not just of his own thoughts and actions but of the immediate surroundings, of others and then, the world beyond.

"The hills are blue and hot." Out in the hermitage, Merton is awake to the world of creation, to the need to protect the environment. He knows all the birds that are his neighbors, the snake in the outhouse as well.[25] "The woods and the foxes," the natural world, make for the "cool" that is his immediate existence, over against the "hot medium," in McLuhan terms, of the monastery. This "hot" world is one of "ought" and "must" and "should," despite St. Benedict, who saw the best thing to do was to "cool it." Merton says his life is one in which he does not have to "bundle up packages and deliver them to myself."[26] These "packages" are the trends, the traditions, the

---

[24] Daggy, *Dancing in the Water of Life*, 177–78.
[25] Merton, "Day of a Stranger," in Cunningham, *Thomas Merton: Spiritual Master*, 215.
[26] Ibid., 217.

selves with which we are obsessed and obsess over with others.

Up on the hermitage hill, the air is clean, the Spirit is the wind that comes through the trees. Merton sensed that it had been blowing through his life for years, clearing away a lot of debris. Before his days' end, three years ahead, even more would be cleaned out, revealed, made simple. In that small hermitage, in the simplicity of keeping a house, everything that was necessary became clear.

Throughout his writings, Merton used the natural world to talk about contemplative prayer. He saw all of creation full of the presence of God, all the world a sacrament in our terms. Contemplation was simple silence before and with God. A God "out there," or "up there" or anywhere else but in and with oneself too, was impossible for him. In *Thoughts in Solitude*, he says the sky, birds, and wind in the trees have become his prayer.[27] All through *New Seeds of Contemplation* we hear much the same.[28]

---

[27] Thomas Merton, *Thoughts in Solitude* (New York: Farrar, Straus and Giroux, 1958), 92, also 99, 101, 114.

[28] "A tree gives glory to God by being a tree. For in being what God means it to be, it is obeying Him. It "consents" so to speak, to His creative love. It is expressing an idea which is in God and which is not distinct from the essence of God, and therefore a tree imitates God by being a tree. . . . The forms and individual characters of living and growing things, of inanimate beings, of animals and lowers and all nature, constitute their holiness in the sight of God. Their inscape is their sanctity. It is the imprint of His wisdom and His reality in them. The special clumsy beauty of this particular colt on this April day in this field under these clouds is a holiness consecrated to God by His own creative wisdom and it declares the glory of God. The pale flowers of the dogwood outside this window . . . the little yellow flowers that nobody notices on the edge of the road are saints looking up into the face of God. . . . For me to be a saint means to be myself. Therefore the problem of sanctity and salvation is in fact the problem of finding out who I am and of discovering my true self." Thomas Merton, *New Seeds of Contemplation* (New York: New Directions, 1961), 29, 30, 31.

By 1965, in "Day of a Stranger," the more pious and theoretical tone is gone, while the substance is perhaps even more formidable. He doesn't waste his time with "spirituality" or "love" or Zen. "I am working on knowing myself, becoming myself, my true self," Merton seems to say, encouraging us to do the same. The "false and private self" that tries to exist outside God, reality, and life is an illusion.[29] It is in the "love and mercy of God" that the secret of identity is hidden and where it is to be found.[30] We have to empty ourselves, radically simplify daily activities, possessions, even thoughts and prayer so that we can be in and with God. As Merton describes his prayer to Abdul Aziz: "Strictly speaking I have a very simple way of prayer. It is centered entirely on attention to the presence of God and to His will and to His love."[31]

I think this simplicity of prayer is one of the most important gifts of Merton to us today. Prayer is never just a formal, obligatory activity. Here he knew from hard experience. When he entered the monastery, not only did the Trappists sing the Canonical Office, all the seven hours in Latin every day. They also did the Office of the Blessed Virgin Mary, and often, the Office of the Dead. On some days the hours in choir for this formal prayer could have been six or seven if one also included the Mass. For Merton the prayer of the church was deeply integrated in his life. Even on his final trip, to Asia, he was praying the daily psalms and readings.

So too did these prayer "hours" define his "day" at the hermitage. From the middle of the night— he rises at 2:15 a.m. for night vigils—the day is framed by prayer. He quotes from just one psalm, but there a hundred and forty-nine others he sings,

---

[29] Ibid., 34.
[30] Ibid., 35.
[31] Thomas Merton, *The Hidden Ground of Love*, ed. William H. Shannon (New York: Farrar, Strauss and Giroux, 1985), 63–64.

along with Alleluia in the Gregorian second mode.[32] At the time he writes this account of his daily activities, he is still trudging down to the monastery to finish his teaching of the novices, to take part in the daily community liturgy. He returns, water bottle filled (this is before his plumbing and power have been hooked up) and notices a bumblebee humming in the eaves, the larks singing as they rise from the tall grass. There is quiet for reading and reflection in the afternoon. He says he's married "the silence of the forest."

> The sweet dark warmth of the whole world will have to be my wife. Out of the heart of that dark warmth comes the secret that is heard only in silence, but it is the root of all the secrets that are whispered by all the loves in their beds all over the world. So perhaps I have an obligation to preserve the stillness, the silence, the poverty, the virginal point of pure nothingness which is at the center of all other loves. I attempt to cultivate this plant without comment in the middle of the night and water it with psalms and prophecies in silence.[33]

For all the quiet of the woods, the companionship of the animals and the release from all the demands of monastery life, Merton was no slacker in his "day." He continued to produce—reviews, articles, essays, and letters; hundreds of them. I counted over thirty authors mentioned in the various drafts of the piece, from Isaiah and Jeremiah to Auden, Camus, and Sartre. There are great voices of the tradition as well as doubters and critics of the same, visionaries, and realists.

Merton's "day" was a continual nourishment of inner life. He was writing like crazy. Through his talks at the monastery, he connected his confreres to a really diverse selection of writers

---

[32] Merton, "Day of a Stranger," in Cunningham, *Thomas Merton: Spiritual Master*, 221.
[33] Ibid., 219.

and themes. Scripture and the monastic tradition were important, but he was constantly introducing authors and issues that made his listeners part of the larger world. The recordings of these talks over many years reveals the sheer breadth of Merton's learning, all of which he carefully shared with his community. There are the classical spiritual writers as well as lesser-known Cistercians. He introduced Sufism and Buddhism to his fellow monastics. He spoke on literary giants like Blake, on whom he wrote his master's thesis, Donne and Nietzsche, as well as Beckett, Camus, Joyce, Auden, Kafka, Weil, and Foucault, among others. The death of John F. Kennedy is discussed as well as contemporary Russian writers like Pasternak, Bulgakov, and Berdyaev, various approaches in Marxism, racism in the South and throughout the country, and the work of Martin Luther King Jr. This is just the audio portion. Readers know well the enormous correspondence, all the reviews, essays, and articles and then the many volumes of notes and comments in his journals. Merton was a walking university. The hermitage may have been rural peacefulness, solitude, and silence, but the world of ideas blazed there too.

"Paradise Is All Around Us and We Do Not Understand . . . the Gate of Heaven Is Everywhere"[34]

If simplicity is a crucial gift Merton gives, then commitment to work, to service of others and the world are others. In his "day," there is no valuing of one action over another. All have their place—the psalms, Scriptures, liturgy, the reading from all the writers mentioned and many more, the talks for the novices and Gethsemani community, and then the work of writing about trying to find God and God's way, in the civil rights and antiwar movements, in the Vatican II renewal in the church, and much more—the laundry, making coffee on rising

---

[34] Merton, *Conjectures of a Guilty Bystander*, 132, 158.

or supper at day's end, sweeping, stacking wood, cutting grass and weeds, and the rest. What I want to present as Merton's vision is summed up beautifully in a passage of a letter to Etta Gullick.

> As for spiritual life: what I object to about [the phrase] "the Spiritual Life" is the fact that it is a part, a section, set off as if it were a whole. It is an aberration to set off our "prayer" etc. from the rest of our existence, as if we were sometimes spiritual, sometimes not. As if we had to resign ourselves to feeling that the unspiritual moments were a dead loss. That is not right at all, and because it is an aberration, it causes an enormous amount of useless suffering. Our "life in the Spirit" is all-embracing, or should be. First it is the response of faith receiving the word of God, not only as a truth to be believed but as a gift of life to be lived in total submission and pure confidence. Then this implies fidelity and obedience, but a total fidelity and a total obedience. From the moment that I obey God in everything, where is my "spiritual life"? It is gone out the window, there is no spiritual life, only God and His word and my total response.[35]

God is everywhere and fills all things. Merton learned to pray differently, in his own struggles, in his disappointments, in his hope. Prayer found a way into his concerns for ecology and peace. Describing his day as a stranger, one marginal but yet still present in his community and world, he unwittingly echoes an ancient, scriptural perspective, namely that we are always strangers and pilgrims, that our real home is heaven.

Understanding heaven not to be "up there" or "after" this life, but here and now, Merton's own search for home, orphan that he was as a child, was not just for a street address and a building. "Home," for this "stranger" was finding once again,

---

[35] Merton, *The Hidden Ground of Love*, 357.

the world and his "true self."³⁶ And in so doing, Merton left for us a path, a way of seeing the world and our lives in it, as sacramental celebration—and a foretaste of the feast to come.

---

³⁶ Montaldo, "Loving Winter," 117: "Merton gradually abandoned hope for a suddenly perfect life in some perfect place always elsewhere than where he actually was. He surrendered himself instead to the slow heart-work of seeking God one day and one night at a time in the place where his eyes opened and shut every morning and every evening. He got up and fell down, he got up and fell down, and he got up all over again. Merton's journals are a confession of the necessity for us all to move insistently forward through our daily experiences of both absence and presence to that Voice of Love calling each of us to Love's Self."

Marilynne Robinson
Photo from the University of Iowa.

Chapter 8

"I Sense a Sacredness in Things": Marilynne Robinson and the World of *Gilead*

> I don't like categories like religious and not religious. As soon as religion draws a line around itself it becomes falsified. It seems to me that anything that is written compassionately and perceptively probably satisfies every definition of religious whether a writer intends it to be religious or not. . . . [A] mystical experience would be wasted on me. Ordinary things have always seemed numinous to me. One Calvinist notion deeply implanted in me is that there are two sides to your encounter with the world. You don't simply perceive something that is statically present, but in fact there is a visionary quality to all experience. It means something because it is addressed to you. This is the individualism that you find in Walt Whitman and Emily Dickinson. You can draw from perception the same way a mystic would draw from a vision.[1]

Marilynne Robinson's work is not only beautifully crafted. It is truthful. As she told an interviewer, writing for her is not so much "craft" as it is "testimony," witnessing to what is there all over creation. Someone has said she is constantly looking for grace working in people's lives. I believe this is another

---

[1] Marilynne Robinson, "The Art of Fiction no. 198," *Paris Review* 186 (Fall 2008), http://www.theparisreview.org/interviews/5863/the-art-of-fiction-no-198-marilynne-robinson.

way of saying she perceives all of life and the world as sacrament.

"A lot of people who actually believe in the sacredness of life, they write things that are horrible, desolating things," Robinson said. "Because, for some reason, this deeper belief doesn't turn the world. . . . It comes down to fear; the fear of making self-revelation of the seriousness of 'I sense a sacredness in things.' "[2] Her books are entrancing. After her first novel's publication in 1980, it took twenty-four years for the next one to come out.[3] That was *Gilead*, the first in a trilogy. She of course did not stop writing in that period—there are numerous essays and a nonfiction volume published in those years.

In what follows, I am not going to take apart the trilogy volumes or inspect closely the plot lines and characters. Readers need to allow themselves the opportunity to experience these splendid and well-received books themselves. I do, however, want to show that Robinson deserves a place with the other writers we are listening to here, precisely because she shows us the grace and mercy all around, because she is convinced of the world as sacrament. Moreover, her characters do just spit out theology. Rather, the good people of Gilead are instances of God at work, what I have elsewhere called "living icons."[4]

---

[2] Wyatt Mason, "The Revelations of Marilynne Robinson," *New York Times Magazine*, October 1, 2014, http://www.nytimes.com/2014/10/05/magazine/the-revelations-of-marilynne-robinson.html.

[3] Marilynne Robinson, *Housekeeping* (New York: Farrar, Straus and Giroux, 1980).

[4] Mother Maria Skobtsova, as noted in the chapter about her here, used this description of persons of faith. See *Mother Maria Skobtsova: Essential Writings* (Maryknoll, NY: Orbis Books, 2003), 81; see also Richard Rohr, *Things Hidden: Scripture as Spirituality* (Cincinnati, OH: St. Anthony Messenger Press, 2008), 35; and Michael Plekon, *Living Icons: Persons of Faith in the Eastern Church* (Notre Dame, IN: University of Notre Dame Press, 2002).

Gilead and Its People

To enter the trilogy—*Gilead*, *Home*, and *Lila*—is to walk into a world of parables, a kind of sacramental microcosm. But this is not obviously so. The place is a small town in Iowa. *Gilead* is set in 1956. *Home* is at roughly the same time, while *Lila* starts back decades before. In *Gilead*, in 1956, television is new, and even the Boughton and Ames households acquire sets. Memories of the Great Depression and its misery are fresh, also of the war. There is even more distant history—that of Rev. Ames's grandfather and father, during the Civil War and after—recalled. The civil rights movement is just making the national news. The Montgomery bus boycott is viewed on TV, and not positively. The names of Stevenson and Eisenhower are mentioned.

It is a small, dusty town set amid farms. The model for it is Tabor, in southwest Iowa, a center of abolitionist activity and the home of the Rev. John Todd, on whom the figure of John Ames's pastor-grandfather is based. In several interviews, Robinson notes that she did extensive historical research into the migration from New England to the Midwest, Iowa in particular, of the patriarch Rev. Ames. He was originally from Maine. John Ames's father, also a pastor, became a pacifist during World War I. In *Gilead*, John Ames does spiritual combat with both of these larger-than-life men. The grandfather tore apart his congregation on the abolition issue, left them to serve as a chaplain in the Union army and was wounded there. John's own father remained a parish pastor but suffered through the miseries that the First World War inflicted on young men.

The grandson and son, John Ames, spends all his life, from childhood to senior years, in that small town. Every street, all the corners of his church, are home. On sleepless nights, he wanders the lanes, sometimes spends the earliest morning hours in the sanctuary. It could seem confining, suffocating. But it is not. His reading, and then radio and television, link St. Louis and Memphis and the rest of the country and the world to Gilead. Ames is absolutely at home in them all. Grace is everywhere.

Most of the villagers of Gilead, though, remain nameless, even faceless in Robinson's account in the three volumes. The center of the three very different but related narratives are the Rev. John Ames, the town's Congregationalist pastor, his much younger, mysterious wife Lila, and their young son, Robby. The other pole is the household of the town's Presbyterian pastor and a childhood companion and lifelong friend of John Ames, the Rev. Robert Boughton, his daughter Glory, who's returned home to care for him, the returned prodigal son, ne'er-do-well of the family, Jack, actually named John Ames Boughton for the Rev. Boughton's lifelong friend.

In Jeremiah 8:22, the prophet asks "Is there no balm in Gilead? Is there no physician there? When then has the health of my poor people not been restored?" Gilead means "hill of testimony/witness" (Gen 31: 21). In the African-American spiritual, the trust is that indeed healing is there. And Robinson makes of this sleepy town a kingdom of grace, of God's mercy showing up where one least expects it, alongside where you'd think you'd find it—in the Bible, often quoted, in hymns, in the sermons spun by the two aging preachers. But the wonder of grace, the astounding goodness of God is found even more powerfully in the broken lives as well as the enduring faithfulness of the Gilead folk.

> There is a balm in Gilead
> To make the wounded whole;
> There is a balm in Gilead
> To heal the sin sick soul.

There is healing in Gilead, not sudden, miraculous healing, but the slow, gradual, almost imperceptible healing that occurs when people are moved by God's mercy to change, to forgive, to deepen their acceptance of the other who is different, who is damaged, who is handicapped by shame and discouragement.

The Pastors and Their Families

Among the principal characters we encounter and get to know well, there is plenty of suffering and spiritual depth to go around, and then some. John Ames has spent decades in faithful service to his parish, growing old alone, his young wife and only infant child having died shortly after birth many years earlier. Robert Boughton has buried his own wife of many years by the time we meet him and remains grieving her and one of his eight children, who has lost himself in drinking and misery. Named for his friend, John Ames Boughton, or Jack, has been incarcerated, bouncing around towns. Given the segregation and racism of the time, he is unable to live with his wife, the African-American pastor's daughter who is mother of his only surviving child. He fathered another child, a daughter, with a Gilead girl from the other side of the tracks, but she died young.

In the trilogy, Jack's homecoming as the severely damaged prodigal is narrated from both the suspicious, even hostile perspective of Rev. John Ames and Jack's also broken sister, Glory. Abandoned by her fiancée, she leaves a teaching position in her grief to return home to care for her failing father, the Rev. Robert Boughton. There is much about Glory's past that we never get clear on. Despite an entire volume devoted to her, this is also the case with Lila. Decades younger than John Ames, Lila becomes his second wife and the mother of their small son, Robby—named for the Rev. Robert Boughton. It is to Robby that the entirety of *Gilead* is written, as a long letter, really a book of letters, by which to remember a father who most likely will be dead before the boy is grown.

Abandoned herself as a small child, rescued from near abandonment and abuse, Lila is taken, removed by a drifter and sometimes migrant worker, Doll. Doll becomes a surrogate parent, and Lila knows no sense of home or enduring affection save that shown by Doll. Eventually, Doll disappears after an act of violent self-defense. Left alone, Lila survives by cleaning and doing laundry—she is a total failure in a St. Louis bordello. Able to scavenge from the fields, fish, find shelter in a shack outside Gilead, and do a little work, Lila might have kept drifting had she not sought shelter from a huge rainstorm in the town's Congregational church.

At first sight, John Ames falls in love with this woman years younger than he, younger even than his dead daughter would be. He is 67, diagnosed with angina, aware that his days are numbered. She is close to or just thirty, but with a lifetime or more of wandering and hard knocks. Lila talks like a nearly uneducated country girl. Yet we hear that she learned to read and write in one fall and winter where Doll put her into a local school. She continues to learn by meticulously copying out passages from the Bible, wondering what this strange collection of stories and teachings means. Ames will become, at first, her principal religious teacher, until it becomes clear how deep her own spiritual life is. One of their first exchanges begins with difficult lines from the book of the prophet Ezekiel.[5]

Lila first is welcomed by Ames, then courted by him. Eventually, despite her fears about being tied to a house or town, she astonishes Ames by telling him, "You ought to marry me."[6] Both Ames and Lila have their own versions of this important moment of her agreement to marry him. In a beautiful scene of affection and tenderness, he baptizes her down by the river where she has been fishing after an intriguing theological exchange about what baptism means. It is the only love scene

---

[5] Marilynne Robinson, *Lila* (New York: Farrar, Straus and Giroux, 2014), 125–35.

[6] Marilynne Robinson, *Gilead* (New York: Farrar, Straus and Giroux, 2006), 209.

I know of that consists in a sacrament being celebrated. Later on she attempts to wash this baptism off in the river, alien as religion of the traditional sort is to her. Yet somehow she intuits what faith is really about.

Words and Sacraments

In *Gilead*, Lila is only named once, referred mostly as "your mother" to the son who is receiving all the letters from Ames, his father. We are led to think Lila not only has been distant to religion but even suspicious of it. Her spiritual discernment, however, is disarming. What she intuits about grace and how we receive the mercy of God is truly stunning. At the end of a communion service, with the remnants of the elements still on the holy table and the candles still lit, she tells Ames, "You should give him some of that." She's referring, likely motioning to their son, still a small boy. Ames then responds.

> You're too young, of course, but she was completely right. Body of Christ, broken for you. Blood of Christ, shed for you. Your solemn and beautiful child face lifted up to receive these mysteries at my hands. They are the most wonderful mystery, body and blood.[7]

This is but one example of Lila's insight and of the unusual sacramentality throughout the trilogy. But it is not imposed upon this little town and its inhabitants. There is no straining to locate the holy in the everyday. It is exactly the opposite. There is a drawing on the tradition but only when the moment opens up. Only then is the word recognized, welcomed. Often, John Ames cites the Scriptures or Calvin or brings in a sermon text on which he's been working. And just as often, Lila, for all her supposed unbelief, will ask a question of real depth and

[7] Ibid., 69–70.

vision. We are amazed at just how much she has intuited from her own experience. Lila needs no instruction to figure out much of what goes on in church on Sunday, though like her surrogate mother, Doll, she sometimes questions the efficacy of praying or the point of following Jesus. But as just noted, she instinctively grasps the Lord's Supper and the need for her son to receive communion, not at all the common practice then for a small child.

Ames himself shows a most discerning sense for both word and sacrament, far beyond catechism definitions. He connects the bread and the cup of communion to his own father feeding him a piece of biscuit, not in church at the communion table but as he and other children watched the demolition of an old Baptist church.[8] There is no getting hung up on doctrine, on what the sacrament is, real presence or memorial, not even the rules of waiting until a child is rational, confirmed until he can commune. John Ames has experienced what the bread and cup, and for that matter, the water and the word, indeed are—something his Lila knows in her bones. These elements are the bridge between God and ourselves and between us and our neighbors, no matter the denomination or politics or color. Even when set inside the church building itself, they retain the earthy, material feel they have elsewhere—on a dinner table, in a bucket of water taken from a river.

Especially that sign of water, of cleansing and new life, appears throughout the books. At the very start, Lila herself, decrepit, dirty, her hair matted and full of mites, is bathed, cleaned, by Doll who took her, saved her. At the very end, Rev. Boughton has a hard time with the water when he sort of baptizes Ames and Lila's baby, just after his birth. This is a happy repeat of the sad baptism of the first child who was to die, along with her mother so many years before.

---

[8] Ibid., 102–3, 114.

Later, in church at the formal christening, it seems that Boughton also baptizes Lila, again, touching her head with water after he has baptized her son. "I don't really know what I'm doing here," he stammers. "I should have asked you first. But I wanted you to know that we couldn't bear—we have to keep you with us. Please God."[9]

What a dive into depths of the sacrament! The water is not only cleansing and new life but communion, connection, belonging too. I cannot help but connect this to Lila's own musing on how the old black coat her husband always used to preach in was the one he wrapped around her shoulders as they walked in the evening coolness. The coat had his warmth still in it, and the coat became the love, the care in which he wrapped her. They were not married when he wrapped her in the coat, but the act of caring for her was the beginning of her discovering his love for her, and hers for him.

Despite her qualms about baptism and being a Christian and the wife of a pastor, Lila is herself accomplished, experienced in ministering to others. We see this in how she responds to the other girls in the bordello, even to her boss there. Though she is repulsed by the parishioners reaching out to her, she tries to help a desperate young man, fleeing the law after likely beating his father to death or something close to it. She gives him her coat, walks home pregnant and freezing. Lila tries to feed him and gives him the little cash she has. What became of him shortly after, in a brutal blizzard, haunts her, so close to her own marginal, drifting life he is.

Though we hear the story from the vantage of an unseen narrator, it appears that somehow Lila, for all her social challenges, is able to relate with ease to the prodigal Boughton son, Jack. Early in *Gilead*, John Ames writes to his young son that he believes our Lord would have chosen to spend some time with Lila if she had lived in his time. He tells the boy that his

---

[9] Robinson, *Lila*, 248, 257.

mother has a familiarity with the world, with poverty, pain, and longing and also love, much more so than he ever had.[10]

It is a wrenching, slow conclusion to the last book in the trilogy, as Lila approaches the birth of her son, torn by doubts about staying with Ames, tortured by the thought she and the child might die in the birth event, also thinking through the devastation to John Ames if she were to one day disappear, like Doll, with their little boy. Ames shared with her a sermon written during a sleepless night in which he also ponders how sorrow has turned into joy without the sorrow ever slipping away. Lila has planted gardens around the parsonage, turned an empty widower's rooms into a home again, even cultivated roses on the graves of Ames's first wife and daughter.

There is a particularly powerful scene in which Ames and a very pregnant Lila ride out a ferocious late winter blizzard, huddled in bed together for warmth, hoping that birth will not come in the storm when they would be left completely on their own.[11] The scene is like others of their intimacy, their age difference somehow transcended, a very strong attachment growing between them, binding them and then, the child together. We almost forget that as this last book, a prequel to *Gilead*, ends, that in the first book of the trilogy as well as the second, *Home*, their son is already seven or eight, capable of playing ball, is at school, and being befriended by the prodigal Jack Boughton, much to the Rev. Ames's alarm.

Despite remembering what his father and grandfather taught about encounter with the neighbor being encounter with God, part of Ames cannot forgive Jack for the years of misery he has brought to his father. Nor is he able to trust that somehow Jack will not make a mess out of the lives of his sister, Lila, and their son and others in Gilead. Here is one of Ames's many, nearly obsessive reflections on this.

---

[10] Robinson, *Gilead*, 30.
[11] Robinson, *Lila*, 232–45.

Now here is the point I wish to make, because this is the thought that came to me as I was putting all this before the Lord. Existence is the essential thing and the holy thing. If the Lord chooses to make nothing of our transgressions, then they are nothing. Or whatever reality they have is trivial and conditional beside the exquisite primary fact of existence. Of course, the Lord would wipe them away, just as I wipe dirt from your face or tears. After all, why should the Lord bother much over these smirches that are no part of His Creation? Well, there are a good many reasons why He should. We human beings do the real harm. History could make a stone weep. I am aware that significant confusion enters my thinking at this point. I'm tired—that may be part of the problem. Though I recall even in my prime foundering whenever I set the true gravity of sin over against the free grace of forgiveness. If young Boughton is my son, then by the same reasoning, that child of his was also my daughter, and it was just terrible what happened to her, and that's a fact. As I am a Christian man, I could never say otherwise.[12]

Over and over again, in the homes and streets of Gilead, people collide with anger and loss, with selfishness, stupidity, and hurt. But the aging pastor cannot, in all the Scriptures or the commentaries or catechisms, find reasons to condemn or speak of punishment. It is perfectly the same vision that Pope Francis has and that we have come upon in so many of the writers here. Like that old, comfortable black coat placed around Lila's shoulders, like the babbling, fading old Boughton who keeps hoping his wandering son will stay and heal, like Lila and her uncanny sense for what is inside a person—all these Gilead people keep reminding us of the gift of grace.

Despite her efforts to wash her baptism away, despite her difficulties with the details and necessities of small town life, even more so, those of being the pastor's wife, Lila in the end

---

[12] Robinson, *Gilead*, 189–90.

reveals the miracle of grace incarnated. So do the bumbling, often ineffective gestures of the Revs. Ames and Boughton and their children. Ames tells Lila that religion, indeed, all his preaching, the singing, the praying, the sacraments are about existence. He does not need to try to illumine her. For all her impoverishment and abuse in life, Lila instinctively knows the forgiveness and mercy of God and its incarnation in the lives of women and men.

A Parable Reenacted

Then there is the parable of the Prodigal Son, the loving father, the good brother, and others surrounding them. It is enacted mostly in *Home* but partly, from John Ames's point of view, in *Gilead*. We watch the aging, physically failing father, Rev. Boughton. For years he is hoping, waiting for the return of Jack. Jack was a troublemaker growing up, someone who seemed to smirk when caught stealing or doing other mischief. He gets a local teenage girl pregnant. But her family will accept no help whatsoever from the Boughtons, completely cutting the mother and child off from them. Tragically, the little girl dies, further grieving Rev. Boughton and his wife.

Like the boy in the gospel parable, off Jack goes to the city, to school and work and a life of turmoil and unhappiness. We hardly get to know any other of the seven Boughton children except Glory, who has become her father's caregiver and who becomes much the same to her troubled brother Jack. Another "good boy," Teddy, is a physician not far away and he reappears to check on the old man's failing health as well as the returned prodigal.

When Jack finally does return home, to be cared for by his sister, he returns in great personal loss and grief. In some ways the pain is even worse for the old man. For he must watch as this child of his reveals not only his alcoholism, but also the pain of being separated from his wife, and their child, because of race. Her father, also a pastor, absolutely forbids their living together, likely seeing both Jack's problems and the deep racial divide in the Midwest in the 1950s.

We anguish through weeks and weeks of Jack's struggle to recover back home. His heart is elsewhere, with the woman he cannot be with and their child. He writes and waits for letters in response, but none come. Bright and, when sober, capable, he also struggles with depression bordering on despair. Robinson opens up the New Testament parable in contemporary setting. Somehow, the transition of the parable forward to the twentieth century in Gilead, Iowa, is not so neat. The nobility of the Middle East farmers of the first century CE of the parable is nowhere to be found in the Boughton house. I think Robinson is showing us here that there is more complexity, actually, more messy humanity, in Jesus' parable than churchgoers ordinarily perceive. Try as Rev. Boughton might, it is impossible for him to connect with his lost boy. Glory is allowed closer, deeper into his darkness. When his namesake and surrogate parent John Ames confronts the distasteful task of conversation with Jack, it is enormously painful for both of them.

Not only as his father, Rev. Boughton's closest friend, but as a pastor, Ames should have experience and the spiritual tools. And yet, there is a resistance to cracking the shell on both Jack's and Ames's parts. Though they come close, they never really connect. And without spoiling the narrative, it is nevertheless necessary to say that the parable of Jack and his father does not have the closure and happier ending of the parable in Luke's gospel. As with almost every one of the main characters, Robinson leaves us with imperfection, with a further step or act that could have been taken and was not. Gilead may be a kingdom in which parables play out, it may also be a paradise in the moment, but it is no Eden of everything right and in its place.

Not only here, primarily in *Home*, but through the trilogy, there is a contemplation of the layers of "father," all the ways in which both presence as well as absence, admiration, and repulsion come into play in this parental relationship. It is no coincidence that the relationship with God—"Our Father"—is also at issue and in play. And I could not help but see that the figure, the status, role, and meaning of the pastor is entwined in all the other characters and their lives.

The Rev. John Ames comes to visit and bring communion to his fading friend, Robert Boughton. It is more than a pastoral and friendly visit. It is a leave-taking, sad and at the same time full of peace and acceptance. It is the reconciliation that cannot happen with Jack. Glory receives communion along with the old pastors, though Jack declines. After Jack leaves, with no forwarding address, no plans, quite unexpectedly his estranged wife, Della, arrives at the Boughtons, with their son, Robert looking for him. Once more the timing is wrong. Things do not work out to a happy ending. Glory promises to give Jack Della's note with some numbers and names. She does not, however, know when or even if she will ever see him again. The prodigal had come home. His father, waiting for so many years, did get to see him and spend some time with him, though without healing or real reconciliation. Just as with the last communion, Jack was present but did not partake. He had returned home, but not to stay. And yet, as Glory ponders all of them and the homecoming that was not permanent, the healing not completed, the pain not relieved, she wonders if Jack's son might one day return. She would herself be old, her father gone, but in the return of the son's son, the prayers of a father would be answered. "The Lord is wonderful" is her confession as the book comes to its end. It is not at all a conventional expression of piety either. Robinson has provided in the Gilead villagers a stark, sometimes disappointing depiction of human striving and suffering. Painful memories are not just blotted out. They continue to figure in people's lives. But there is, for all the loose ends, healing.

Balm, Mercy in *Gilead*

All the biblical citations, all the discussions of Calvin and other theologians, all the baptisms and communions, all the tangled, messy lives of these people who end up in Gilead—Doll and Lila, John Ames, the son Robby, Rev. Boughton, the prodigal Jack, Teddy the dutiful boy, and Glory the dutiful daughter—all of them find a balm, find forgiveness, find mercy unexpected and undeserved there.

In the very last pages of the book named for her, Lila muses on the tremendous sadness she might inflict on her husband, the good pastor Ames, were she to leave with her son. As much as Rev. Boughton's second helping of baptismal water was a prayer and hope she would stay, Lila's past can never leave her. She will always remember being alone, having to rely only on herself, finding it always a challenge to trust or love another. The open road is a pull on her, a wild call to freedom, even though she has come to appreciate the sheltering love of a husband and a house she has very much turned into a home. She often refers to him as "the old man," but she weeps at the touch of his hand on her hair, is warmed by the spread of his coat around her. After her son's baptism in church, sitting down to rest in the study off the sanctuary, the baby in her arms, her thoughts wander.

> The old coat he had put over her shoulders when they were walking in the evening was as good to remember as the time when Doll took her up in her arms. She thought it was nothing she had known to hope for and something she had wanted too much all the same. So too much happiness came with it, and happiness was strange to her. He said, We have to keep you with us. In that eternity of his, where everybody will be happy, how could he feel the lack of her, the loss of her? She had to think about that.[13]

---

[13] Robinson, *Lila*, 258.

And think on she does, about Doll and Mellie, Doane and Marcelle with whom she drifted, of the boy she tried to help who likely had killed his father, of people she thinks no one would miss when they were gone, but yet all of them swept up along with all of China in Rev. Boughton's expansive and inclusive eternity.

> In eternity people's lives could be altogether what they were and had been, not just the worst things they ever did, or the best things either. So she decided she should believe in it, or that she believed in it already. How else could she imagine seeing Doll again? If any scoundrel could be pulled into heaven just to make his mother happy, it couldn't be fair to punish scoundrels who happened to be orphans, or whose mothers didn't even like them, and who would probably have better excuses for the harm they did than the ones who had somebody caring about them. It couldn't be fair to punish people for trying to get by, people who were good by their own lights, when it took all the courage they had to be good. . . . That's what she was thinking. The Reverend couldn't bear to be without her. Nothing against Mrs. Ames and her baby. Eternity had more of everything kind of room in it than this world did . . . There was no end to it. Thank God, as the old men would say. . . . All the tangles and knots of bitterness and desperation and fear had to be pitied. No, better, grace had to fall over them. . . . That's how it is. Lila had borne a child into a world where a wind could rise that would take him from her arms as if there were no strength in them at all. Pity us, but we are brave, she thought, and wild, more life in us than we can bear, the fire infolding itself in us. That peace could only be amazement, too.[14]

Heaven is there, in the town of Gilead. Paradise can be touched in the moment. One can encounter a sacrament in the world or the world as sacrament—how unusual, how exquisite, the

---

[14] Ibid., 260–61.

vision of this for Lila, a young woman for whom life has been a battering, a struggle. Somehow, without seminary training or most Sundays of her life in church she intuits what the Scriptures and all those teachers and preachers and their sermons were struggling to say.

Her devoted husband, John Ames, himself an everyday theologian, is constantly amazed not only at her questions but also in what she says she's rolled over in her thoughts. She tells him she does not know how to pray, may not even see the point of it, but he, spiritually discerning, knows better. Lila, as he says, is exactly the person the Lord would have taken time to be with. With all the difficult, miserable parts of her past, those we never really hear of, she is the one who somehow has heard the word spoken to her, kept it and lived it.

Marilynne Robinson can and does write scholarly prose, challenging essays on realism, the Reformation, Christology, experience, and what we end with here—grace everywhere.[15] But as we have seen here, a gift beyond her scholarship is that of what I think could be called incarnational sacramentality. She is able to express some of the most powerful truths of the faith, not by well-constructed, elegant propositions, but by the experience, the lives, and, yes, the words, both halting and articulate, of Lila, John Ames, and their fellow citizens of the kingdom of Gilead.

---

[15] Marilynne Robinson, *The Givenness of Things: Essays* (New York: Farrar, Straus and Giroux, 2015).

Father Richard Rohr, OFM
Photo from the Center for Action and Contemplation.

Chapter 9

"Everything Belongs": Richard Rohr's Active Contemplation

Our identification of God with the past has done the present and the future no favor. Old mistakes are still mistakes, and we do not need to keep repeating them. For much of the world, this preoccupation with the past comes across as a divine approval of everybody else's death (non-Christians, heretics, Native peoples, "sinners," women, the poor slaves, and on and on), and never our own. Many people have lost all interest in our grand spiritual talk and our Scriptures because they too often have been used by people who are themselves still small (who are stuck in their False Self).
 It does not help to deny that we are stuck, and yet it does not help to stand arrogantly above it all either—as if we do not share in the one great human crucifixion of reality, the one "world sorrow" (*Weltschmerz*, the Germans call it). We Christians affirm the communion of saints in the Nicene Creed, but I think there should be an equal belief in the "communion of sinners." We are fully a part of both groups.[1]

Another "Francis"

There is seldom a day when Pope Francis does not feature in our intense world of information and media coverage. Even Donald Trump found his extreme positions challenged by

---

[1] Richard Rohr, *Immortal Diamond: The Search for the True Self* (San Francisco: Jossey-Bass, 2013), xviii–xix.

Francis as less than Christian. But the name "Francis" was also deliberately chosen by the Jesuit Jorge Mario Bergoglio to bring to mind Francesco, the "little poor man" of Assisi, Giovanni di Pietro di Bernardone; a man I would wager is the best known of Christian saints.[2]

But there is yet another "Francis" on the scene of religious writers and spiritual guides, even though his name is not actually "Francis." If you were to view him lecturing or being interviewed on YouTube or other venues, Richard Rohr is riveting. He rattles off sentence after sentence and often appears as though he is embracing his audience or interviewer with his own excitement and passion. There are many good reasons that Rohr's work has made him a sought after, carefully attended voice among spiritual writers today. He does several conferences and online streaming series each year. There is a daily meditation to which you can subscribe online from his Center for Action and Contemplation.[3] And there are his many books and guided online courses. You know that he is listened to when he appears for an hour with Oprah, as he did last year on her series, Super Soul Sunday, February 8, 2015.[4]

Rohr has become a kind of multimedia pastor; an ecumenical one and, unlike most, a learned one. But he is as different from the likes of Joel Osteen and other televangelists as could be imagined. His credentials immediately distinguish him from the "industry" of spiritual celebrities. Whether in the brown Franciscan habit or ordinary clothes, there is no doubting his authenticity. He is a "little brother" of St. Francis of Assisi, member of Our Lady of Guadalupe Province. He has

---

[2] See Jon M. Sweeney, ed., trans., *The Complete Francis of Assisi* (Brewster, MA: Paraclete, 2015).

[3] Center for Action and Contemplation, "Daily Mediations," https://cac.org/category/daily-meditations/.

[4] See Oprah Winfrey and Richard Rohr, "The Search for Our True Self," *Super Soul Sunday*, Season 6, Episode 523, February 8, 2015, http://www.oprah.com/own-super-soul-sunday/Oprah-and-Author-Richard-Rohr-The-Search-For-Our-True-Self.

been a friar for almost fifty years and a priest for over forty. He has had years of pastoral experience—teaching, parish assignments, as a chaplain in corrections, part of the development of an experimental community, New Jerusalem, in 1971. In 1986 he founded the Center for Action and Contemplation and is the dean of its "Living School," which provides online as well as conferences in the Albuquerque area.[5] Up until very recently, Rohr traveled widely, lecturing and preaching. He now stays closer to home and has continued to publish. Constant in his career has been the dual vocations of membership as a friar in the Franciscans and active parish ministry—he regularly presides and preaches at a nearby church, Holy Family.[6]

His recent book on the Franciscan tradition as an ongoing "alternative orthodoxy," clearly sets out how the vision of Francis of Assisi and his collaborator, Clare, shaped the work of the brothers and sisters of the various Franciscan families.[7] We also come to understand why Jorge Mario Bergoglio, when elected bishop of Rome—as he prefers to be called—became the first pope ever to take the name of Francis of Assisi. We have now heard the central theme of compassion, of God's mercy and the need for our own mercy toward each other over and over in his tenure. The newest collection of Pope Francis's talks takes its title from what he himself has repeatedly said, to some resistance, namely, that mercy is God's defining characteristic and is thus the heart of the Gospel.[8]

---

[5] There is biographical information as well as a description of the various educational programs at https://cac.org/. I have also used material from other of Richard Rohr's books for the overview presented.

[6] Rohr's homilies at Holy Family Church are accessible at: https://cac.org/category/homilies/.

[7] Richard Rohr, *Eager to Love: The Alternative Way of Francis of Assisi* (Cincinnati, OH: Franciscan Media, 2014).

[8] Francis, *The Name of God Is Mercy* (New York: Random House, 2016). See also Walter Kasper, *Mercy: The Essence of the Gospel and the Key to Christian Life* (Mahwah, NJ: Paulist Press, 2014).

Richard Rohr is not only an insightful interpreter of Francis of Assisi's vision. He also has been uniquely able to connect it to the conditions of our world in the early twenty-first century, many hundreds of years removed from the "little poor man's" own era. I have to admit that as a former friar myself—I was a Carmelite—I have a soft spot for the outlook that the "mixed life" brings.[9] The very name of Rohr's Albuquerque institute, the Center for Action and Contemplation, captures it. The friars, whether Dominican, Franciscan, Carmelite, or Augustinian, in addition to their distinctive heritage, shared a common approach, one best captured in the phrase derived from Thomas Aquinas and the motto of the Dominican Order—"to give away to others the gifts of one's contemplation/prayer" (*contemplata aliis tradere*).[10] Their purpose was to be in the world, for the life of the world, as authentic preachers of the Gospel. At the same time, they valued the life of prayer in their own houses and communities, not only *lectio divina* or the prayerful reading of Scripture but also the Divine Office—the prayer of the hours and the celebration of the Eucharist. Thus, to their active work of pastoral care, study, and other activities was connected the unceasing presence before God, the prayer of contemplation. Though himself in the Benedictine tradition as a Cistercian or Trappist, Thomas Merton nonetheless greatly valued the witness, work, and spirituality of the friars, as Daniel Horan, another Franciscan writer, has argued.[11] Merton himself first sought to enter the Franciscans after his time on the faculty of St. Bonaventure University.[12]

---

[9] See Michael Plekon, *Saints as They Really Are* (Notre Dame, IN: University of Notre Dame Press, 2012), 105–49.

[10] Thomas Aquinas, *Summa Theologica*, II, II, q. 188, a. 6.

[11] Daniel P. Horan, *The Franciscan Heart of Thomas Merton* (Notre Dame, IN: Ave Maria Press, 2014).

[12] Michael Mott, *The Seven Mountains of Thomas Merton* (Boston: Houghton Mifflin, 1986).

Rohr has consistently made clear the sources from which he draws inspiration. He describes a broad "wisdom lineage" which has formed his faith and life. He also locates himself within a "perennial tradition" that connects divine reality with the world and our experience.[13] The critics who are troubled by Rohr's ecumenical eclecticism usually fail to note how heavy his list is with the mainstream Christian tradition—the Hebrew Scriptures and New Testament, the writings of the Desert Mothers and Fathers, then the post-apostolic and later fathers, particularly the Eastern ones. Of course the Franciscan tradition is dominant, with focus on Francis himself, Bonaventure, and Duns Scotus. What troubles some is the same broadening of inclusion that Thomas Merton employed—classic and contemporary Buddhist sources like Pema Chödrön and Thich Nat Hanh. Ghandi and Martin Luther King Jr. also figure as important contemporary writers. Rohr's pastoral experience has led him to add Jung and the Twelve-Step movement as well as integral theory of Richard Wilbur.[14]

Action and Contemplation: Major Themes

Some of the leading themes, both of Rohr himself, based on his own spiritual development, and of the Center for Action and Contemplation, should be noted. These include action over doctrine, an emphasis on the humanity of Jesus/God, resistance to equating the Gospel with the institutional church, and a refusal to seek only ecclesiastical formulations and solutions in favor of a more secular, everyday way of living the Good News. He has also tried to identify the major perspectives of his work despite the different focus of his books.

---

[13] Rohr, *Immortal Diamond*, 213.
[14] See Rohr's *Breathing Under Water: Spirituality and the Twelve Steps* (Cincinnati, OH: Franciscan Media, 2011).

Rohr values tradition. But like many other contemporary thinkers, he reads tradition as inclusive of the world and our experience—this is why he is such an important voice on the world as sacrament, on spirituality in the everyday. For him, tradition is never just a body of doctrines, a collection of theological statements as traditionalists so often make it. Tradition is living.[15] Tradition must be experienced, must be validated in practice in one's life. This does not mean a merely subjective or selective approach, picking what one likes from the tradition and ignoring or rejecting what is not attractive.

Rohr values the trinitarian God. In the Trinity, we have the unity as well as community of the Divine, God as the relationships of love among Father, Son, and Spirit. In the Franciscan heritage, Rohr is profoundly incarnational. The humanity of God (also valued by Russian theologians from Solovyov to Bulgakov) is consequential for faith and life.[16] Jesus is the face of God. God entered creation, became part of, subject to time and space in the incarnation. Jesus then shares everything we have in this world and life except sin. The gospels make clear, before the onset of Hellenic conceptual impositions, a more worldly, earthy character to the life of the kingdom of which

---

[15] Russian émigré thinkers in Paris between the wars also saw tradition as living. It was the focus of their manifesto, published in 1937, called *Zhivoe predanie (Living Tradition)*. And see a partial translation of these essays from 1937: *Tradition Alive: On the Church and the Christian Life in Our Time, Readings from the Eastern Church*, ed. Michael Plekon (New York and Lanham, MD: Rowan & Littlefield, 2003). See also Paul Valliere, *Modern Russian Theology* (Grand Rapids, MI: Eerdmans, 2000); Antoine Arjakovsky, *The Way: Russian Religious Thinkers of the Emigration and Their Journal; 1925–1940*, trans. Jerry Ryan, ed. John A. Jillions and Michael Plekon (Notre Dame, IN: University of Notre Dame Press, 2013). Several of the writers featured in this book were associated with the "living tradition" stream among the Paris "émigrés"—Evdokimov, Gillet, Skobtsova, Afanasiev. Behr-Sigel and Men are also shaped by this experiential, incarnational vision. See also, Michael Plekon, *Living Icons: Persons of Faith in the Eastern Church* (Notre Dame, IN: University of Notre Dame Press, 2002).

[16] See Valliere, *Modern Russian Theology*, 11–15.

Jesus spoke.[17] All the parables are set squarely in the everyday of baking, cooking and cleaning, farming, fishing, and maintaining a family. Rohr often observes that returning to the Scriptures, the sources, is often a disturbing, challenging experience, for we have been long turned into overly spiritualistic and moralistic believers. Death and life are central. The heart of Christianity is the paschal mystery of the cross and the empty tomb of Jesus. The resurrection of Jesus is the truth of God's triumph and the promise of what we are given—grace and transformation.

The distinction between the divine and the human, the sacred and the profane—the former being viewed a superior to the latter—is not valid in the Christianity of the New Testament. First the creation and then the incarnation witness to one reality. All things are made by God, humans beings reflect God's image and likeness. The Spirit of God is present and active everywhere in the world. Everything that is, is holy. And "everything belongs," everyone belongs, as Rohr says it in the title of one of his most important volumes, on how prayer is to be found in life.[18] Nothing is excluded from God's transforming action. No one, no matter her or his identity and situation in life, is excluded. This truly encompassing or catholic inclusion is, of course, contrary to centuries of the behavior of the church and its members.

Lastly, all of God's work in Christ is "for us and for our salvation," and "for all." Christ is not the possession of Christians, Christ is cosmic, universal. The gospels make it clear that we are changed by descending as Jesus did and then rising. Failure, disappointment, and loss are our teachers, along with the good that we experience, the grace that carries us

---

[17] See Richard Rohr, *Things Hidden: Scripture as Spirituality* (Cincinnati, OH: St. Anthony Messenger Press, 2007).
[18] Richard Rohr, *Everything Belongs: The Gift of Contemplative Prayer* (New York: Crossroad, 2003).

along. It is not that we become personally perfected, rather, that as we fall and rise, we enter communion with God and each other. The search for the "true self" is one in which we "fall upwards," as the title of another of Rohr's books calls it. Shaped by rules and structures, compliant with institutions and standards in the first half of our lives, we become our true selves as we are able to let go of what formed us.[19]

In Franciscan terms, we best criticize the bad by the practice of the better. Contemplation, as Merton came to realize, cannot be acquired for itself or just for me, but only as it opens me to others, urges me to action and not just reflection.[20] Merton's famous "epiphany," "In Louisville, at the corner of Fourth and Walnut," was that we grow in contemplation, in prayer and self-knowledge. Like Merton, we too see the world and all those people as beautiful, walking around, shining in the sun.[21]

This brief overview will frustrate some who prefer more systematic thinking. Rohr is no more a systematic spiritual writer than the likes of Marilynne Robinson and Mary Karr, poets Mary Oliver and Christian Wiman, writers Barbara Brown Taylor or Kathleen Norris. But I will tell you why Rohr is read and respected. He is able to talk about the spiritual life in numerous languages—those of psychology and anthropology, the languages of Franciscan spirituality, as well as the broader Christian language of the Eastern and Western churches and the best of other world religious traditions—Buddhism, Sufism, Hinduism, Judaism. Like his spiritual father, St. Francis, who journeyed to the Middle East for encounters

---

[19] This is the focus of Rohr's *Falling Upward: Spirituality for the Two Halves of Life* (San Francisco: Jossey-Bass, 2011).

[20] Of Merton's extensive writings, see *New Seeds of Contemplation* (New York: New Directions, 1961); *Contemplative Prayer* (New York: Doubleday, 1969); and *The Springs of Contemplation: A Retreat at the Abbey of Gethsemani* (Notre Dame, IN: Ave Maria Press, 1992).

[21] Thomas Merton, *Conjectures of a Guilty Bystander* (New York: Doubleday, 1968), 156–58.

with Muslim leaders, Rohr not only consults a raft of writers and their works but also constantly integrates important contemporary spiritual teachers into his programs, live and online—Shane Claiborne, James Finley, Mirabai Starr, and Simone Campbell, among others.

Rohr draws on the Christian tradition creatively. The language of falling and rising, dying and coming to life is a central theme in so many of his writings. One also hears in Rohr from a community of beloved teachers, from the Desert Mothers and Fathers; from Meister Eckhart, Julian of Norwich, Thomas Merton, Irenaeus of Lyons, and Bonaventure; from Matthew Fox, Marcus Borg, Ilia Delio, Kathleen Dowling Singh, and Rob Bell, among contemporary voices. The inclusive nature of tradition as well as its diversity, the ecumenical character, is evident as the thinkers Rohr draws on.

Drawing on Jung and Wilbur, Rene Girard, John Polkinghorne, and Cynthia Bourgeault, among other sources in psychology and philosophy, Rohr is adept at connecting experience to what the Christian tradition has to offer us. Or to put it in a way very familiar here by now, he sees the world as sacrament—the possibilities for encounter and transformation not only in our personal struggles but also in our observing and engaging in events around us.

Rising—The Path to God and to the True Self

Rohr's extended meditation on the search for the true self—really how our spiritual lives unfold in our daily existence—is titled, from a Gerard Manly Hopkins poem, *Immortal Diamond*. Hopkins was never one to deal in familiar pious words, hence the imagery is for most of us, not one we immediately connect with God. All the better though, for it forces us to give up assumptions both from psychology and religion. And the approach Rohr takes, though we will only overview it briefly, makes clear how the sacred cannot be cut off from the ordinary.

Our falling and rising with Christ is the motif that holds the book together. Rohr wants to address the personal journey each of us is on, the path of becoming who we were intended to be, our true selves. But this process always involves Christ. God is within, closer to us than our hearts, as Augustine said.

Despite the centrality of the resurrection in the gospels and in all of Christian tradition and liturgy, the yearly celebration of the "feast of feasts," as hymns call it, we are never at ease with it.[22] I know that in my own Eastern church tradition we know, supposedly, how to "do" Easter. Most who attend it are struck by the light and joy of the Paschal Vigil—the procession outside, the wonderful paschal hymns, the Eucharist, and then the wonderful food fest afterward early in the morning as people share the contents of their overflowing Easter baskets. Truth be told, though, there is much more psychic energy spent on Lent, on the self-abasement and groveling in our ever-present, ever-destructive ways. An Eastern church hymn summarizes this in the most mournful of lines: "When I think of the many evil things I have done, wretch that I am, I tremble at the fearful day of judgment, but trusting in thy lovingkindness, like David I cry to thee, have mercy on me O God." Unlike Lent in the Western church after Vatican II and the larger liturgical renewal, there is no resurrectional or baptismal character to Lent in the East. It is for the most part focused either on the cross and suffering of Christ—the principal theme in Holy Week, or on the depravity and guilt of the human self.

This is not just an interesting and esoteric liturgical detail. Skilled healer that he is, Rohr notes in this book, as well as throughout his talks and other writings, that we are better at identifying what is wrong with ourselves—and fixating on it. Having been a pastor for decades, he knows all too well Christians' obsession with sin and guilt, with the need for judging and penance, the suffering more than the risen Christ. It is an

---

[22] Rohr, *Immortal Diamond*, xi, xiv.

echo of what you hear from many experienced therapists, namely, that many of their clients prefer remaining in their neuroses, in their distorted visions, and struggling with them rather than rising up through change. Freud and Jung both observed how much of traditional religion is concerned with guilt and the definition of sin rather than healing, which is what the very term, "salvation" means.

Now, both in Christian tradition as well as in the human sciences that are concerned with diagnosis and healing, there has to be a sense of sin, of personal weakness, selfishness, delusion, blindness. Yet I think Rohr quite rightly observes that we are much better at this ransacking of ourselves and self-condemnation than we are at accepting the new life of resurrection we are given. This is grace which, despite all our falling away, never disappears and constantly seeks to raise us up. The false self takes it that God is other, elsewhere, up or out there. But as Paul notes, the mystery is Christ within us, our hope of glory[23] (Col 1:27).

Not only in the book *Immortal Diamond* but also throughout his writing and lecturing, this is one of the most frequently emphasized themes—that of God's presence in us and of our "original blessing" and continued hosting of God within us. Rohr is also correct in noting how difficult this is for us to accept. We would rather have God at a distance. Crucial to finding the true self then is this realization, namely, that it is easier to want to stay with a god who is distant and a self mostly made up of the trappings of our existence—what we own, have bought, what others think of us, and the like.

Rohr has some insightful comments to make about what most therapy does for us—strategies for coping with our own and all the false selves around us.[24] It's not that we can get away without such a false self—it is what we are given, then

---

[23] Ibid., 5.
[24] Ibid., 30–36.

make our own, early in life—what we need to get by. But how limited if we only become the self we think we are or want to be![25] Is it any better with spiritual direction, with religion? No, and Rohr holds out his experience of over forty years as a priest as witness.[26] Only healthy, authentic religion can assist, accompany one in the transformation that allows the true self to emerge.[27] When you actually work through Rohr's text, you may be amazed at how often "resurrection" or the "risen Christ" is mentioned in this reflection on what spiritual life is about, the path toward the true self. And he gives credit to the writer who put the true/false selves back on the table, namely Thomas Merton.[28]

So, here is Richard Rohr's contribution to living the spiritual life in the everyday, to the world as sacrament. Our very identity, our selves, is where God dwells. The great paschal mystery is not just for Holy Week and Easter but for every day, as we fall and are raised, as we strive to become one with God and each other, as we move from false to true selves.[29]

Dying with Christ and Communion with God and Others

Rohr launches into what might appear as a detour but what turns out to be a very useful reflection on how we process information, not only about the empirical realities of our world but also about God. Our Enlightenment demand for fact, for validity fades. It fails us when we come to the realm of God, ourselves, and others. Here the language is that of metaphor and symbol, the richness of poetry.[30] Both fundamentalist and

---

[25] Ibid., 43–52.
[26] Ibid., 39–43.
[27] Ibid., 48–52.
[28] Ibid., 38.
[29] Ibid., 59–66.
[30] Ibid., 67–77.

"Everything Belongs" 177

atheists demand literalism, which is why the central symbol of resurrection does not work for either. The resurrection cuts into us, our lives, hence Rohr speaks of the "knife edge of experience."[31] Jesus' resurrection is no mere piece of doctrine, not just a line in the Creed or the New Testament or an event from the distant past. The earliest texts we have, from Paul, make it clear that the resurrection is part of our own experience. Here is the perspective that one finds in virtually everything Rohr writes or says.[32] God is not just revealed truth, and a being wholly other than ourselves, to be cognitively accepted, listened to, praised, and obeyed.[33]

A consequence of this union or communion of God and ourselves is that we are able to put aside moralism as the everyday version of our faith. To be "in Christ" means resurrection, our constant transformation, rather than obeying lists of rules, rather than following the practices of an institution, thus mistaking churchly conforming for living out the paschal mystery with Christ. Of course, one will be challenged by choices, but the motivation and the vision of them is utterly different. Rohr quotes the great Dominican spiritual teacher Meister Eckhart: "The eye through which I see God is the same eye through which God sees me; my eye and God's eye are one eye, one seeing, one knowing, one love."[34]

Another way of saying this is the language of "deification" or *theosis* used by Eastern church teachers such as Symeon the new theologian, a medieval Byzantine monastic writer and mystic.[35] We do not violate any boundaries such as that of

---

[31] Ibid., 77–81.
[32] Ibid., 81–89.
[33] Ibid., 95–102.
[34] Ibid., 106.
[35] Ibid., 107–26; see Symeon the New Theologian: *The Discourses*, ed. and trans. C. J. De Catanzaro (Mahwah, NJ: Paulist Press, 1980); *On the Mystical Life*, 3 vols., ed. and trans. Alexander Golitzin (Crestwood, NY: St. Vladimir's Seminary Press, 1995, 1996, 1998).

essence. Our "becoming God" is participation, communion, what Paul, the very first teacher after Jesus, saw and emphasized. It is not about keeping the law or laws, it is dying and rising with Christ, being "in Christ." It is not necessary to repeat the little trip through religious history that Rohr narrates. It is useful to connect it to our experience, realizing how in both the Eastern and Western churches, over time, it became easy to reduce the life in Christ to obeying rules, performing certain actions, attending services, and assenting to various doctrines. Mother Maria Skobtsova's startling critique of "types of religious life," presented in another chapter here, illustrates what Rohr is arguing.[36] His own quote of what a bishop once told him says it strikingly. "I don't have time for the mystics. We're running a church here."[37]

In a chapter on death, Rohr returns to both the Pauline and Franciscan visions of the foundation of our everyday existence. I could call it the "sacrament" of dying, but I know that most would then consider it the reiteration of classic asceticism, the rejection, even reviling, of all that is delightful, pleasurable—denial becoming more important than the real goal of dying, which is rising. There is, to be sure, much we have to die from, fear being among the most important thing and the source of so much bad religion. Rohr speaks in another book of "necessary suffering."[38]

The real sacrament here is of both dying and rising. Jesus' work is to heal, to give life, and proclaim this as the Good News of the kingdom.[39] And this is not to be a tribal, sectarian gathering but universal, reaching out across supposed boundaries, to all. It is no surprise that Jesus spends so much time with those marginal to the church and official cult of his time—

---

[36] See author's earlier chapter, "The Sacrament of the Brother/Sister: Mother Maria Skobtsova," 34–49 in this volume.
[37] Rohr, *Immortal Diamond*, 110.
[38] Ibid., 144.
[39] Ibid., 148–58.

tax collectors, non-Jews from Samaria and Canaan, a Roman centurion.

Universal, Intimate, Everyday

Rohr's closer examination of the resurrection narratives reveals an intimacy that the risen Christ enters with his friends. He moves through closed doors. There he is, unexpectedly, taken for a gardener by Mary Magdalene. Walking along the road to Emmaus and breaking the bread at the inn for his fellow travelers. He says to put a hand to his side and touch the wound. He asks for something to eat. Later, he appears on the shore making breakfast for them after a night of fishing—broiled fish and bread he has prepared on the shore over a fire.

This is, I think, the best version of world as sacrament that Richard Rohr gives us as he examines the resurrection narratives. It is not as proof texts of resurrection that he presents them. Rather, these are scenes of what dying and rising do to us—we are transformed, given new life. We become who were made to be. These narratives are about the risen Christ. If, however, we look carefully at the other characters in them, these narratives are about us too.

The narratives are about a God who is human, one of us, who has entered life with us in space and time. Jesus is with us as we eat and drink with him. He is there at our work, as on the lakeshore for the ones fishing. He is in our relationships with each other, in our hopes, in our fears. It is profoundly moving to consider all those of Jesus' friends who are there with him after the resurrection. These friends first included the women who come to the tomb to anoint his body, a group of women named Mary, Martha, Joanna, Salome, and Susanna, Nicodemus and Joseph of Arimathea, and others that well may have included his mother and Mary Magdalene.[40]

---

[40] Ibid., 180–81.

Then there is Peter and the disciple Jesus loved, traditionally thought of as John. Jesus engages also with Thomas and his doubts, with the crew of them in the fishing boat who see him on the shore. Jesus talks with the ones walking down the road to Emmaus, possibly Luke and Cleophas or Cleophas and his wife, Mary. Then there are all those gathered who see him ascend.

Once more we are reminded how down-to-earth, how wonderfully mundane the gospels are, even more so than the public teaching in the letters. But the Scriptures are just one source for Rohr, as we have seen. So many other traditions and voices also speak to us about the life of the Spirit in our daily existence, in our time. Rohr offers a distinctive vision of how the life in Christ plays out in everyday existence. For him, the world is indeed sacrament.

Barbara Brown Taylor
Photo by Kerry Simmon from the author.

Chapter 10

"Finding an Altar in the World": Barbara Brown Taylor's Everyday Liturgy

Do we build God a house so that we can choose when to go see God . . . in lieu of having God stay at ours? Plus, what happens to the rest of the world when we build four walls— even four gorgeous walls—cap them with a steepled roof, and designate that the House of God? What happens to the riverbanks, the mountaintops, the deserts, and the trees? What happens to the people who never show up in our houses of God?[1]

An American Original

Time magazine included Barbara Brown Taylor as one of its one hundred most influential people in America for the year 2014.[2] That same year she published *Learning to Walk in the Dark*.[3] This is a rich, wide-ranging series of reflections on darkness, which Taylor calls "shorthand for anything that scares me—that I want no part of—either because I am sure that I do

---

[1] Barbara Brown Taylor, *An Altar in the World: A Geography of Faith* (San Francisco: HarperOne, 2008), 9.

[2] Elizabeth Dias, "The 100 Most Influential People: Barbara Brown Taylor," *Time* magazine, April 23, 2014, http://time.com/70780/.

[3] Barbara Brown Taylor, *Learning to Walk in the Dark* (San Francisco, HarperOne, 2014); see also "In Praise of Darkness," *Time* magazine, April 17, 2014, http://time.com/65543/barbara-brown-taylor-in-praise-of-darkness/.

not have the resources to survive it or because I do not want to find out."[4] As with her other books, her preaching, and her lecturing, Taylor is courageous, but in a most unassuming way. She never hits us over the head with truth; she allows us to discover it gradually, along with her. She brushes away the accumulated material and allows us to see what is there, often hidden, sometimes what we would rather not see or own.

This is the case with darkness. She does not have to force our faces into what scares us, and what is present all the time despite our denials, our usual wanting to be children of the light and of the day, children of joy and peace. In life, in our faith and in our experience, there is more. She is a calming, reassuring guide. We can descend with her into terrifyingly dark, claustrophobic caverns, where we are almost buried in silence and darkness. But she's well equipped and with the headlamp and sturdy shoes and clothing, she will guide us back up and out.

In *Learning to Walk in the Dark*, she actually has a chapter on cave exploration, so this is not just metaphor that I am spinning out about her wise spiritual instruction.[5] In the two other books that make up the trilogy, *Leaving Church* and *An Altar in the World*, Taylor shares with us her own experience as a priest and afterward, when she leaves parish ministry. She chronicles the thinking, decisions, and study that led up to ordination. She very honestly narrates her experiences in ministry, first on the staff of a large Atlanta congregation and then in the parish of her dreams, Grace-Calvary Episcopal Church, in Clarkesville, Georgia.

Leaving Church is an intense, powerful memoir. Taylor wrote it after some years in ordained ministry and after a difficult end to her time at the Clarkesville parish. I think it must have taken a great deal of prayer and counseling as well as inner

---

[4] Taylor, *Learning to Walk in the Dark*, 4–5.
[5] Ibid., 11–132.

work to write. And since discovering it, I have given it to many—seminarian interns at our parish, other friends, and colleagues in ministry too.

I was introduced to the book by a former intern and friend who was given it to read at an institute for clergy recovery and healing. After a destructive conflict in his parish, he recognized the need for help. All those entering the program for recovery were given a copy of Barbara Brown Taylor's unflinching account of her own failure in ministry. They could then use the book to begin their own assessment and recovery.[6] In addition, they would have, as all readers, a discerning look at the toxic, destructive properties of religion. This Taylor continues but also moves beyond in the second book, *An Altar in the World*. I want to focus on what she offers us in that volume here. The crucial location of "world" in the title says it all. This is very much an exploration of the world as sacrament.

I recently completed a book of my own. *Uncommon Prayer* I called it, with *Prayer in Everyday Experience* as the subtitle. I wanted to look at how writers, poets, and others prayed in their ordinary, daily lives, in joy as well as sadness, in situations of home, family, work, nature, and amid the bustle and turmoil of life in our time.[7] Taylor's book was an inspiration.

Having spent so much of her first book in her priestly collar and vestments, in church preaching and presiding at the Eucharist, baptisms, funerals, and weddings, the leave-taking from parish ministry deposited Taylor, one Sunday morning,

---

[6] Barbara Brown Taylor, *Leaving Church: A Memoir of Faith* (San Francisco: HarperOne, 2006).

[7] Michael Plekon, *Uncommon Prayer: Prayer in Everyday Experience* (Notre Dame, IN: University of Notre Dame Press, 2016). See also my earlier books on the search for holiness and persons of faith in our time: *Living Icons: Persons of Faith in the Eastern Church* (Notre Dame, IN: University of Notre Dame Press, 2002); *Hidden Holiness* (Notre Dame, IN: University of Notre Dame Press, 2009); and *Saints as They Really Are: Voices of Holiness in Our Time* (Notre Dame, IN: University of Notre Dame Press, 2012).

on her front porch, just in ordinary clothes. She and her husband built the house of their dreams on a piece of land they bought in that rural Georgia community. There were flowers and vegetables in their gardens to be weeded, watered, and harvested. There were also numerous chores around the property in addition to maintaining the home. So it almost naturally followed that she would start to relocate the practice of faith there, in her house and the village, rather than in the sanctuary with the cross and candles, altar and pulpit and font.

Getting Out of the Church, into the World

An Altar in the World is not really an attack on all that constitutes "church." Earlier Taylor noted that she had to stop marking the date in a message or letter with a feast day or church season as a professor of religious studies at Piedmont College, the position she moved to after she retired from her parish. She no longer donned the uniform of clerical collar and black shirt, was no longer addressed as "Reverend" or "Mother," but as "Professor" or "Ms. Taylor." She had never really left "the world," yet she realized how it had been filtered through a churchly set of lenses.

She rediscovered Sunday again as a real Sabbath of rest from work and quiet—clergy cannot have a Sabbath on Sunday! But having ended her parish work, Taylor indeed was slowed down by the expanse of a Sunday out in the country, at her home. And while fidgeting a bit, not being in church, vested, with the organ prelude going and soon the rest of the service she would be leading, Taylor comes to see that church has artificially imprisoned the sacred.

> *Here is the church; here is the steeple; open the doors and see all the people.* . . . [W]e did things together in those sacred spaces that we did nowhere else in our lives. . . . [B]ut after we stepped into the parking lot we lost that intimacy. . . . Somewhere

"Finding an Altar in the World" 187

along the line we bought—or were sold—the idea that God is chiefly interested in religion. We believed that God's home was the church, that God's people knew who they were, and that the world was a barren place full of lost souls in need of all the help they could get. . . . The problem is, many of the people in need of saving are in churches, and at least part of what they need saving from is the idea that God sees the world the same way as they do.[8]

For a long time it has not been possible to think of faith, worship, and ministry except within the context of the organized church—that is, within historical, institutional churches. The sign of that is the church building, distinctive in architecture (though this is diverse) over history. Recently, research has indicated that the pattern is changing, and rapidly. Demographic change is making its impact felt. Not even 2 percent of mainline denominations say that they are attracting younger people, in the eighteen to thirty-five brackets. And among eighteen to thirty-five-year-olds, over 25 percent describe themselves as religious "nones," not belonging to any religious congregation or participating in one.[9] Congregations are aging and thus each year seeing more members disappear, fewer joining.[10]

While Taylor does not confront these trends directly, her reflection on faith outside the sanctuary is an examination of what might be called a relocation of faith or, better, a rediscovery of it elsewhere. While there are indeed critical things to be

---

[8] Taylor, *Altar in the World*, 5–7.
[9] "The '1 Percent' in Mainline Protestantism? Congregations Attracting Young Adults," http://blogs.thearda.com/trend/featured/the-1-percent-in-mainline-protestantism-congregations-attracting-young-adults/.
[10] In another book, I have gathered a number of first-person reflections on this as well as an overview, the collection entitled *The Church Has Left the Building: Faith, Parish and Ministry in the 21st Century*, ed. Michael Plekon, Maria McDowell, and Elizabeth Schroeder (Portland, OR: Cascade, 2016).

said about remaining trapped in models of parish organization from premodern, agrarian, small-town situations, even such considerations are not the principal focus for her. Neither is the location of worship and prayer within consecrated walls, within ancient liturgical rites and prayer books.

Hers is a more constructive endeavor, one that articulately expresses the central theme of this book. She wants to remind us of a reality deeply set within the traditions of faith, namely the earthy foundations of our faith, its roots in everyday life and experience. If an altar may be seen as established in the world, then it follows that there are numerous possibilities for the world to be sacrament.

Christian worship in general, including the Scriptures and the sacraments, are very much in and about the world. The biblical narratives are about farmers and those involved in shepherding and fishing. The Scriptures tell the story of God's involvement with the world in terms not just of preachers and healers but of kings, military leaders, and massive construction projects such as city walls and the temple. The narrative is about faithfulness to God and the way God's Word sets out a path for living. But it is equally the account of stupidity, selfishness, and cruelty that brings about death, destruction, and suffering. There is surely no argument about this with respect to the Hebrew Bible. And the gospels of the New Testament are paralleled with the nitty-gritty narratives of the conflicts and troubles of the early Christian communities tended by Paul and other apostles.

The very actions, sacred ones, by which one enters the community and by which one is put into communion with God and with others employ the material necessities of life—water, bread, wine, oil, and physical gestures of blessing, forgiving, and healing. The essential medium of communication, language, uses metaphor, symbol, and parable to convey what God has to say and what we need to hear and put into practice.

Practices of Worldly Spirituality

Although it will not be possible to exhaustively examine them, Taylor suggests a dozen practices in which we can encounter God in the world, and she knows there are many more. She thinks of them as ways she has found to answer the question of a trusted colleague and friend who asked what was saving her life—she had previously inquired of him what he wanted her to talk about at his church.[11]

It is immediately apparent that some of the practices, as Taylor says, are so basic, so delightful, that it seemed absurd to set them apart, somehow, as "holy." Making a meal for another, making love, hoeing and weeding a garden, listening to a friend, enjoying the simple delight of one's own body without pain, but also the challenge of enduring pain and suffering.

We could call these practices sacrament with no trouble at all. All bring together the spiritual and the material, the human and the divine. They employ the world around us, life and activity in it as encounters with God, with others, and with ourselves. "No work is too small to play a part in the work of creation," Taylor writes.[12] So, as noted, it is not so much a rejection of traditional liturgy or the sacred texts and rites and the house of prayer in which these are celebrated. It is clear that Taylor did not leave either the priesthood or the church but rather expanded the sacramental vision and field of engagement. And, I would point out, in so doing, she actually returned to the sources.

Consider that in the New Testament, as many commentators have noticed, how little action occurs inside of synagogue, temple, or even early house churches. The altar was commanded by God to be set up first in the tent or tabernacle with

---

[11] Taylor, *Altar in the World*, xv.
[12] Ibid., 115.

which the Israelites wandered, their portable temple, as it were. Then later, when a permanent dwelling for God was described and created, the first Jerusalem temple (and its successor), the altar was to be located there. Yet later on, there was no altar in village houses or prayer, study, and assembly—the synagogues. Even when the Jerusalem temple was destroyed and the priestly led sacrifices and prayers were no more, the "ark" where the sacred writings were kept—not the ark of the covenant from the holy of holies—remained a sign of the presence of God. From it the scrolls were taken out for proclaiming God's word. The *tefillin* or small boxes with lines of the Scriptures were strapped onto the forehead and arm as a sign and commitment to keep the Torah always in and with oneself. Many lines from Scripture echo the ideal. And the many mitzvoth or applications of the Torah to details of daily life and work confirm the sense that no part of life or of the world lacks the presence of the Holy One. Everything that is, is holy, Abraham Joshua Heschel said.

But in the Scriptures themselves, while there are numerous scenes and events that unfold before the ark, within the tent and temple, most of the action unfolds in everyday life—in fields where there are sheep or cultivated crops, in homes and castles, in the marketplace and battlefield. In the New Testament, this seems even more deliberately the case. As Amy-Jill Levine's work recognizes, the Jewish framework and tradition are always present—Jesus reads from the prophet Isaiah in his hometown synagogue and preaches and is almost killed. Jesus visits the temple during the feasts as well as the synagogue in Capernaum. Later, Paul goes to where the people pray, wherever the synagogue meets. Yet so much of Jesus' teaching and ministry takes place in peoples' homes, in village squares, out on the roads and in the fields and on the sea of Galilee. So many parables are about the ordinary—a woman baking, someone cleaning a house, fishing and farm work being done, meals being prepared and enjoyed. The world is where the altar is now, all of it a temple, a place for communion.

"*Finding an Altar in the World*"   191

> I can set a little altar, in the world or in my heart. . . . Human beings may separate things into as many piles as we wish—separating spirit from flesh, sacred from secular, church from world. But we should not be surprised when God does not recognize the distinctions we make between the two. Earth is so thick with divine possibility that it is a wonder we can walk anywhere without cracking our shins on altars.[13]

So Barbara Brown Taylor leads us through a selection of practices in which world becomes sacrament. She does not give us, as some spiritual literature does, recipes, step-by-step instructions on how to experience, for example, pain or the feel of our bodies or the touch of another or the experience of nature as sacred encounters. She really does not need to do so. As in her other trilogy volumes, as well as in her sermons and other essays, she, like a good spiritual mother or father, allows us, invites us to accompany her own experience. I don't know if I have her courage to meditate naked before a full-length mirror! But I can identify the powerful satisfaction of tearing into weeds in our garden, of the smell of my tomato plants as they are popping out fruit in late summer.

You need not be a master hiker of wilderness trails or a daily devotee of the treadmill to benefit from her reflections on walking. She not only listens to monk and writer Thich Nat Hanh on traditional Buddhist walking meditation but also takes us along with herself and her husband Ed on getting lost in the woods at a church camp walking at night, without flashlights and with the moon not as much help as they had thought due to the dense foliage.[14]

Narrated in *Learning to Walk in the Dark*, I greatly enjoyed her account of spending the night with just her dog in a cabin without any light or iPhone or any other technology. The intense silence of a summer evening in the country, or alone in

---
[13] Ibid., 15.
[14] Ibid., 53–56.

the bedroom of an old farmhouse, or lying out on a blanket, gazing up at the stars—what beautiful writing, what gorgeous memories to carry around inside, what convincing examples that the prayer books and cross and icons and hymns are all superb, but not always necessary. She captures other extraordinary moments too—climbing up onto the fire escape of an old Victorian house close by her seminary as a young woman, unsure of where to go with her education and her life. She wondered out loud to God that night what she was supposed to do with her life. Whether for real or wishful thinking—it matters little—Taylor hears the reply: "Do anything that pleases you . . . and belong to me."[15]

She remembers, so vividly, I feel I am there with her, long, seemingly unending summer afternoons in the fields and woods behind her childhood house.[16] You will be moved as I was, by her memories of her father, of her learning to use his tools, cleaning his guns meticulously, and laying out on the deck on a summer night with him as a seven-year-old, watching the planets come out, the moon rise, and stars fall.[17] With these treasured scenes she reminds us of the grace of paying attention to things and people around us, the reverence for the world that needs no catechism question or answer, no defined doctrine. It is also striking that her father, who practiced no formal religion at all, was nevertheless one of the most influential spiritual teachers Taylor had in her life.[18]

Just as poignant is Taylor's description of how she learned that pain, physical pain but also psychic pain, is also a great teacher in the spiritual life. "Pain makes theologians of us all," she writes.[19] And then she describes, in excruciating detail I will not repeat here, the aftermath of a serious injury to her

---

[15] Ibid., 110.
[16] Ibid.
[17] Ibid., 17–20.
[18] Taylor, *Leaving Church*, 22–24.
[19] Taylor, *Altar in the World*, 157.

eye. Her account is horrific, disturbing, and if that is not enough, she goes on to her fear of needles, even that of novocaine at the dentist. For a lifelong dentophobe, lovingly cared for by several compassionate dentists and hygienists, this was almost too much for me to endure. Her further learning from pain is eloquent. A night of pain and the sleeplessness it ensures, "can erase most of what you thought you knew about yourself."[20] Your supposed spiritual depth, your emotional strength, your tolerance levels, patience, even your believed-in compassion for others—stripped away by chronic pain. In her pastoral care experience, Taylor also discovered another kind of pain, that of being unable to relive the pain of another.[21] She offers one of the most insightful, succinct commentaries on the figure of Job as one who suffers not only intensely but also without apparent reason.[22]

Less disturbing, yet just as important, are her reflections on the practice of "wearing skin," that is, of being bodies, not just having them, a reality she connects with great insight to God's incarnation, as the Russian theologians put it, to the significance of "God's humanity"—something that still confronts the ordinary religious mind. Still thinking about pain, it is clear that the body is one of the most demanding of any teachers or spiritual directors we ever will have. If we are not saved, made whole in our bodies—this despite aging, sickness, and death— there is no possibility of salvation, which means therapy and healing. It is not just the world around us that is sacrament, it is also the body that I have, that I am. And so it is clear why the great traditions all see the cleansing power of water to wash us, whether the baptismal water of the Jordan that Jesus himself stepped into or the embrace of Mother Ganges. It is not only funerals that are times of eating and consoling; the breaking

---

[20] Ibid., 164.
[21] Ibid., 160.
[22] Ibid., 161–69.

of bread is sacramental for all persons of faith, whether the Shabbat challah or the eucharistic loaf. Prophets smear oil not only on kings but also on the sick. The traditions recognize the importance of fasting. Yet if they do not also revere feasting, then something is wrong. We know exactly how distorted and unnatural, hence ungodly, is the aversion to but obsession with sex for so many devout people, and it matters little whether they are Muslim, Jewish, or Christian.

Christians cannot claim to be Christians without recognition of and love for the flesh. "And the Word became flesh and dwelt among us" (John 1:14). Taylor speaks of the incarnation not so much as a doctrine but as a daily practice. But we can only do this if we believe that God understands our flesh and blood, speaks the language of the body. Lo and behold, it seems, on closer inspection of the scriptural texts, that the disembodiment and overspiritualization is our problem, not God's. Jesus feeds people with bread and fish. He touches and heals them, listens to them and exchanges often challenging conversations with them. Jesus walks all over the roads of Galilee and elsewhere, drinks when thirsty from a Samaritan woman's jug at the Sichar well. He puts a towel around his waist and washes his friends' feet at their last meal together. And they must have known what he was trying to say by his actions, for we have them preserved in these texts, his showing by doing, his attending to our bodies with his body and whole being.[23]

The Sacrament of Community, the Practice of Being Neighbor

One thing, one practice, leads to another. For me, the greatest way in which the world is sacrament to us is community. Taylor wisely draws on the Desert Mothers and Fathers for the centrality of encountering others as the encountering of God.

[23] Ibid., 43.

These great women and men make it clear that when we see our neighbor, we see God. Elsewhere in the book we have come upon this, especially in Mother Maria Skobtsova's insistence that the commandments to love God and the neighbor cannot be divided or valued differently from one another. To do so immediately starts a distortion of faith, God becoming more important, the divine taking precedence over the human, the body, the ordinary. The incarnation and the community of the sister and brother are what baptism and Eucharist are about.

> I understood that it was not possible to trust that God loved all of me, including my body, without also trusting that God loved all bodies everywhere . . . hungry children and indentured women along with the bodies of sleek athletes and cigar-smoking tycoons. . . . My body is what connects me to all of these other people. Wearing my skin is not a solitary practice but one that brings me into communion with all these other embodied souls. It is what we have most in common with one another. . . . What many of us miss, in our physical dis-ease, is that our bodies remain God's best way of getting to us.[24]

It is not just a commandment to love the neighbor. Taylor reminds us that we really do need the brother and the sister. No theological training is required for compassion, for forgiveness. We know, even if we have never heard the Tertullian quote, that there is no such thing as a solitary Christian. But is this not the great challenge for us at this point in the twenty-first century? On November 8, 2016, those going to the polls elected as president a candidate with no previous experience of public service, one given to reviling whole groups of people. Here are some of his claims: Mexicans are "rapists," "murderers." We need to exclude refugees from Syria because they could be terrorists. We need to exclude Muslims from entering the country and submit those living here, citizens or not, to special surveillance as potential terrorist threats. Undocumented

[24] Ibid., 41–42.

immigrants must be deported rather than integrated. Some people even call for an end to all immigration as the face of America is changing color and religion.

The desire is to return the country to an earlier time that somehow was "greater" because we knew who Americans were then. A governor insists the criminals who push drugs and abuse young women are outsiders. They are from more racially diverse nearby states, and they are even identified by him with African American names. This is poorly veiled racism. Before the lead-up to the 2016 elections, even political pundits would have argued that such extreme positions were those of only a statistically insignificant minority. On the way to the November 2016 election, such perspectives as those of the preceding paragraph had become mainstream, echoes at rallies of thousands of Trump supporters.

Here is the issue of the neighbor as "other" that Taylor raises.[25] It is addressed in the tradition too. Consider the Good Samaritan, the Canaanite woman, and the unnamed tax collector, as well as Zacchaeus and the Roman centurion in the gospels. Mother Maria Skobtsova recognized that the neighbor would often be not the person with whom we'd prefer to associate. Yet the reality of the incarnation is such that no one is excluded from God's humanity. It is easy to be kind to those who are kind to us, Jesus realized, but what of those who are our enemies, out to get us, unlike us, "other"?

Much of what passes for religion seems to direct us vertically, to the kingdom of heaven somewhere else, to a God "upstairs" or "out there." We would rather have a heaven, a church, a community of people in our own image and likeness. Such could not be further from the reality that the Christian tradition holds. You belong, always, to this family or tribe, this city or village. But you belong as well to God, who is everywhere, part of every aspect of life, not just the religious ones.

---

[25] Ibid., 94–95.

"Finding an Altar in the World" 197

And all of the details in the Torah on treatment of the injured slave, the widow in need, the foreigner seeking refuge, the neighbor whose crops have been trampled by your herd, or the one who unintentionally injured your ox—not to mention someone robbed or raped or assaulted or taking a life in self-defense—no matter the specific circumstances, the common truth affirmed in all is we are always obligated to the one before us, that each person and every relationship is important, in fact, sacred.

Here the world and the sacrament collide, the "sacrament of the sister and brother."[26] John Chrysostom and later Maria Skobtsova, Dorothy Day, and others came to see that what we do at the altar has consequences. It needs to be extended beyond the holy table of gold or silver, stone or wood, to the altar that is flesh and blood—that of the sister and brother before us.

Barbara Brown Taylor suggests several other practices that are well worth pondering. If it is the case that we must value and celebrate our bodies, the practice of suffering, of pain, cannot be avoided. Though we cannot consider it, so too the work that a body and living entail. The tough, exhausting practice of work is captured by Taylor's need to carry water into her house when loss of power in a winter ice storm shut off the pump. Work is of our nature. Even when others now perform it for us, there still remain many difficult, boring, and tiring tasks that a world of technology cannot eliminate. Work of this sort is what makes the graceful leap of a dancer, the flash of color on a canvas, the sheen of a glaze on a finished bowl, the deft writing in a book, the exquisite flavor of a dish all possible, capable of our delight. How compartmentalized and, indeed, impoverished are we if we fail to recognize the encounter with the holy in labor involved.

---

[26] See chap. 3 of this book, "The Sacrament of the Brother/Sister: Maria Skobtsova," as well as chap. 7 of *Uncommon Prayer*, "The Prayer of Care."

We devour books and retreats on prayer—how to do it and how to do it better, more effectively. The practice of being present to God helps us to know ourselves and our lives more accurately. Perhaps, it is better stated exactly the opposite. The more we become aware of ourselves and our lives, the better will be our awareness of God.

> When I fretted over people in trouble, so that my worry for them followed me around all day like a hungry dog, was that prayer? When I cooked dinner for people who had plenty to eat at home, thinking about them while I chopped the turnip greens and mashed the sweet potatoes, was that prayer? When I went outside after everyone had gone to bed and moaned at the moon because I could not come up with the right words to say what was in my heart, was that prayer? . . . When I am fully alert to whatever or whoever is right in front of me; when I am electrically aware of the tremendous gift of being alive; when I am able to give of myself wholly to the moment I am in, then I am in prayer. Prayer is happening, and it is not necessarily something I am doing.[27]

In her efforts to not so much leave the church behind, but better integrate faith in her life, Barbara Brown Taylor offers us much about life as prayer, about the world as sacrament. Looking around, we may be startled but, I think, pleasantly surprised to find so much of a cathedral around us—not the massive ones hewn of stones, but put together from so many small pieces, faces, places, and lives.

---

[27] Taylor, *Altar in the World*, 178.

Sister Joan Chittister, OSB
Photo from Robert Ellsberg, Orbis Books.

Chapter 11

"Passion for God, Life, and Justice": Joan Chittister's Prophetic Way

A Life and Breaking Out of It

We have become used to learning from monastic men and women valuable lessons for active everyday existence, for life in the world. Kathleen Norris has contributed a number of books based on her friendships with sisters and brothers in the Benedictine heritage, as well as her experience as an oblate, that is, a layperson with a connection to a specific monastery. The relationship is one in which an individual perhaps visits and stays for retreat at the monastery occasionally. But the more enduring bond is that of prayer and exchange on the spiritual life as one uses the monastic elements as important parts of one's own spiritual striving in the daily round of work, family, neighborhood.

Of course there are the other popular, even stereotypic images of monastics and their lives. On many monastery websites, even on the covers of CDs and books and the wrappers of monastic products like jam, honey, cheese, fudge, and fruitcake, the older images still are used—monks with their hoods up meditating or sisters tending gardens or domestic animals. There are the photo galleries of brothers and sisters in church, chanting the Divine Office. Occasionally it is startling to see the faces of very young monastics, twenty-somethings, clad in the habits from another time. In some cases, I have been struck, in online stories or on websites, by the energetic faces of twenty-something cloistered Dominican nuns or serious bearded Benedictine monks in Norcia, where the monastery has been revived. Hipsters as monks, almost![1]

Paging through Tom Roberts's riveting, wonderfully thorough biography of renowned Benedictine Joan Chittister, there is a progression of photos from the full wimple, veil and long black habit in which she was professed to the much-simplified suit and veil and the ordinary dress to which the sisters of her community have now transitioned. Not only in his biography but also in many of her own books as well, her life becomes a most revealing text.[2] But the images of Joan in the last thirty or more years, what she became, what she did, and especially all that she has written leave this young veiled and coiffed sister and more behind.

In reading this biography, I thought a lot about the path that had been paved even further back by Thomas Merton. He made himself the target of attack both from conservative readers and his own superiors with his courageous writing about the civils rights and anti-Vietnam War movements as well as the dire need for reform and renewal in religious life. Merton was, by Joan Chittister's own account, the principal inspiration of her own spiritual development in her early years as a Benedictine. And in remarkable symmetry with him, her own vision came to be rooted not only in prayer and contemplation but also in many active directions. I suspect many will fixate on the revelations of the difficult childhood Joan experienced, most specifically the harsh, abusive treatment of her mother by her stepfather.[3]

---

[1] The Monks of Norcia, http://osbnorcia.org/en/.

[2] Tom Roberts, *Joan Chittister: Her Journey from Certainty to Faith* (Maryknoll, NY: Orbis Books, 2015); see also *Called to Question: A Spiritual Memoir* (Lanham, MD: Rowman & Littlefield, 2004); *Scarred by Struggle, Transformed by Hope* (Grand Rapids, MI: Eerdmans, 2003); and *Following the Path: The Search for a Life of Passion, Purpose and Joy* (New York: Random House, 2012).

[3] Roberts, *Joan Chittister*, 11–28.

Thomas Merton often had sarcastic things to say about such "caricatures" of monastics as those mentioned above, not a few of which appeared in publications from his own monastery, Gethsemani, in his lifetime. He understood that these images corresponded to how a great many "out in the world" wanted the cloistered women and men, the monastics, to look and also to sound and behave. Thus, while writing about the civil rights and antiwar movements of his time, as well as about the need for reform and renewal of monastic life, Merton was not surprised at all to find himself attacked by readers and criticized, even censored, as it happened, by his monastic superiors. He was told that such concerns of social justice and the political order, issues of war, violence, and discrimination, were not appropriate concerns for a monk! Until today, almost fifty years after his death, Merton is suspect and the target of attack by conservatives who deplore his progressive stances on war and racism, not to mention his criticism of the hierarchy and his support of reform in the church. One only has to think of the backlash already launched against another preacher of God's mercy, Pope Francis.

Whatever the case was for male monastics and clergy back before Vatican II, things were far worse for religious women. The figure and the life story of Benedictine Sister Joan Chittister encompasses this in startling, powerful terms. Chittister lived through the pre–Vatican II period of American Catholicism. She grew up and encountered the lack of any connection or compassion, even on the part of priests, for those outside the church, for non-Catholics. The story of Joan Chittister's life captures the culture of preconciliar Catholicism in America in which Chittister was raised. It deeply affected her parents as her non-Catholic, Presbyterian father was effectively cut out of the picture by Catholic clergy, this rift only one of many that made the marriage of her parents a battlefield. Many of the writers profiled in this book had similar experiences. Thomas Merton and Richard Rohr have both documented their encounters with this fortress mentality, a kind of religious imperialism.

Chittister's was a hardscrabble family life and childhood. She often observed that all she was able to do—finish her doctorate, teach, publish so prolifically, be invited to speak at so many venues, be elected as superior of her community for three terms—that all this and so much more she did was "not bad for a kid from Seventeenth and Peach," her home address in a then very poor neighborhood in Erie, Pennsylvania.[4] Her first years in the Benedictines were no less challenging and difficult. Religious life for women before Vatican II was often rigid, legalistic, and sometimes bluntly inhumane. Religious women, hard as it may be to believe, were often brutal with each other. Kathleen Norris's essays on Benedictine nuns have to be among the most powerful accounts of these women confronting their past in the church, especially in their formation.[5] There are plenty of striking instances described here in Roberts's account, based on Chittister's memoirs and interviews with her. But there was as well the rich liturgical life of Daily Office, Mass, and a communal existence shaped by Benedict's Rule. The Erie Benedictines' principal ministry was education, and Joan had her start here, working as a teacher, eventually tagged for graduate studies because of her gifts as a writer. We learn of the senseless, almost irrational decision making of superiors, often by emotional shifts and the need to control subordinates. A woman with Joan's obvious gifts for communication and leadership singled her out as a target for authoritarian treatment. It is no surprise that early on, she became committed to reform and renewal, not only of her own Benedictine community but also, as the years progressed, of the wider church.

---

[4] Ibid., 180–82.
[5] Kathleen Norris, *The Cloister Walk* (New York: Riverhead Books, 1996), 249–63, 317–28.

A Life Transformed into Passions

I think the rest of Chittister's story, brought into focus by this powerful narrative, is amazing in itself. As the biography documents, Chittister's wish to pursue a vocation with the Benedictines was valued and supported in the 1950s. She entered the novitiate (as I did for the Carmelites) directly from high school. That's what you did in those days if you were testing a vocation, and generally you had support from family and your parish clergy. She had already had, through secondary education at the Benedictine's academy, almost a "minor seminary" experience of preparation for later religious formation.

All the details are there—this kind of black stockings and shoes, this black dress as a postulant, and then the black habit and the complicated wimple and veil the women Benedictines wore. What comes across strongly in Chittister's memoir notes, in interviews, and in this biography itself is the internal culture of ruthless top-down authority from superior to the rest of the community—those in formation in particular. The scene in which Joan is ordered to toss her diary into the fire of a furnace by her superior is stunning. Such self-awareness and self-reflection on the part of a still very young but ambitious writer and teacher—Joan as novice—was incompatible with the faceless, selfless ego then the model for members of religious communities. I can witness, as a Carmelite novice and student friar back in those days, that the impossibility of having any strong opinions or ideas of your own was indeed the prevailing point of view of religious superiors.[6] You also were to have no close, as they called them, "particular" friendships either. For necessity, of course, you had just functional ones with your superiors and peers. What was more, no one cared what you thought

---

[6] Michael Plekon, *Saints as They Really Are* (Notre Dame, IN: University of Notre Dame Press, 2012), 105–50.

or how you felt and if you were so unwise as to express your ideas and feelings, you would be told such were signs of pride and selfishness. Thus, as a writer, keeping a working notebook and daily journal were, in the view of her superior, absolutely incompatible with being an obedient novice and junior monastic.

Rather than obliterate herself, as the order to burn the journal suggested, Joan Chittister did the exact opposite. She grew, learned, developed, and came into her own as a person, an intellect and a discerning spiritual leader and teacher. For years she followed the path that endured, even after Vatican II, of women religious being the underpaid rank-and-file workers of Catholic schools, hospitals, and other care institutions. She dutifully served as a teaching sister, the primary ministry of her community. But her superior intellectual gifts were recognized and she was sent on to graduate work and degrees. In time, her leadership skills were also appreciated, and she was elected by her community to several terms as the prioress, the major superior.

What stands out most is that as a leader in several Benedictine associations, then in her own community, then in the Leadership Conference of Women Religious and beyond, and finally in the larger American Catholic Church, she became an outspoken, fearless voice. While at first careful and cautious, she eventually shed these restraints and became the most candid and the most defiant voice among women religious up until Sister Simone Campbell and the recent "Sisters on the Bus."

Clearly, the tension between the Vatican Congregation on Religious and American sisters has drastically dissipated as the ministry of Pope Francis progresses. Threats of sanctions are gone, though clearly some Curia deeply distrust American Catholic women religious whom previously they condemned as being rebellious and not sharing core Catholic values.

Joan Chittister was an important force, over the decades, in shaping the sisters' commitment to reform and justice and their defiance against church harassment. Chittister has urged renewal and reform, but not just within religious life and the Catholic Church. Her efforts have moved to the larger social and cultural landscape to questions about immigration reform, the opposition to military conflict in Afghanistan and Iraq, climate change, and the status of women, to mention just a few. Chittister's engagement grew and became more sweeping through the 1980s and into the twenty-first century. While she continues to write and speak, her schedule has been scaled back in recent years (she has reached the age of eighty!). What is clear from Roberts's biography is how much resonance there has been from Chittister's fidelity to her Benedictine roots, her commitment to change and justice and to the effort of Pope Francis to lead with mercy toward the same ideals.

Passion for God

Joan Chittister's longtime friend and colleague, one of the editors of a collected volume of her writings, fellow Benedictine Mary Lou Kownacki, is responsible for describing Chittister's threefold vision as "passion for God," "passion for life," and "passion for justice." Tom Roberts follows a similar path in his biography. You can also see these patterns in Chittister's publications.

While it might not seem apparent at first view, it is nevertheless the case that an activist like Joan Chittister offers us some important perspectives for our concerns here in this book. I think there are ways in which Chittister shows us how to live the life of the Spirit in the ordinary, how to encounter the world as sacrament. Both her biographer and the editors of her writing suggest these different aspects of her thinking and life.

The first of these has to do with her own lifelong journey from what Tom Roberts calls "certainty to faith." It is her changing but deepening understanding of God. Chittister's recollection of her mother's Catholic priest's categorical rejection of her Presbyterian father and his faith remains vivid well over a half century later.[7] The intransigence and arrogance of the Catholic outlook then did great damage to her parents' marriage and, in turn, to her childhood and later years as a young adult in the church and the Benedictine order.

Chittister has written a number of reflections on how profoundly her vision of God has changed, probably the most powerful coming in a lecture/essay from a millennium conference, "God at 2000."

> What I have learned about God after a lifetime of seeking is that, first, God must be sought in the light, and that, second, God does not have to be found. If there is anything in the world, however, that may deserve our pity, it may well be the very idea of "God." What else in the history of humankind has been more reviled as fraud, more ridiculed as unprovable or, on the other hand, more glorified out of existence—more condemned to unattainable remoteness—than the notion of God?[8]

The radical rethinking of so basic a part of faith, really at the very heart of it, is shocking to many. How could a nun, one who has spent most of her adult life in prayer, spiritual reading, religious community, come to question the most essential element, God? But Chittister says it most succinctly when she says that for her, God in 2000 is not the God she knew in 1950, a lifetime ago. Did God change? Did Joan Chittister change? It's complicated. Yet all of you reading this can identify with the transformation Chittister is describing. Her early upbringing and later religious formation gave her a very restricted image of God as judge. This was the God with one eye on the law and another on all of us constantly disobeying it. This was a God of wrath and punishment, before whom we were always

---

[7] *Joan Chittister: Essential Writings*, Modern Spiritual Masters Series (Maryknoll, NY: Orbis Books, 2014), 222–224; Roberts, *Joan Chittister*, 16–26.

[8] *Joan Chittister: Essential Writings*, 38.

in the wrong. Further, this was an omnipotent God with little mercy." I know I have experienced such a transformation. Remember the fresco and then the stained-glass window images of God the Father in the churches of my childhood, mentioned in the prologue? As my grandmother warned, this was the God who was "always watching me." I think this was a constant image of God in the lives of many Christians of our time.

> I have used the God of judgment and been judgmental of others. I have used God to get me through life. I have called the intolerable "God's will" and called our failure to stop evil God's failure to stop evil. I have expected God to be the crutch that would make the unbearable bearable. As a result, I often failed to take steps to change life either for myself or others when injustice masked itself as God's will and oppression as God's judgment.[9] . . . I learned as life went by that the God I make will be the God I seek, the spiritual life I live, and the quality of my own heart. Until I discover the God in whom I myself believe, then, until I unmask the God who lives in my own heart, regardless of the panoply of other God-images around me, I will never understand another thing about my own life.[10]

The education and experiences of Chittister's life as a Benedictine, as a teacher, as head of a community, and as an activist exploded the aggressor God with whom she'd begun her life. She credits the Rule of Benedict as pivotal in her transformation. In addition, the larger spiritual tradition, personal encounters, science, globalism, and feminism played important roles.

Paul Evdokimov raised the question for us—who is our God? He pointed to the God who loves us so much that he wants to share our existence and our suffering with his "foolish" love.

---

[9] Ibid., 39.
[10] Ibid., 40.

Lev Gillet showed us that the identity of God, or better, the names we give God, the images we employ, can do exactly the opposite of what they ought to. They can drive a person away from God, or worse, confirm for them that God is "up there" and apart from them, a fearful potentate who is really more in our image and likeness, a projection of our own sense of order or retribution. When you consider how often religion has been used by governments and leaders to legitimize their own goals, their own visions, then the need for what Chittister experienced becomes evident.

I think it would be fair to say that every writer listened to in this book experienced a basic transformation in his or her vision of God. Barbara Brown Taylor had to leave church in several ways in order to again find that God was already present outside, in the world. Lev Gillet's years of encounters with troubled, suffering people led to his dropping "God" in favor of "Love without limits," or simply, "Love." His friend and coworker Maria Skobtsova noted all the cultural and social forms religiosity takes without facing the reality, and a liberating one it is, that it is all about love—for God, for the neighbor before us. In his hermitage, Merton finally recognized the simplicity of it all, of God's presence in and with us, something that Richard Rohr constantly stresses. Marilynne Robinson allows us to see and hear the movements of grace and forgiveness constantly at work, in the very ordinary inhabitants of the small Iowa town of Gilead. Joan Chittister put it poignantly—she came to realize, but only gradually, with effort and pain over years, that sin was not the center of life, that life was anything but "one slippery slope away from God," but quite the opposite.[11] All is grace, as Teresa of Avila, Dorothy Day, and Marilynne Robinson attest.

---

[11] Ibid., 224.

Passion for Life and for Justice

Though she does not explicitly speak of the world as sacrament, Chittister says that several forces propelled her out of a kind of Catholic "ghetto" and faith into the arena where God calls us all to work. The texts of the Scriptures and the world spiritual traditions, along with the Christian heritage, were for her important sources, as were science, globalization, and the women's movement. The Rule of Benedict in particular, ancient as it is, nevertheless identified essentials of life in and with God for her. This was a life not only of creative work but also of holy leisure, of silence, and reflection. For this life, Benedict saw community as essential, and Chittister further saw in Benedict's encompassing vision a responsibility for the world, a stewardship of the environment, a mandate to care for those in need. Finally, Benedict shows that the way of Christ is one of humility. We defer to the other, welcome the other, the guest, as Christ.[12] In all of this, we experience peace, not the negotiated settlement of armed conflicts but life as God wants and sees it.[13]

Joan Chittister's life is like a canvas on which the expansion of spiritual openness and vision can be read. Too much to describe in detail here, her career is decades rich with learning, teaching, writing, with important leadership roles, with active participation in peacemaking, in action for justice. An important aspect of her activism is the rediscovery of what it is to be human. It may sound strange that such a rediscovery was necessary for a woman who grew up in a tumultuous but loving home, with a devout mother, and then was surrounded by dedicated Benedictine women of work and prayer. Yet repeatedly in her writings, Chittister herself makes it clear that, like Merton and Taylor and Rohr and so many others here, she

---

[12] Ibid., 66–76.
[13] Ibid., 84–89.

too had to move beyond the religious structures and perspectives in which she was raised and in which she was formed. The formalism and legalism of her "first half of life" were ill-suited to the challenges she faced later—exactly what science, globalization, feminism, and social injustice taught her. Remembering an intense childhood incident, one in which the loss of a beloved pet completely overwhelmed her, Chittister described how her mother and father crawled in on either side of her in bed and hugged her close in her grief.

> [B]eing human meant to enter into someone else's pain. And that is what we have lost. We "defend" ourselves by threatening the globe and our own level of civilized humanness with it. We have chosen technological progress and financial profits over the needs of human beings. We have bartered the quality of our own souls; we live the denial of Reverence for Life. But we have become a society of machines and business degrees, of stocks and bonds, of world power and world devastation, of what works and what makes money. We train our young to get ahead, our middle-aged to consume, and our elderly to be silent. . . . We talk about our ideas for getting ahead rather than about our ideas for touching God. . . . We have forsaken the good, the true, and the beautiful for the effective, the powerful, and the opulent. . . . So what do I believe in? What do I define as human? I believe in the pursuit of the spiritual, in the presence to pain, and the sacredness of life. Without these, life is useless and humanity a farce. . . . To be human is to listen to the rest of the world with a tender heart, and to learn to live life with our arms open and our souls seared with a sense of responsibility for everything that is.[14]

Joan Chittister makes it clear, as do Dorothy Day, Elisabeth Behr-Sigel, Maria Skobtsova, Barbara Brown Taylor, and the rest, that there is no such thing as activism in general or for "causes" that are "trending." Entering another's pain, standing

[14] Ibid., 118–19.

"*Passion for God, Life, and Justice*" 213

up and speaking out for her, are traced back to very particular experiences of being comforted, loved, held.

Chittister's Benedictine community was threatened by the Vatican with "appropriate punishment" if she went ahead with a lecture at a conference on women and ordination in Dublin in 2001.[15] Of course she did, only one of many talks that would be considered radical, insubordinate, provocative, disobedient, heretical. Her tenacity and her integrity has made her partner with some of the finest prophetic voices of our time, all of them sanctioned and attacked, some censored, others driven away—Küng, Rahner, Congar, Schillebeeckx, Guttierez, de Chardin and Courtney Murray, Elizabeth Johnson, Matthew Fox, Charles Curran, and Roger Haight, to mention only a few. After nearly unanimous support of her despite this threat, the community remained singled out for a visitation and scrutiny.

Chittister has reduced her number of lectures but continues to write. The prodigious list of books she has published include commentary on the Rule of Benedict, also a classic assessment of the state and future of religious women and men, reflections on the Creed, on aging, on prayer, on prophetic action, and on *lectio divina*, and much more.[16] There is no Benedictine author more prolific! As with the other writers listened to in this book, the invitation and the suggestion is to enter into the literature each has produced, in Chittister's case a rich, formidable collection.

---

[15] Roberts, *Joan Chittister*, 159–79.

[16] Joan Chittister, *The Fire in These Ashes: A Spirituality of Contemporary Religious Life* (Kansas City, MO: Sheed & Ward, 1995); *Wisdom Distilled from the Daily: Living the Rule of St. Benedict Today* (San Francisco: HarperCollins, 1990); *The Rule of Benedict: Spirituality for the Twenty-First Century* (New York: Crossroad, 2010); *The Radical Christian Life: A Year with St. Benedict* (Collegeville, MN: Liturgical Press, 2011); *In Search of Belief* (Liguori, MO: Liguori Publications, 2006); *The Gift of Years: Growing Older Gracefully* (New York: BlueBridge, 2008); and *The Breath of the Soul: Reflections on Prayer* (Mystic, CT: Twenty-Third Publications, 2009).

Over the last several decades, Chittister went to stand with and support the Leadership Conference of Women Religious, the International Union of Superiors General. She participated in the UN Conference on Women gathering in Beijing in 1995 and later worked with the Global Peace Initiative of Women with Joan Campbell. She was part of the 2000 UN Millennium World Peace Summit of Religious and Spiritual Leaders. Like Richard Rohr, she too appeared on Oprah Winfrey's "Super Soul Sunday" series, on March 1, 2015.[17]

God, Neighbor, and the World

There is no need to make a case for Joan Chittister's record both as a teacher/writer and as a leader. As with the other writers to whom we listen here, I encourage the reader to seek out her publications, numerous and diverse and well-received. Chittister's own life became her classroom. I can well identify with the pre–Vatican II church in which she spent her childhood, surely an institution of "certainty," but also one from which most had to move in order to remain in church. Throughout both her biography and writings, Joan Chittister is open about her profound doubts and intense questioning of the church, her order, and the Christian tradition. Like Merton, she has steeped herself in the spiritual traditions of other world religions and explicitly cites Buddhist and Sufi mystics and parables. She is a remarkable spiritual leader and writer, one whose difficult experiences opened her compassion and discernment even further.

While more thoroughly documented in the new biography, some of the family of origin details have been reported earlier

---

[17] See Oprah Winfrey and Sister Joan Chittister: "A Life of Passion, Purpose and Joy," *Super Soul Sunday*, Season 6, Episode 601, March 1, 2015, http://www.oprah.com/own-super-soul-sunday/Oprah-and-Sister-Joan-Chittister.

"Passion for God, Life, and Justice" 215

by Chittister herself. But this more recent book documents, among other things, the difficulties of her parents' marriage, the abusive treatment of her mother by her stepfather and her presence amid this until her parents separated and she and her mother relocated. But Chittister is courageous and honest enough to narrate more, including some extremely oppressive treatment within the Benedictines. Meg Funk has likewise provided such accounts, both narratives coming from religious women who remained and who were leaders in their communities as well as well-known authors.[18]

What is significant here is that like many of our other writers, Chittister provides numerous points of connection for us to the course of her life, intersections that enable us to relate our own journeys with hers. More than other writers here, she also presses the identity of women and the place women should have not only in society but also in church.[19]

Among the authors surveyed here, only Barbara Brown Taylor's intense memoir, *Leaving Church*, comes to mind as comparable. There are, to be sure, others who share with stunning honesty—Mary Karr, Christian Wiman, Sara Miles, Darcey Steinke.[20] This is a kind of spiritual text—the personal accounting of one's life.

Chittister echoes points of view we have heard elsewhere in this volume. She sides with those who urge us to listen more carefully to our own tradition, that of the Hebrew and then earliest Christian Scriptures. There we see God not as distant, transcendent judge but "closer to us than our own hearts," in

---

[18] Mary Funk, *Into the Depths: A Journey of Loss and Vocation* (New York: Lantern Books, 2010).

[19] *Joan Chittister: Essential Writings*, 199–235.

[20] I have covered a number of these and more in *Hidden Holiness* (Notre Dame, IN: University of Notre Dame Press, 2009); *Saints as They Really Are: Voices of Holiness in Our Time* (Notre Dame, IN: University of Notre Dame Press, 2012); and *Uncommon Prayer: Prayer in Everyday Experience* (Notre Dame, IN: University of Notre Dame Press, 2016).

Augustine's well-known words. From the rule of her community, that of Benedict, one that has had nearly universal appeal, she derives what are really aspects of the world as sacrament—lived holiness, forgiveness, simplicity, hospitality.[21]

Chittister, like other masters of the life of prayer, applauds the traditional tools of reciting the psalms and pondering the scriptures and other texts. But as Barbara Brown Taylor, she insists we see all the texts beyond those in our Bibles and prayer books, all the prayer that cannot be described or taught that occurs in everyday life.

Lastly, she puts into practice the adage we heard from Paul Evdokimov, namely, that we need to become what we pray.[22] Recognizing the decline in lifetime vocations to the religious life, Chittister has dedicated herself to the oblate or associate connection of laypeople with monastics as well as to an online program called "The Monastic Way."[23]

Merton, who stumbled and struggled his way through life, finally realizing it was all prayer, all the time, shared that in his journals and letters. It took twenty-five years for us to be able to track his pilgrimage and it changed our entire appreciation of him. Joan Chittister has already shared with us a great deal of her life and the lessons learned from it. Like her fellow monastic, Merton, it is a different path than what most of us travel—more focused, intense, with the accompaniment of community but not that of spouse or family. Yet in sharing her family of origin experiences and then those of her Benedictine family, we are allowed to see that the need to rediscover, to grow, even to reinvent ourselves is a common challenge of

---

[21] *Joan Chittister: Essential Writings*, 125–29, 130–33, 144–46, 151–52.

[22] Ibid., 88–92. See the chapter here on Paul Evdokimov and *The Sacrament of Love*, trans. Anthony P. Gythiel and Victoria Steadman (Crestwood, NY: St. Vladimir's Seminary Press, 1995), 61–62.

[23] Roberts, *Joan Chittister*, 229; see also *The Monastic Way by Joan Chittister*, www.monasticway.org; see also Joan Chittister, *The Monastery of the Heart: An Invitation to a Meaningful Life* (New York: BlueBridge, 2011).

trying to live the spiritual life in our time. She shows us exactly how God, the neighbor, and the world are sacraments of encounter for all of us.

Kathleen Norris
Photo from the Steven Barclay Agency and the author.

Chapter 12

"Quotidian Mysteries": Kathleen Norris and the Struggle with Everyday Demons

It is a quotidian mystery that dailiness can lead to such despair and yet also be at the core of our salvation. We express this every time we utter the Lord's Prayer. As Simone Weil so eloquently stated it . . . the "bread of this world" is all that nourishes and energizes us, not only food but the love of friends and family, "money, ambition, consideration . . . power . . . everything that puts us in the capacity for action." She reminds us that we need to keep praying for this food, acknowledging our needs as daily, because in the act of asking, the prayer awakens in us the trust that God will provide. But like the manna that God provided to Israel in the desert, this "bread" cannot be stored. "We cannot bind our will today for tomorrow," Weil writes; "we cannot make a pact with [Christ] that tomorrow he will be with us, even in spite of ourselves." Each day brings with it not only the necessity of eating but the renewal of our love of and in God. This may sound like a simple thing, but it is not easy to maintain faith, hope or love in the everyday.[1]

Living Each Day

Kathleen Norris has defined herself as a poet, but she has done many other superlative kinds of writing, as the passage

---

[1] Kathleen Norris, *The Quotidian Mysteries* (Mahwah, NJ: Paulist Press, 1998), 10–11.

just cited attests. There is a notable memoir of her undergraduate years at Bennington College and her coming of age in the tumultuous 1960s.[2] Her encounters thereafter in New York with literary luminaries such as James Merrill, Jim Carroll, Denise Levertov, Stanley Kunitz, Patti Smith, and Erica Jong are also narrated in the volume. She has become best known for absorbing, thoughtful writing on the spiritual life. She crafted a poetic, poignant account of the move, with her husband, from New York City to the small town of Lemmon, South Dakota, to her grandparents' house.[3] There she discovers both the monotony and complex depth and beauty of life on the prairie.

This was in many ways the start of a new kind of existence as a writer. Not only was it a major cultural relocation, it was also concurrent with a renewal in her own spiritual life. It involved her going to church again, becoming an active member of the local Presbyterian parish in town, and eventually, also, a regular lay preacher there. The revival was even more profound for it involved her discovering monastic life, specifically that of Benedictine monks in a local monastery. And this led to her becoming an oblate or associate connected to a nearby Benedictine abbey, something unusual for a not very observant adult raised in a Presbyterian heritage.

In *The Cloister Walk*, Norris vividly describes monastics and their lives and also her attraction to the pattern of their daily existence.[4] These derived from Norris's stays at several Benedictine monastic houses. The essay on Benedictine women monastics and the changes through which they have gone since the Second Vatican Council is extraordinary. Norris came to deeply know and understand these sisters and was thus able

---

[2] Kathleen Norris, *The Virgin of Bennington* (New York: Riverhead, 2001).

[3] Kathleen Norris, *Dakota: A Spiritual Geography* (Boston: Houghton Mifflin, 2001).

[4] Kathleen Norris, *The Cloister Walk* (New York: Riverhead, 1997).

to present their situation more accurately and sympathetically than any author I know of. In *Amazing Grace*, Norris uses the framework of a dictionary/encyclopedia to delve into the "vocabulary" of religious faith, connecting the internal, intricate meanings of "salvation" and "grace" and many more standard terms with the lives of those who are trying to live them out.

A more recent major effort combines both her reflective writing and memoir in describing a number of years' hiatus from publishing.[5] These were the years in which her husband's physical and emotional health declined dramatically. She chronicles her efforts to stand by and care for him through severe depression, suicidal periods, and disappearances, culminating in his death from cancer. She also describes most lucidly her own struggles with depression, at the same time (and most unusually), doing a historical study of the understanding of *acedia*—the spiritual dryness and despair described in detail in the ancient world among the earliest monastic mothers and fathers. She offers a provocative case for the presence of this old affliction camouflaged in our time. She sees it behind the inability of many to feel sympathy or compassion for others, perhaps a defense mechanism against the onslaught of images and information of pain and misery that cannot be remedied. One thinks of the spectacle of the civil war in Syria and the continued destructiveness of terrorist attacks, particularly the media-bloating atrocities perpetrated by ISIS.

The Glory of the Ordinary

As early as the book *Dakota*, Norris displayed a poet's sensitivity to the minutiae of everyday life. Her poetry contains numerous meditations on the exquisite glory and beauty of

---

[5] Kathleen Norris, *Acedia & me: A Marriage, Monks, and a Writer's Life* (New York: Riverhead, 2008).

such mundane tasks as hanging laundry on lines outside, preparing a meal, tending gardens. From the Benedictines she learned the famous motto of their order, *Ora et Labora*—"pray and work." I have written about a series of presentations she did along these lines called "Holy Realism." There is an image there that is almost an icon of the world as sacrament. It is the kitchen scene of a poet, Kate Daniels, holding onto a small child, leaving her poetry aside to brown ground turkey to combine with store-bought sauce for the family's dinner.[6] Daniels writes: "Try as I may, and I do, I have a hard time browning the ground turkey I'm planning to mix with canned spaghetti sauce for the glory of God. I try to find the poetry that exists, even here. . . . I know that God is here, but in the chaos and the noise, I can't seem to find him." But God indeed found her and her meal, just as God steps into the village oven where the woman is baking so much bread that all in the village go home with bread, not from heaven but free, a gift (Matt 13:33). Maybe it is the bread of heaven.[7] The world is a supper for her husband and children of inexpensive pasta and meat sauce put together by a busy mother. The sacrament needs no explanation.[8] The same attention to the small graces and epiphanies of everyday life appear in *The Cloister Walk* and *Acedia & me*.

These epiphanies were the principal focus of the Madeleva Lectures she delivered in 1998, sponsored by the Center for Spirituality and St. Mary's College, Notre Dame, Indiana. Her selection for this prestigious series put her in the community of previous and past eminent figures such as Elizabeth Johnson, Sandra Schneiders, Lisa Sowle Cahill, Mary Boys, Joan

---

[6] Kate Daniels, "Poetry and Presence," *Louisiana Literature* 16, no. 1 (Spring/Summer, 1995).

[7] Amy-Jill Levine, *Short Stories by Jesus: The Enigmatic Parables of a Controversial Rabbi* (San Francisco: HarperOne, 2014), 107–25.

[8] Kathleen Norris's talk, "Holy Realism: Living Life as It Matters," from the April 28–29, 2003, Trinity Institute Conference, "Shaping Holy Lives." The text is at http://www.explorefaith.org/holiness/life1.html.

Chittister, Margaret Farley, M. Shawn Copeland, and Wendy Wright, to name only a few. Norris titled the lecture "The Quotidian Mysteries: Laundry, Liturgy and 'Women's Work.'"

All these categories are significant. Years ago Norris wrote a piece on doing laundry, seeing in it much more than removing dirt. Doing laundry is a sacred ritual, a source of great delight, a generous service done for someone loved.[9] She also discourses on laundry and hanging clothes in *Dakota*, as well as a number of other places in her writings. Laundry is a task both necessary and never really finished. No sooner do the folded washed clothes get put away into dresser drawers when yet another worn item flies toward the hamper—if you still have one! In my house, soiled things are hurled down the basement stairs to pile up at their foot, closer to the washer and dryer.

Work, like the food of daily bread mentioned above, relocates us in the real world of God's creation. God really does have a sense of humor, Norris observes. Work is not punishment but the constant invitation to experience the leisure of mindless tasks, like dishwashing and laundry. It is, even more importantly, a chance to play, not to accomplish great things but just to be part of a necessary task that has to be done over and over again. Immediately, but surprisingly (at least to me), Norris connects this repetitive activity to worship, not spontaneous prayer, but the celebration, again and again, of a set liturgy, text that does not change. In her writing, Norris returns many times to how prayer and work, the great mainstays of the Benedictine tradition, figure in everyday existence.

In commenting on her poem, "Housekeeping," Norris launches into a revealing account of how the release and liberation of the springtime in South Dakota often worked exactly

---

[9] "Hers; It All Comes Out in the Wash," *New York Times Magazine*, August 22, 1993, http://www.nytimes.com/1993/08/22/magazine/hers-it-all-comes-out-in-the-wash.html.

the opposite on her. She and her husband, as noted, lived in her grandparents' house there for years, the setting of *Dakota: A Spiritual Landscape*. The return of warm weather, the melting of piled-up snow, should have made her heart thrill, leap. But being able to venture back outside not bundled up terrified her. She would resist the thaw by staying inside as if it were still blizzard season. Eventually all this would dissipate and she would be able to hang clothes on the line, work in the garden, experience heat and sun once more.[10]

While dealing with her depression in much greater detail in a later book, *Acedia & me*, Norris mentions this frequently in *The Quotidian Mysteries*. Her perceptive understanding of the most ordinary, repetitive tasks of keeping a house comes from the poet's craft—taking care to look, listen, experience. Thus she reminds us that in addition be being a form of prayer, these necessary activities, this drudge work is also important as therapy. The Greek term for depression's emptiness, dryness, is *acedia*, and it is telling that it means "lack of care." One has stopped caring about most everything—washing one's hair, clothes, rising to the tasks of the day. Then, the tools to struggle against this depression and its grasp Norris found in the desert mothers and fathers of the third and fourth centuries. They used prayer—very short doses of it, as well as physical work and Scripture, again in small doses, along with the counsel of wise, experienced elders. Last of all, they knew how crucial community, some kind of interaction with others, relationships with others, was to health, to therapy.

What Norris gives us in *The Quotidian Mysteries* is her profound sense of the sacred present in the smallest and most boring of daily detail. "Quotidian Mysteries" is really another way of saying the world as sacrament. The root of the word "mystery" is *mysterion* in Greek, what Eastern Christians use, even in English, as a synonym for "sacrament." She also gives

---

[10] Norris, *Quotidian Mysteries*, 36–39.

us a look inside the spiritual toolbox, at what practices she learned and employed.

Struggling with *Acedia*

Later on Norris produced a memoir that also seeks to explore the Greek term *acedia*, which comes close to the complex today we call "depression."[11] In this memoir, Norris again uses much of what she earlier described as the "holy realism" of religion, the certain presence of God in the mundane and repetitive chores of daily living, from laundry to housecleaning to throwing together a meal for a tired, stressed-out family.[12]

The memoir is a brutally frank look at her early life, her later student days at Bennington, and her marriage to David Dwyer, a complicated and (I think) tormented person and a talented poet. He was an Irish-Catholic New Yorker, Jesuit educated, but fallen away, in dramatic fashion, from everything churchly. Thus Norris's own religious revival at first troubled him. He was even more disturbed with her attraction to the monastics and her becoming a lay associate of the monastery. Eventually some of the Benedictines nudged him into overcoming his own religious phobia. This enabled him to accept Norris's regular visits to monasteries, praying of the Daily Office, and many essays and lectures and conferences on the ways in which monastic life offers much to nonmonastics.

All of the years of their life together, their work, and their troubles are entwined with Norris's explorations of *acedia*, its symptoms, causes, and the ways spiritual masters have confronted it. We learn greater details about her life as writer as well, how she and David first lived in the intense literary world of New York City, only to make the dramatic transition to Lemmon, South Dakota. She lovingly remembers her emotionally

---

[11] Norris, *Acedia & me*.
[12] Ibid., 178–98.

troubled husband David's struggles with depression and his failing health due to pulmonary issues. Early in life he'd suffered both a mental breakdown and near death from a misdiagnosed intestinal condition. As the years progressed in their marriage, his condition slowly but cumulatively deteriorated.[13]

There were bouts of depression and drinking, a breakdown and psychiatric hospitalization, and a terrifying disappearance from home with a suicide note left behind.[14] He died at only fifty-seven.[15] Soon after, Norris was called to help with her developmentally disabled sister, beginning postsurgical treatment for breast cancer.

She concludes her memoir with reflections on being a widow, being without children—a choice they had made as a couple—and being middle-aged, all the while coming back, over and over, to the reality of the *acedia*/depression with which she struggles. I can think of other writers involved in the search for God who likewise faced their depression and truly challenging situations in their lives—Elisabeth Behr-Sigel, Dorothy Day, Maria Skobtsova, Barbara Brown Taylor, Thomas Merton. It's not that I selected them for this book solely on that account either. Rather, these writers give us the gift of sharing how they dealt with pain and disappointment and depression in lives that were also immensely creative and productive.

Spiritual Practices and Tools

While this is not a "self-help" volume, Kathleen Norris probably offers more practices for surviving and thriving despite spiritual dryness and discouragement—*acedia*—than anyone else except Barbara Brown Taylor's worldly spiritual practic-

---

[13] Ibid., 102–11.
[14] Ibid., 67–82, 223–28.
[15] Ibid., 238–48.

es.[16] Norris forages the Desert Mothers and Fathers and later monastics and other writers to fill her basket with beautiful, healing practices. Among them she holds out the "purity of heart" path, one beloved of the ancient writer Evagrius as well as medieval mystic Julian of Norwich. Purity of heart was also a focus for Kierekegaard and for John Eudes Bamberger. Bamberger was a psychiatrist who had been a novice under Thomas Merton and was later Merton's friend and confidant. He was an Evagrius scholar as well.[17] This is both a simple yet radical practice, one in which we strip away thoughts, feelings, and actions that falsify, distort, or kill love in us. Love here is the image and likeness of God in us. This is not a recipe, and to try to turn it into a format for everyone would be to destroy the possibility of it bringing insight and healing.

Norris hunts down other ancient practices that remain amazingly effective. In *Amazing Grace*, an earlier volume, she dwells on many of them, from salvation and eschatology and the incarnation to several meditations on conversion and a number of perceptive reflections on prayer and reflective spiritual reading or *lectio divina*.[18] Familiar with psychotherapy, group therapy, and antidepressant medications more recently available, she nevertheless tries the old ways, and though often frustrated, she also came to recognize their authenticity and effectiveness. Naming the demon/sin is tried and true even in therapy today.[19]

As a writer, Norris naturally cherished the work of other authors. So she found the reading of Scripture and reflection on it for prayer to be a powerful way of ordering one's day, one's feelings. Such spiritual immersion even gave definition

---

[16] Barbara Brown Taylor, *An Altar in the World: A Geography of Faith* (San Francisco: HarperOne, 2008).

[17] Norris, *Acedia & me*, 29–32, 164–69, 208–12.

[18] Kathleen Norris, *Amazing Grace: A Vocabulary of Faith* (New York: Riverhead, 1998).

[19] Norris, *Acedia & me*, 33–38.

to one's cognitive map. In visits to the monasteries, documented throughout *The Cloister Walk*, she easily, eagerly slipped into the daily cycle of services in the morning, at midday, in the evening, and before retiring.

The guidance of an elder, the giving of a "word" of discernment rather than elaborated theory, was perhaps the principal way in which the ancient monastics were formed. It was also the way in which they sought healing, by a deeper understanding of their suffering given by another.[20] She also held on to the struggle with the demon afflicting as necessary to knowing one's disease and eventually living through it.[21] The grief with which she grappled in the months after David's death became another occasion for encounter, this time with doubt about all she had clung to in a reborn faith. David, despite an intense religious upbringing and education, came to doubt everything to which he'd been exposed.[22] As traumatic as the death of a spouse is for the survivor, the grief does open to moments of gratitude, to the realization of the gift of the relationship and of the years together.

A spirited celebration of prayer as the practice most effective against *acedia*/depression is what Norris provides toward the end of the memoir. "God talk" worked for her, she asserts. Despite the development of more sophisticated antidepressant medications, even the psychiatric profession has come to recognize the limitations of such treatment.[23] She cites Thomas Merton as one who recognized the need to fight back, in confronting depression, with oneself.[24] From the ancient desert monastics to contemporary healers, Norris traces the practices that can be put to use over a lifetime. She notes the strength

---

[20] Ibid., 87–94.
[21] Ibid., 95–101.
[22] Ibid., 255–65.
[23] Ibid., 269–72.
[24] Ibid., 272.

from a community with whom one prays, eats, studies, and works. There is use of texts to draw one out of oneself, toward another point of view. She cites the psalms in particular. The ancients also recognized the power of tears, of allowing one's feelings out to express frustration, sorrow, and guilt.[25]

Coming to Terms with Oneself

As Barbara Brown Taylor teaches us in her most recent book, learning to accept darkness and all it means as part of our world, our lives, is profoundly transforming.[26] Throughout her books, Norris never flinches when it comes to the dark, painful aspects of our relationships and existence. Whether in describing her own awkward experiences—even the ways her Bennington peers captured her idiosyncrasies in nicknames like "pope," or her own insecurities starting out as a writer in New York—she is never afraid to let us see her difficulties. Even more than her own collisions with classmates and fellow writers, she allows us into her marriage. There we recognize the profound bonds of affection between Kathleen and David. But we are also allowed to experience the depression that afflicts both of them, and the even more painful failure of David's health, both physical and emotional. We confront the loss of a spouse and widowhood with her, no event more life-altering, as she says. As large and imposing as these life events are, she does not spare us the other disappointments and frustrations writers face. And she shares with us the joys of her friendships with Benedictine sisters and monks too. Throughout her work, she depicts life as the landscape of encounter with God. The daily or quotidian mysteries are indeed the experience of living in the world as sacramental in innumerable ways.

---

[25] Ibid., 274–82.
[26] Barbara Brown Taylor, *Learning to Walk in the Dark* (San Francisco: HarperOne, 2014).

Norris also notes that we should be able to allow ourselves to fail, to do less than superior work regularly, another very useful practice—lowering standards and just getting by. Norris looks to some of the great women in the Scriptures as icons of struggling and living on—Sarah and Leah, Hannah and Mary and Elizabeth. With Merton and so many others, some of whom we have listened to in this book, she concludes, "Prayer and love are learned in the hour when prayer has become impossible and your heart has turned to stone."[27]

Throughout her writing, Kathleen Norris keeps returning to tools of the spiritual trade. While some of these, like persistence in working, attentiveness, reflection, the need to revise and rework, were "tools of the trade" for her as a poet and as a memoir writer and essayist, she also acquired a number of others from her time with monastics. Putting these practices of meditative reading, contemplation, and prayer together with her reverence for the encounters of the everyday—doing laundry, cleaning house, and making supper—surely witness to the world as sacrament, to the constant possibility of spiritual engagement in the most ordinary of tasks and settings.

But in the end, it is not a book of "recipes" for the spiritual life that Norris gives us, surely not a "how to be spiritual" handbook. Taken as a whole, her writings are much more. In them we are able to trace her own growth and deepening. As a poet, she is able to pull us into the not-so-obvious corners of monastic life. With her we get to know how this life shapes women and men. In following the people and practices Norris documents, there is much for us to take away. Though few are called to be monastics for a life's profession, the order and awareness of their life is, as other writers have noted, most useful for all of us.

---

[27] Thomas Merton, *New Seeds of Contemplation* (New York: New Directions, 1961), 221.

But even more, Norris is ruthlessly honest in allowing us to see her own personality, her own stumbling in relationships with others, and not only her dreams but also the large disappointments she has faced, all the way from her undergraduate time, narrated without any self-pity or sentimentality, to the last days of her husband's illness and her first as a widow. Perhaps, for one who might appear to be terribly private, we receive more of Norris's own journey than even some others who have much to say about their experiences. And from these, we again see how much of the spiritual journey and its struggles take place in the blur of everyday activities, in our work and closest relationships, the world being charged with sacramental possibilities.

Michael Plekon
Photo from Baruch College–CUNY.

Epilogue

"The Liturgy after the Liturgy": Michael Plekon, Learning to Be a Pastor

Scenes from Ministry

In a book about a more worldly spirituality, about the world as sacrament, all the other chapters have been encounters with some remarkable women and men from the Western and Eastern churches. All of them wrote about how they understood their faith and about how they tried to put it into practice—how they tried to love both God and neighbor, stand up for the marginal, and help those in need.

They are especially important persons of faith as their holiness is most ordinary, taken up with everyday life, with the issues that concern many of us in our time. Now, I do not at all place myself in their class as an exemplary writer and actor. I thought, however, that to their words and witness I could add a few examples from my own experience, things I have seen and done that also contribute to a sense of the world as sacrament, a place where God is active. What I want to offer here, in a reflection on a worldly, everyday spiritual life, are a few "scenes," moments in which I have learned a great deal not only as a believer but also as a spouse, parent, and child, as well as a teacher and pastor. At the start, as a prologue, I described a little of the diverse experiences I have had of the churches growing up and in adulthood. I want to end with a bit more of that.

I was prepared as a kind of "late vocation" candidate for ordination in the Lutheran Church in a manner strikingly similar to what I would experience almost fifteen years later, when being scrutinized for ministry in the Orthodox Church. Given my time in the Carmelites, the undergraduate program with three majors and almost enough credits for a master's degree, then my graduate training and subsequent work as a scholar and professor, I was given a series of sessions with faculty at the Lutheran seminary in Philadelphia. These examined me in everything from church history and Scripture to preaching and pastoral care. Then I was apprenticed to the senior pastor of the parish to which we belonged and where I would be serving for pastoral training and supervision.

For a year I did a kind of pastoral internship. I took a turn preaching at services, did supervised pastoral visiting in hospital and homes, and taught church school and adult education classes. I had already done some of this kind of pastoral work with the Carmelites. But in preparation for ordination, I did roughly what a deacon could do. I also met regularly, over the course of more than a year, with the candidacy committee and advisors. When my supervisor approved my internship work, I was voted on by the synod assembly and executive council and ordained on June 3, 1983, the commemoration of Pope John XXIII, the "pope of love" and great ecumenical leader who convoked the Second Vatican Council and now has been made a saint in the Catholic Church.

After I was ordained, among the first non-Catholic ordinands ever at Fordham University Church, I began what would be almost a decade as associate pastor at Trinity Church in Brewster, New York, and two other parishes. I was again ordained in order to function as a priest in the Orthodox Church, this in 1996, but I count 1983 as the start of my ordained ministry. Trinity Church's gifted senior pastor, H. Henry Maertens, envisioned me as a member of a team ministry rather than as his subordinate assistant—this was the new way of structuring the pastoral division of labor when there were multiple staff clergy. We participated in numerous workshops for those engaged in team ministry. We alternated preaching and presiding at the Eucharist, the one concelebrating assisting in the distribution of communion. Otherwise, I attended parish council meetings and reported at them on my pastoral work. I continued to take part in church school, confirmation classes, and adult education. While we alternated visiting at the local medical center, I was given responsibility for the pastoral care of the elderly, especially those shut in at home and in area nursing facilities. I was also assigned the visitation of inactive members.

I should also note that I was always a "non-stipendiary" pastor. That means I was not paid a salary or other benefits by the parishes in which I served. Put another way, I was a "worker priest," though not employed in factory work as those who were called by that description some years ago, mostly in postwar Europe. Otherwise, my pastoral service was governed by the canons or constitutions of the larger church body in which I was on the roster of the ordained. I also followed the parish constitutions as well as the wishes of the rector or senior pastor. Everywhere I served I was accepted as part of a team or collegial ministry, even though the senior had full responsibility to the bishop and the parish council.

Years later, I am grateful for the formation and support Pastor Maertens gave me as a mentor at Trinity Church, Brewster. In retrospect, I realize how much I absorbed from his experience, not only at Trinity, but also in earlier parish assignments, both as an associate and as senior pastor. He was a teacher for me in pastoral work, but in an indirect manner. Recognizing my training earlier in the Carmelites and in graduate work in religious studies and theology, he focused more on pastoral practice, providing me opportunities to do ministry of all kinds. One area he gave me in which to learn by practice was pastoral care of the homebound and the elderly. This included those in institutional settings. During the decade we worked together in that parish, we learned from and complemented each other.

In the early 1980s, there was significant ongoing transition from more traditional patterns of parish life and organization. While there were still a very active youth group, children's choir, adult choir, and women's group, there was a recognition that these were no longer sufficient. The direction in which most parish programs was directed was connecting discipleship with everyday life. There was still exposure to the Scriptures and church teaching, but the aim was to empower and equip Christians to serve in their neighborhoods, jobs, and schools as witnesses of the Gospel. We were not a town/village parish and were not based on a shared ethnic/language culture. We were a regional and inclusive parish community. At the same time, the diocese had developed a program for training lay deacons to assist in education, youth work, social outreach, pastoral care, and preaching and to assist at the Eucharist.

Also during this time, Pastor Maertens and I worked at renewing the liturgical life of the parish. Primary was returning to the weekly celebration of the Eucharist as the principal service, also making baptism part of the Sunday liturgy. The services of Holy Week were enhanced as was attention to the commemoration of holy women and men in the church calendar and the observing of important seasons such as Advent and Lent.

Founded just before the Second World War, Trinity was in my time there a parish of close to eight hundred members. It was a diverse regional parish as well. I recall numerous conversations with a member who was a national church staffer, the Rev. John Hesford, in which the three of us clergy pursued what this regional character meant for our pastoral work there. For one thing, it meant that as the only Lutheran congregation in Putnam County, and at some distance from the nearest other ones in nearby Connecticut and northern Westchester County, we had members in numerous municipalities and school districts, as well as three counties and two states. This was also quite another kind of parish community in the religious and

Epilogue: "The Liturgy after the Liturgy" 237

ethnic diversity of the members. Trinity could not be categorized as predominantly German or Swedish, Norwegian or Danish, as was the case with numerous congregations in Brooklyn, the Bronx, and Manhattan. Like other exurban and suburban parishes on Long Island and in New Jersey, we did not realize that many of the demographic trends that would redefine congregational life were already present, though more dormant, in our parish. For example, at least half in the community were not cradle Lutherans. Neither was it a village parish. It was founded as such, in the village of Brewster, in a single family home—chapel downstairs, pastor's apartment upstairs—a frequent mission model. By the 1950s, migration from the city north into the northern Westchester and Putnam County areas made the original building too small for the community. A starter or "first unit" building with sanctuary upstairs and fellowship hall and classrooms downstairs was erected not in the village but out on the highway between Brewster and Carmel, very close to the then-newly established Interstate 84.

The first new members in the early 1960s were raised in Bronx and Brooklyn parishes where there was still ethnic identity and a number of conscious efforts to maintain denominational identity. Intermarriage and the move to the near-rural exurbs soon diminished those patterns. They were almost gone by the time we arrived in 1981. In the early 1980s, we were still using a model of parish activities and scheduling that had committee and council meetings and various activities—choir rehearsals and youth group meetings and classes on most weekday evenings. This became unsustainable, even in my decade there.

Looking back now, with both of us parents working and two young children, I am not sure how we managed, Jeanne and I. Most weeks, in addition to full-time teaching at the City University of New York's Baruch College, I had twenty to thirty hours of pastoral work, including Sunday services and classes. I find it hard to believe that our schedule of work and then my church work could be fit into the time of feeding and caring for kids, doing laundry, and grocery shopping. Only about halfway through almost a decade at Trinity did the ministry committee and council start setting aside a small stipend for our children's education each month. This was a small way to recognize my contribution, but out of the thirty-five years of pastoral service, it was in place, perhaps, only in my last five years at Trinity.

Location, Location, Location

During the years I served at Trinity, the community was exclusively white, drawn largely from former New York City dwellers who were drawn to lower taxes, an escape from blacks and Latinos, and bigger houses and better schools in what previously had been a rural, dairy-farming area. The Harlem Line of Metro North as well as Interstates 84 and 684 made commuting south to lower Westchester and the city for work possible. Numerous corporations like Pepsico, IBM, *Reader's Digest*, Grolier's, Texaco, and Union Carbide, among others, offered employment there at that time (all of these have since disappeared or dramatically declined in size). The school systems were good—plenty of sports for kids. Trinity exploded in growth in the 1970s and 1980s under such favorable demographics. The church school was booming, with close to 150 children. The confirmation classes were two dozen or more in those years. The demographic trend toward most women working had begun, so one of the first signs of change was the inability to attract younger adults out to weekday evening choir rehearsals, classes, and meetings.

Eventually, the continued surge of children at the parish resulted in many drop-offs and pick-ups for Sunday church school, held between the two services necessary to fit the congregation into the first, small worship space built in the early 1960s. We knew that with parents simply bringing kids to

Epilogue: "The Liturgy after the Liturgy" 239

church school and not staying to attend one of the services with them, there was no future for a congregation that seemed to have grown so rapidly. While all these families were counted as members, there was neither the personal participation in the parish's life nor financial support that went along with such active belonging.

Even in the late 1980s, as we built a new sanctuary and church school space, the demographics were changing. Finances were always difficult and became more so as the stagnation of wages and outsourcing of jobs bit into the suburban and exurban population from which the parish drew. By the start of the 1990s, service attendance, along with participation in various activities like choir, church school instruction, the women's group, and other committees was beginning to shrink. This was a pattern repeated almost everywhere—minimal parish attendance, especially in preparation for first communion and confirmation—and then "graduation" from church, not only for the young people but also for their parents as well. I dwell on this because while there is great attention now focused on the continued shrinking of belonging to religious communities, the rise of the religious "nones," I saw the pattern emerging very clearly almost thirty years ago. Having been invited back to preach on a Sunday for Trinity's seventy-fifth anniversary year in 2014, I saw a community of about a hundred or so, less than a fifth the size of what it had been when I served there from 1982 to 1991.

I learned all the varied aspects of pastoral ministry there at Trinity—visiting, counseling, crisis intervention, teaching, administrative oversight. With an experienced senior pastor as mentor, I was supervised, directed, often corrected but also encouraged and provided opportunities to do more. I learned what it meant to be a pastor in addition to all these specific skills in ways I never expected. One Sunday, on exiting a service, I received an emotional request for prayers for an ailing parent from a congregation member. I completely forgot this particular request later on in the week. The only time I remembered the sick parent was the moment I was asked to pray for her. The joyous news, the very next Sunday, of how powerful my prayer must be, given the dramatic improvement in the sick mother's health of course, gladdened but also just mortified me. And it prompted me not only to construct a prayer list, which I now refer to daily, decades later, but also to confront the fact that I had no prayer life, habit, or rule whatsoever. I began reading at least morning or evening prayer from the Book of Common Prayer then and still today follow the same practice most days.[1]

Slumber Service

What I have described so far does have a great deal to do with the world as sacrament. From the very start of my years of ordained service, across the churches there was the realization that the postwar era of enormous religious activity and church expansion was over. Both the political and cultural changes in the 1960s and 1970s contributed to the gradual detachment of "baby boomers" from active membership and participation in congregational life. The response of the mainline churches was to turn attention to living out one's faith in service, in the world, not so much in parish programs but in one's workplace, neighborhood, and family. This is not to say that traditional parish groups and programs suddenly disappeared. They continued on as important ways of sustaining belonging to the parish. But I think we both sociologically and theologically were trying to put into practice the rediscovery of parish as "the people of God," as community, and of church membership not as ethnic or merely social cohesion but a vocation of discipleship.

---

[1] I have written about prayer, remembering, and a prayer list in *Uncommon Prayer: Prayer in Everyday Experience* (Notre Dame, IN: University of Notre Dame Press, 2016), 95–119.

I had a lot of adventures in what one would think would be fairly predictable afternoons of pastoral visiting around Putnam County in the early 1980s. I recall the activities directors of the Putnam Medical Center and of one of the larger skilled nursing facilities asking me to step into their offices. These were the days when the boxes of index cards with patients' names and personal information, including religious affiliation, were there for all clergy to peruse. Privacy restrictions ended this. Clergy now need to have ID badges, to have been previously vetted—all very good developments, as some enterprising evangelical clergy would use the cards to attempt to convince patients they had not yet taken the Lord as their personal savior and had not yet experienced the true faith.

I was approached for something quite different. Apparently some funding had appeared, where there were longer-term skilled nursing patients, for social and educational activities, namely, the addition of noncounseling engagement for their afternoons. The directors, being active churchgoers themselves, independently had come upon a short service with singing as a mode of this newly funded social-educational engagement. Neither offered me a stipend but asked if I could, with other local clergy, start offering, once a month at least, a short service for all interested residents. They did not use the label "ecumenical," but this was exactly what they had in mind.

So began a run as the celebrant at a distinctive liturgical service for residents of skilled nursing centers. My first services taught me quickly that such celebrations had to be adapted to local needs and circumstances. The first ones were in the winter, about 2:00 p.m., after lunch, in the more than adequately (actually overheated) activities room. Slumber time for the little congregation gathered. Several were snoring away when wheeled into the activities room. I knew that singing just one verse of a very familiar hymn, like "Holy, Holy, Holy" would be enough to begin. I found that any Scripture reading or prayers read would need to be spare indeed. Within a few verses of a psalm and a very brief reading from one of the gospels, there was already snoring and groaning, many eyes shut with heavy breathing. The short, loud, energetic homily I'd prepared went out to a peacefully slumbering twenty-five or so mostly elderly women in wheelchairs and walkers nearby. Oh, there were a couple of bright-eyed hearers, one lady of color who "Amened" me after every sentence.

I did a short prayer of the people, then went round and, as it turned out, awakened a few by exchanging the greeting/peace. I had looked at a couple of orders of service for special circumstances in both the Lutheran *Book of Occasional Services* and the *Book of Common Prayer*. These books both had very brief services for visits to hospitals and nursing homes. That is exactly what I decided to do—very short services for the slumbering, with the consecration of the bread and cup, ending in the Our Father.

One of my epiphanies, after being surprised to hear so many singing "Holy, Holy, Holy," was saying the Lord's Prayer. Even with eyes closed, many in the congregation there in the far-too-warm activities room joined in, reciting the Our Father all the way through the doxology at the end, "For thine is the kingdom . . ." I decided to bring around both the bread and wine—I was using unleavened wafers. I intincted each one, that is, dipped a small piece of the communion wafer into the small chalice and usually placed it on the tongue, with the words: "The body of Christ, broken for you. The blood of Christ shed for you." Now what happened next I had beheld, in awe, earlier on visits to the homes of very ill parishioners. Even though seemingly not awake or attentive, the distribution words triggered the memory of receiving communion. In some cases, eyes opened, the sign of the cross was made, hands joined as for prayer, and in most cases they opened their mouths and, as taught and practiced for many years, put out their tongues to receive the Lord. A few held out open hands in post–Vatican II style.

When done, I said the postcommunion prayer, gave the final blessing, but then went around with the holy oil to anoint for healing. Most often, the anointing formula evoked the folding of hands after the sign of the cross was made. These profound, moving liturgical actions were made by the same elders who were dozing in the cozy warmth, postprandial, listening to the few hymn verses sung, and the calming words of Scripture and prayer.

Having participated in big liturgies in the cavernous Cathedral of St. John the Divine, large gatherings at diocesan and national church assemblies with soaring voices and multiple bishops, this less than half hour liturgy in the activities room remains among the most memorable, whether at Putnam Medical Center, Putnam Nursing and Rehab, Waterview and Salem Hills, or a couple of other local skilled nursing centers.

I routinely came away from these nursing center services feeling that the service had been celebrated for me rather than the other way around, that I had come as a chaplain of sorts to have a service for the residents. I also am as amused today as I was years ago then to hear the well-intentioned directors assure me that these services were funded as "enhanced social and educational opportunities" for residents. I suppose a good magician or singer or instrumentalist could have done even better. Whenever a string or keyboard player came in, it was magical, seeing where the playing took these elderly, incapacitated people.

Home Church, the Sacrament of Visiting

Another scene was one played out so many times I lost count, always in the homes of elderly folk and others from the parish I was assigned to visit. I was asked to work my way through a list of inactive or minimally active individuals who at one time had been engaged enough to actually be listed on the parish rolls. What was intriguing here was that these names were counted as active members in order to maintain our profile as a close to one thousand–member congregation, as the senior pastor put it, wildly overestimating the actual numbers. Since our assessment to the national church body and the synod/diocese was a set percentage of the overall parish budget, we did not have the problem of being "taxed," as it were, by head count, as in the assessment plans of other church bodies.

I have diverging, often ambivalent memories of these "inactive" lists and visits. This was before the days of internet communication. I never did on-site "cold calls" like the Mormons or the Jehovah's Witnesses. But even calling ahead to see if a visit could be scheduled was not always effective. I found that in quite a few cases, the number was no longer in service. The individual or family had relocated. In other cases, calls were answered either with an abrupt, "not interested," or there was an account of excuses for why they could not come to church or support the parish. There were cases in which past grievances, in some instances with a pastor long since gone from the parish, were repeated. The inactive members who allowed me to visit turned out to be a very mixed group.

I remember two families, both roughly my present age, in their sixties—with no obvious physical problems other than those of aging couples, but with profound, wrenching stories of a permanent and severely handicapped and long-institutionalized child, now an adult in later forties. The shame of having such a child, the social stigma they experienced—that everyone at church knew and felt sorry for them, pitied them, but wanted to keep their distance. I asked if they had actually been treated this way or simply feared or imagined it. To my surprise and sadness, the mother of the institutionalized patient said she'd been avoided and distanced at a church women's social event—the curse of middle-class and small-town manners. What do you do with someone who does not fit in?

But in some other cases in which a child had died young in an accident or from cancer, it was inconsolable grief that turned the parents into recluses. They were healthy enough to mow the grass, rake the leaves, tend a garden, shop for groceries.

But they dreaded social contact with others and, after years of avoiding it, did not know any longer how to carry on socially, either with neighbors or strangers. Thus in a couple cases, my visits became a novel and nonthreatening connection with the outside. And I was welcomed, though told they were not so badly off or sinful to need communion that much. In a few other cases, after several visits, one of the partners took me aside at the door on leaving and expressed gratitude for the visits but that they were just too much for the other one to handle. I could just pray for them, send a card, maybe call by phone occasionally.

One visit struck me as odd in that while I was politely greeted by an elderly man with a hard-to-identify European accent, I was clearly suspect, frightening even, though, as always, I was wearing my clerical collar, had identified myself as a pastor in the phone call, and offered communion and prayers. All these he declined. He thanked me for stopping but preferred I not call or try to visit again, all of this he stated at the front door. A year or two later this man's name and photo was splayed across the local papers as a former concentration camp guard. Soon to be tried if he did not leave the country, he died before either deportation or trial, after being denaturalized. Despite the German surname, he was from Ukraine, the place of my own family's origins.

I do not mean to suggest that visiting either inactive parish members or the shut-ins was tedious and distasteful. In looking back at my folder of notes and lists, these I can say, without a doubt, were the most wonderful of my early pastoral activities. I was allowed to enter the joys but also the heartbreaking disappointments of people's families, their marriages, and children's lives. I discovered just why the gospels were full of Jesus visiting the homes of the sick, the desperate, of his encountering those even outside the religious community of his time, determined to have a child or servant healed. I came to understand, mostly with coffee and cookies rather than dried or broiled fish and bread, why Jesus made meals for people who were hungry, how he saw the kingdom captured in the faces of those sharing a supper.

But I have saved the best for last here, the visits and people who were like the sunshine, absolute gifts of grace to me. I may have been proceeding on the senior pastor's plans to visit these folks, a chore he did not much enjoy himself, but as it turned out, the tables were turned. I was the one gifted, graced by their presence. Since she is long since deceased, I can speak of Elvira. She was nearly one hundred years old when I first visited her, and a few years later I was privileged to be at a birthday lunch her neighbors and friends threw for her at her favorite place, the local Chinese restaurant. Elvira was a long-time widow, her husband having died before the Second World War. All of her children were also gone when I met her, though she had a few grandchildren and great-grandchildren who did not visit her very often. In typical Scandinavian fashion, difficult matters were left in silence, and her lack of contact with family was among these. Her next-door neighbor, herself a remarkable saint of everyday life, an attorney, mother, and spouse in a troubled marriage, knew Elvira better than anyone—she was a second daughter to her. Elvira had migrated to New York, to Brooklyn. She came from Sweden shortly after the turn of the century. With her husband she ran a small business for many years, a stationary/candy store. She continued to run it for as long as she could, for decades after his death until her own deteriorating health made it impossible. She was able to sell and then relocate to Putnam County where she and her family had a small place on a lake for weekends in the summer. Now long since settled as a suburb, the immediate area around Trinity Church had formerly been the county seat of a largely agricultural economy—mostly dairy farms, with several rail lines, including the old NY Central, coming straight through for the shipping of dairy products as well as ice. The cutting and storing of ice for New York City was the second-largest industry. Once cars became more widespread, particularly right after the war, Putnam County became a working-class resort area, there being several large, dammed-up lakes.

By the time I started visiting her, Elvira was crippled with arthritis. She was still able to live by herself but not without the care of her neighbors, who checked in on her daily, made meals for her, cleaned the house, and took her to medical appointments. Whenever I called her—the phone was her lifeline and TV a virtual companion—she was always bubbling with laughter. She had a special volume control that made it possible to hear her callers better. When I arrived, she would put on water for tea and bring out a plate of cookies, apologizing that she could no longer bake her own sweets. I always brought her communion and did a little service with a reading and prayers as well. She was alone now, most of her family gone and those remaining only coming to visit sporadically. She no longer could get out to the store or to church and confided that she worried that she would have to sell her house and move into some facility for the elderly. She did not want to give up her independence—after all, she had worked and managed for decades after her children left home and her husband died. Her home was dear to her too, a small cottage but cozy, filled with her favorite china, plants, and photos of loved ones.

I cannot say I ever heard anything profound or, for that matter, troubling from her. There was discretion about personal and family matters that prompted her to breeze through questions both about her past and her family at present. The truth was that her real family were her neighbors, in particular Joyce, a young woman who had returned to law school at night and on the weekends, a dream she had to postpone until her children were older. I was touched by how deep was the trust and affection between Elvira and Joyce, a kind of surrogate child. And I could always get Elvira worked up by asking about Joyce. She would light up and tell me that without Joyce, she could not see how she could go on. But with her, there was a reason for living.

So, as a new pastor, Elvira was one of the shut-ins I was to visit regularly, for communion and prayer as well as contact. There was storytelling and reminiscing about the past. I used to look forward to visiting Elvira and a few other elderly parishioners—Elizabeth, Florence, Martha, Bertha, Millie—more than any other pastoral work. I can still hear their heavy Brooklyn, Queens, and Manhattan accents, all from another time. They all had stories about coping with loss, surviving the Great Depression, terrified years waiting for husbands to return from World War II. Some told utterly fascinating stories about the past. Florence described a working farm on which she grew up in Westchester County, now one of the highest income suburban areas in the country. Another described taking the old IRT subway to the end of the line and then walking or hitching a ride up to a farmers' market at the Racetrack in Yonkers, just blocks from the house in which I grew up—this in the early years of the twentieth century. Every one of these women were widows, most all of them grandmothers and great-grandmothers. They told the story of living through much of a century of enormous change. None made it past high school. Many remembered when women could not vote. And they remembered very well the wars, both of them, then later, Korea and Vietnam. There was storytelling and reminiscing about the past or better, reliving the past.

Without a formal program to train me, what I have described here as the pastoral care of inactive members and of the elderly, both at home and in skilled nursing centers, became, over the course of a decade, a demanding formation for me. In retrospect, I realize what a skilled, experienced, and discerning mentor I had in Pastor Maertens. Thus, having done the academic preparation in both undergraduate and graduate theology courses, research, and writing, I experienced what new presbyters or pastors must have in the first millennium and a half, before seminaries and theological schools were established as the location of formation for pastoral ministry.

I had the parish community and its seasoned pastor with whom to consult and from whom to learn. This training formally started in the first six months of a pastoral internship I served before ordination. It continued, however, for the near-decade I was there as assistant, then associate, pastor.

I should also mention clergy colleagues from neighboring parishes in my diocese who listened to my accounts and offered their experience and reflections. I realize now that my learning how to be a pastor, in the first ten years of my ministry, was a return to the most ancient patterns in which a mentor helped an apprentice learn the craft.

I cannot adequately convey how vivid the faces of the people I visited as a fledgling pastor are even now. Over thirty years later, I remember what they offered me in the afternoons when I stopped by. I remember exactly where they lived and how overheated their homes were in winter. In returning to them, I have tried to show how the world they presented to me was truly a sacrament, just as much as the communion and anointing I brought to them—maybe even more so.

Heaven around Us

There is much more to my story of learning to be a pastor, but it must wait for another occasion. To what I have described here, there is another pastoral experience (over twenty years' worth) working with my longtime friend and colleague Alex Vinogradov in St. Gregory Parish in Wappingers Falls that needs to be explored. There was an ecumenical wrinkle in this relationship insofar as it meant returning to the Eastern or Byzantine church tradition in which I had been baptized, confirmed/chrismated, and raised in early childhood. All the Eastern church writers to whom we have listened in this book I came to know through intensive reading, translation, and writing in the years I have been at St. Gregory church. I mentioned that I actually did meet and got to know Elisabeth

Behr-Sigel as well as others who personally knew Evdokimov, Afanasiev, Lev Gillet, and Alexander Men. I am also privileged to have as a friend Thomas Merton's secretary and assistant in his last years, Brother Patrick Hart of the Abbey of Gethsemani in Kentucky.

And even as I look at retirement both from the City University and from active ministry in the near future, there is more to learn, more to integrate, more to, I hope, pass on.

The narrative I have given here, in the end, is not so much about me or my pastoral formation. Rather, it is my experience, earlier on in my life, of what this volume focuses on, namely, the world as sacrament, of how we encounter God in the most ordinary circumstances of everyday life. Thomas Merton wrote, "Paradise is all around us and we do not understand. . . . [T]he gate of heaven is everywhere."[2] As much as I see that this is true, like many others, it does not undo years of thinking and being formed in other ways.

In other places, I have described how I have experienced my students' conflict with their families of origin, with the religious traditions of their childhood, and their struggles with their own identities. All of these, very often powerfully expressed in classroom discussion, was learning, to be sure, but it was also prayerful exchange.[3] We still keep penning up the sacred into a churchy, spiritual preserve. We then look down on the rest of everyday life as profane, worldly, secular, less than holy. This is a distorted vision to be sure, not worthy of being attributed to monastic exaggeration. For authentic monasticism is deeply incarnational, thus is at root humane, able to inculturate itself into Egyptian, Syrian, Ethiopian, Greek, and numerous other cultural settings. An extreme, world-

---

[2] Thomas Merton, *Conjectures of a Guilty Bystander* (Garden City, New York: Image Books, 1968), 132, 158.

[3] Plekon, *Uncommon Prayer*, 201–21.

denying vision did emerge, however, and given the dominant role of monasticism, came to affect the rest of church life.[4]

Nor can one blame the Scriptures for so much of the alienation of religion from life that we see, a dislocation that turns many young people away. Both in the Hebrew Bible and the New Testament, the sacred and the everyday are permeable. Amy-Jill Levine's recent marvelous examination of Jesus' parables shows this over and over again. She takes one through so many scenes from ordinary life where the power and goodness of God break through—from extraordinary platters of rising dough and then baked bread to profligate and faithful sons and their fathers to all kinds of outsiders to the Covenant finding God very near.[5]

Not a few have noticed that very little of the New Testament takes place in traditionally sacred space. There is one scene in the Nazareth synagogue and some indirect hints that Jesus might have taught and discussed at other such locations. Surely he did within the precincts of the Jerusalem temple. Paul seems to have looked for where other Jews were gathering for prayer in his journeys. Yet the general sense is that the way of Jesus mostly led through the details and demands of daily life. Sick people and farmers, fishing folk and tax collectors, people baking and cleaning—this is where the kingdom is located and received its metaphors.

The writers to whom we have listened here surely present a varied set of lives, ideas, and perspectives on the spiritual life, on trying to find God and live out the Gospel in our time. Though there are common aspects of their vision—inspiration from Scripture and liturgy—they are distinct personalities,

---

[4] Philip Zymaris, "Marriage and the Eucharist: From Unity to Schizophrenia," in *Love, Marriage and Family in the Eastern Orthodox Tradition*, ed. Theodore Grey Dedon and Sergey Trostyanskiy, Sophia Studies in Orthodox Theology, vol. 7 (New York: Theotokos Press, 2013), 134–51.

[5] Amy-Jill Levine, *Short Stories by Jesus: The Enigmatic Parables of a Controversial Rabbi* (San Francisco: HarperOne, 2014).

with their own experiences in life. They are thoughtful and educated, very much women and men of our time. They felt compelled, in their own ways, to reflect on and draw attention to the challenges of our era—of war, migration, poverty, even of disillusionment with the church and faith.

As different as their personalities and experiences, I have tried to listen carefully to them and, in so doing, hope that I have conveyed what I have heard. They experienced the world as the place to meet God, most often through the neighbor, and with much that challenges traditional certainties of belief and practice. As we hear their accounts though, the presence of God, the sureness of mercy is always there. I also hope the few scenes from my own experience added to their wonderful accounts of ordinary, everyday life as the sacrament of God's presence and work in the world.

www.ingramcontent.com/pod-product-compliance
Lightning Source LLC
Chambersburg PA
CBHW051939290426
44110CB00015B/2032